RAJARAJA CHOLA

Interplay Between an Imperial Regime
and Productive Forces of Society

RAGHAVAN SRINIVASAN

ISBN 978-93-54581-14-4
Copyright © Raghavan Srinivasan, 2021

First published in India 2021 by Leadstart Inkstate
A Division of One Point Six Technologies Pvt Ltd

Sales Office:
Unit No.25/26, Building No.A/1,
Near Wadala RTO,
Wadala (East), Mumbai – 400037 India
Phone: +91 969933000
Email: info@leadstartcorp.com
www.leadstartcorp.com

Disclaimer: The views expressed in this book are those of the Author and do not pertain to be held by the Publisher.

Editor: Roona Ballachanda
Cover concept & design: Mrityunjoy Paul
Layouts: Kshitij Dhawale

To Late Professor K.A. Nilakanta Sastri, whose pioneering work in South Indian History inspired this book.

CONTENT

MAPS AND ILLUSTRATIONS

1. Map showing the extent of the Chola Empire of Rajendra Chola I (c. 1030 CE)

2. Map showing Chola Mandalams in the 11th century

3. Chronology chart of the Chola Dynasty

4. Royal seal of the Chola Dynasty

5. A typical inscription from Brihadeeswara Temple in Thanjavur

6. Statue of Rajaraja on horseback

7. The 13-storeyed *Sri Vimana* (tower) of the Brihadeeswara Temple

8. *Sri Vimana* of Brihadeeswara Temple – Outer wall detail

9. Decorative elements on the outer wall of the *Sri Vimana* of Brihadeeswara Temple

10. Coins of Uttama Chola

11. Child *bhakti* saint Sambandar

12. Queen Sembiyan Mahadevi

13. Kailasanathar Temple at Kanchipuram

14. Statue of Nataraja, Chola style

15. A mural painting at Brihadeeswara Temple

16. Image of Tripurantaka

Acknowledgements

This is an attempt to write a short, readable and at the same time authentic account of an important period in the history of South India, the time when Rajaraja Chola established an empire of awesome proportions and when the productive forces of the southern region flourished with stunning results.

This reconstruction of the period stands on the shoulders of works by distinguished scholars such as Nilakanta Sastry, Kamil Zvelebil, Romila Thapar, AL Basham, Champalakshmi, Burton Stein and other eminent historians and commentators of that early period. This book is only a humble tribute to existing documents and analyses of the period. While paying serious attention to their analyses of the period, I have ventured to offer my own interpretations and conclusions on some aspects. I hope that while doing this I have not misrepresented or distorted the viewpoints of these prominent scholars.

I have not adopted a chronological treatment as many traditional historians would have. The structure under which I have assembled the material is my own creation. If this structure and treatment of the subject have missed some crucial elements, then the blame would lie with me alone.

While writing the manuscript, I went through a considerable number of documents in both English and Tamil. Reading some of the original stone and copper plate inscriptions and a sizeable collection of literary works of the period cutting across many genres, gave me immense pleasure. Though I have tried to refer to the original documents whenever I included excerpts and translations in English, I might have missed a few. It was heartening to note that many popular Tamil works of the period along with their translations and commentaries are freely available on the web.

I profusely thank all those who wished me well in this venture and enquired now and then about its progress with expectation and concern. Firstly, I thank my wife Vidya and my son Srinath for the constant understanding and support they gave me when I sat glued to my table for days on end. They provided very useful feedback on my initial drafts which must have been as boring as a construction without doors, windows and paint.

My special thanks to Prof Sharada Srinivasan for reviewing the draft and providing a review blurb for the back cover page. My thanks are also due to Dr Manu V. Devadevan, Prof R. Mahalakshmi, Prof T.R. Govindarajan and others who reviewed the draft in part or full and gave their critical and valuable comments. I also extend my thanks to Sonali Mukherjee for her thoughtful observations on the draft. They helped me to draw a clearer picture of the target audience in my mind.

Copious thanks are due to Leadstart Publishing who guided me through the publishing process in a very professional and systematic way. The painstaking and meticulous editing done by Roona Ballachanda has improved the readability of the book to no small extent. I am grateful to her for her thoughtful suggestions and critical comments which made me scamper to my bibliographic sources now and then. I have greatly benefited from the gentle guidance provided by the Leadstart team including Malini Nair, Pooja Dutt, Trupti Sawardekar, Ananya Subramanian, Bhavika Bharambe, Kshitij Dhawale, Walid Jalal, Vijay T and others. Ananya particularly had been in constant touch throughout the making of this book.

Many images have been reproduced here from the Wikipedia Commons along with attribution to the original creators. My friend and classmate, GV Balasubramanian, Engineer by Qualification, Banker by Profession, and Photographer by Passion has contributed some of the images. A few are from my own personal collection.

Thanks are also due to Mrityunjoy Paul for his excellent conception of the cover, capturing the essence of the book.

ABOUT THE AUTHOR

Raghavan Srinivasan is a graduate in Chemical Engineering from Madras University and a post-graduate in MBA from McMaster University, Canada. After working as a systems analyst for a few years, he was a freelance IT professional before deciding to become an entrepreneur in the social development sector. At present he is a professional consultant in this area. He lives in New Delhi with his wife and son. He has written and edited a number of documents for governments and the UN system. He has also been editing a magazine called *ghadar jari hai* for several years now (http://ghadar.org.in/gjh_html/?nocahce). He has written several cover stories, articles and travelogues for print and online newspapers.

Raghavan is passionately interested in Indian literature, philosophy and history. He believes that the past of our sub-continent has many clues to help us find our way in these confusing times.

His first historical fiction, 'Yugantar: The Dream of Bharatavarsha Takes Shape 2300 Years Ago' has been published by Leadstart.

He can be contacted at:

Email: raghavansrin@gmail.com

FB: https://www.facebook.com/raghavan.srinivasan.12

Instagram: https://instagram.com/rags.srinivasan

Goodreads author: https://www.goodreads.com/ragssrini

Map showing the extent of the Chola empire during Rajendra Chola I (c. 1030 CE)

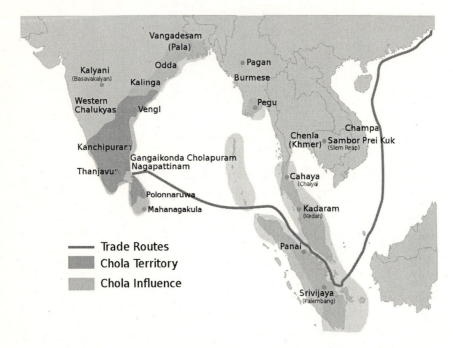

Fig. 1 - Map showing the extent of the Chola empire during Rajendra Chola I (c. 1030 CE)

MAP SHOWING CHOLA MANDALAMS IN THE 11TH CENTURY

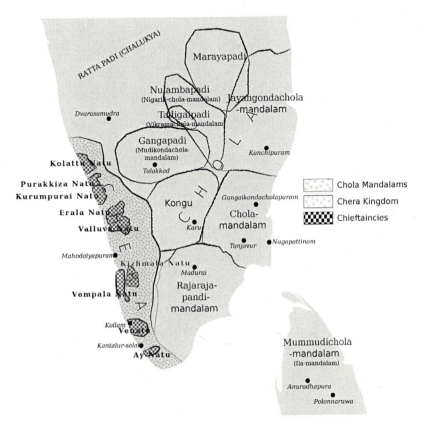

Fig. 2 - Map showing Chola Mandalams in the 11th century

CHRONOLOGY OF PRINCIPAL EVENTS NARRATED IN THE BOOK

Early Cholas: At least before 3rd century BCE

235 BCE – Invasion of Lanka by the Chola king Ellalan (Sembiyan) mentioned in Mahavamsa

848 CE – Capture of Thanjavur by Vijayalaya Chola from the Mutharaiyars

850-871 – Reign of Vijayalaya, the first king of the imperial line of Cholas

871-907 – Reign of Aditya I

879 – Battle of Thirupurambiyam – turning point for the Cholas

890 – Conquest and annexation of Pallava territory by Aditya I

907-55 – Reign of Parantaka I

915 – Battle of Vellur where Parantaka defeated a joint Pandya-Lanka invasion

947 – Birth of Rajaraja Cholan

949 – Reign of Rajaditya

948-49 – Battle of Takkolam between Rajaditya, crown prince and eldest son of Parantaka I, and Rashtrakuta king Krishna III (939–967).

949-957 – Reign of Gandaraditya

956-57 – Reign of Arinjaya

957-73 – Reign of Parantaka II (Sundara Chola, father of Rajaraja)

969 – Assassination of Aditya Karikalan, elder brother of Rajaraja

970-85 – Reign of Uttama Chola

985 – Ascension of Rajaraja

993 – Invasion of Lanka

994 – Rajaraja destroys fleet of the Chera King Bhaskara Ravi Varman Thiruvadi in the Kandhaloor war

997 – Satyasraya takes over western chalukyan kingdom from his father Taila II

998-999 – Rajaraja captures Gangapadi, Nolambadi and Tadigaipadi (present day Karnataka)

1000 – Rajaraja defeats the Telugu Choda Chief Jata-Choda Bhima and installs Saktivarman I on the throne of Vengi

1000 – Rajaraja initiates a project of land survey and assessment

1006 – Western chalukyan king Satyasraya invades Vengi

1007 – Invasion of western Chalukya by Rajendra I

1010 – Completion of construction of Brihadeeswara Temple at Thanjavur

1012 – Rajendra (son of Rajaraja) installed as yuvaraja

1015 – Rajaraja dies

1012-44 – Reign of Rajendra I

CHRONOLOGY CHART OF THE IMPERIAL CHOLA DYNASTY

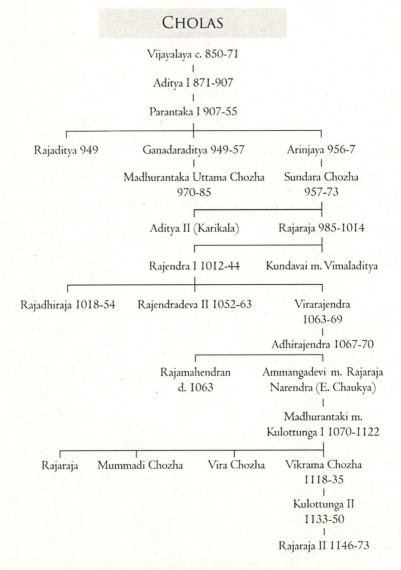

CHOLAS

Vijayalaya c. 850-71

Aditya I 871-907

Parantaka I 907-55

Rajaditya 949

Ganadaraditya 949-57

Madhurantaka Uttama Chozha 970-85

Arinjaya 956-7

Sundara Chozha 957-73

Aditya II (Karikala)

Rajaraja 985-1014

Rajendra I 1012-44

Kundavai m. Vimaladitya

Rajadhiraja 1018-54

Rajendradeva II 1052-63

Virarajendra 1063-69

Adhirajendra 1067-70

Rajamahendran d. 1063

Ammangadevi m. Rajaraja Narendra (E. Chaukya)

Madhurantaki m. Kulottunga I 1070-1122

Rajaraja

Mummadi Chozha

Vira Chozha

Vikrama Chozha 1118-35

Kulottunga II 1133-50

Rajaraja II 1146-73

Fig. 3 - Chronology chart of the Chola Dynasty

PREFACE

Many novels and books have been written on Rajaraja, or Arulmozhivarman, as he was called before his ascension to the Chola throne. Films and TV serials have been made on a modest scale. In the 1950s, novelist Kalki Krishnamurthy published *Ponniyin Selvan* as a weekly series in the Tamil magazine Kalki. Even today, the novel has a cult following and a massive fan base among readers across several generations. A popular film on Rajaraja Cholan with thespian actor Sivaji Ganesan in the lead role was released in 1973 and received critical acclaim. In 2010, a spectacular celebration was organised to celebrate the 1000th year of the Brihadeeswara temple, built by Rajaraja in Thanjavur. A film is also reportedly under making by director Mani Ratnam based on Kalki's magnum opus. Several history books, particularly Nilakanta Sastri's *The Colas*, a landmark volume on the Chola dynasty, and Champakalakshmi's *Trade, Ideology and Urbanisation* provide a good narrative on the reign of the emperor, as a part of a larger setting. Yet they are not enough, considering the colossal changes that took place in *Thamizhagam* during the 25 years of his reign from 985 CE and beyond. Till today, there is no publication in English, to my knowledge, that comprehensively covers the regime of this illustrious empire builder, almost subscribing to the anguish of the people of the South that their history has been given second place.

In 2010, the Tamil Nadu government organised a well-advertised event in Thanjavur to celebrate the 1000th year of the Brihadeeswara temple, which has survived as a living testimony, notwithstanding its inanimate stone and granite structure, of the grandeur of the Chola Empire. The event and the glittering display of the relics of the empire only whetted one's appetite for a ringside view of Rajaraja's exploits and rule and the massive economic, cultural, political, administrative and spiritual transformations that took place during his eventful regime.

My own interest in Rajaraja Cholan dates back to the sixties when my sister and I used to wait anxiously for the paper boy to deliver the weekly *Kalki* magazine every Sunday morning. The clamour to have a first look at the week's episode often led to a fist fight!

It was much later in life, when I started editing the magazine called '*ghadar jari hai*' which focused on bringing to the readers a non-Eurocentric view of Indian history, that I got a chance to study and write a few critical articles on the culture, administration and value systems of the Chola Empire.

I guess my bedtime reading aloud of *Ponniyin Selvan* and other historical novels to my son, transmitted to him large doses of the passion I had for Indian history. His graduation days in History (Honours) — it's a mystery to me how the word 'Honours' adds solemnity to a degree course — gave me an opportunity to pour through history books recommended in his syllabus.

A massive amount of information is undoubtedly available on Rajaraja Chola from stone inscriptions, copper plates, coins, manuscripts and architectural findings, though historians have noted the disappearance of several literary works belonging to his period with gloom. But the challenge was to present the story of Rajaraja in an interesting way, particularly to the millennials, without in any way undermining the authenticity and veracity of the narrative. This is easier said than done. Even well-established historians differ violently, in the academic sense, on their interpretation of historical facts surrounding his imperial rule. Rajaraja's regime has been variously categorised as 'tyrannical' at one end to nothing less than a 'golden age' at the other and more often as a chronicle of 'plunder and piety'.

In a way, I envied Kalki, the author. He was an incomparable storyteller who could weave a web of conspiracies and romance around Rajaraja to win an exalted place for the emperor in the hearts of his readers. As a writer of fiction, he could idealise the past, and write his weekly episodes in absorbing style. He could steer away from the social and political upheavals during

Rajaraja's regime and write long and captivating pages around conversations of lovers in the palace gardens and the escapades of spies and conspirators. Many of those who attended the 2010 celebrations at Thanjavur, and most importantly the organisers, would have patently harboured this romantic picture of the emperor. We often fall into the trap of hero worship as easily as a honeybee falls into sundew. Added to this, governments often love to talk about the grandeur of the past to lull people into forgetting their existential problems.

At the other extreme, there are many who dismiss history as irrelevant in today's changing world. For them, the society that existed 1000 years back and events connected to it are feudal, backward and anachronistic. But a civilisation which forgets its history has nothing to build on for its future. Negating one's heritage opens the door to subjugation by some other 'superior culture' of an 'advanced' civilisation. This is what happened during the colonial conquests when a section of the freedom movement failed to draw inspiration from our rich heritage and instead succumbed to western thought.

One way to write history is to acknowledge that the chariot of time is being drawn by men larger than life, before whom ordinary mortals scatter away in fear and the world's thoroughfares bend themselves to the compulsion of its wheels. The rise of an empire and the exploits of a king are portrayed as the roaring of the ocean as it sweeps away everything in its path inexorably, as an orchestra master whose wave of the wand ensures perfect harmony.

The other way to present history is to argue that it is the broad thoroughfares of the world, which in the first place, let the chariot of time be driven by chosen men and women. It is to acknowledge that the rise and fall of kingdoms are not the result of the strengths and weaknesses of kings and queens alone but an inevitable outcome of the greater rhythm of world events. It is to accept that it is the laughter and tears, the sleeping and eating, and the fortunes and hardships of the productive forces of society which determine the rise and fall of an empire.

It is from the second outlook that I have approached the history of Rajaraja Cholan, as one shaped by the expansion of agriculture, the rise of centres of production, the *nagarams*, and the development of a web of internal and external trade networks. The development of art, architecture, sculpture, poetry and literature to their sublime heights is not attributed to the emperor's genius alone. Having made this point, one has to give credit to Rajaraja for uniting the entire South under his tiger sigil, for erecting the *dakshina meru*, the centre of the cosmos, in the form of the Thanjavur temple, at his capital and developing the brilliant iconography of Saivism, without which the Chola imperial empire could not have survived for more than four centuries.

I have tried to present the chapters in this book in a way that is easy on the reader. Each chapter represents a particular aspect of the reign of Rajaraja, not necessarily presented in a chronological order. An effort has been made to address points of divergence, controversies and allegations about the period as objectively as possible.

There are huge expectations among the youth today to learn more about our rich heritage from authentic sources. I hope this book encourages them on their illuminating journey.

1

THE GREAT ONE
WHO MEASURED THE EARTH

The Mauryan emperor Ashoka and the Chola emperor Rajaraja have many things in common though they were separated by a thousand leagues and 1300 years. Ashoka swept the entire northern part of the Indian subcontinent with his massive army to build the first imperial empire of the subcontinent through fire and sword. Rajaraja assembled a marauding army, no less audacious, to build the first imperial empire of the South after reducing several cities to ashes and charred bones. The black deed once done, both the emperors sheathed their respective swords and turned into sober men to propagate peace and religion. Ashoka called himself *devanampiya*, the beloved of the Gods, while Rajaraja lent his name to the main deity, Rajarajeswara, of the Thanjavur temple, apt names for the union of the sacred with the secular. The canonisation of Saivite hymns by the southern emperor paralleled the code of Dhamma that Ashoka composed and propagated with passion. Grim thoughts about past deeds notwithstanding, both the monarchs revitalised architecture and built imposing temples and stupas. While leaning closer to a particular religion or sect, both of them accepted and encouraged other religious and philosophical sects. Ashoka recorded details of his reign in stone edicts while Rajaraja improvised the method of recording inscriptions on stone, both of which have lasted centuries. Both believed in recording their histories in the language of the people. In the final analysis, their good deeds were remembered more than their bloody past. And undeniably, the Mauryan Empire was the largest that India had known while the Chola Empire was the longest. It is from the inscriptions of the Mauryan empire that we come to know that the beginnings of the Chola lineage goes at least as far back as 300 BCE if not a couple of centuries earlier. In fact, there is ample evidence that southern India had a flourishing commerce with western countries and with those in the East as far as China[1]. And the Cholas never disappeared from the pages of history until the end of the 13th century CE.

In this entire period, very few would contest the fact that it is with the accession of Rajaraja Chola that the land of Tamils entered upon centuries of grandeur. Aside from ruthless conquests and a regular stream of income from fealties, this was made possible by many other factors: expansion of agriculture, the rise of *nagarams* – the trading and craft centres with their new productive forces, the maturing of self-governing corporate bodies such as the *sabhas* and *urs*, increase in inland and overseas trade networks, and overall strengthening of the administrative and military apparatus. No less important to the stability of his empire was the compelling iconography of Saivism[2] and the *bhakti* movement[3].

According to tradition, the Chola country comprised the land locked between two rivers, both called Vellaru in the north and the south, and bounded by the sea in the east and Kottaikarai in the west[4]. 'The Cholas adopted the tiger as their crest; the same animal was configured on their banner'[5], while there is evidence that another branch of the ancient Chola lineage adopted the lion crest[6]. But more purposeful than the royal banner was 'the special banner of the just Chola race', the river Kaveri, 'for she never failed them in the most protracted drought'. Those who controlled the river basin, controlled the South, just as those kingdoms which held sway over the Ganges basin, also ruled over the North. The earliest mention of the Cholas comes from records of an abortive attempt by a Mauryan invasion led by Bindusara, the father of the illustrious monarch Ashoka, eloquently described by the Sangam poet Mamulanar[7]. The Mauryas cut for their chariots a new path across rocky mountains and launched an invasion with their feudatory, the Vadugars, in the vanguard, but were stopped in their tracks by the Mohur chieftain at South Arcot district[8]. Later inscriptions make it clear that this was indeed a one-time misdirected adventure, quite uncharacteristic of the great emperor. That seems to be the last time that South India faced a major invasion from the far north. Ashokan edicts distinctly admit that the Tamil kingdoms were never subject to him. The emperor of the Gupta dynasty, Samudragupta, came down as far as Kanchipuram reportedly, 'but was wise enough to accept pretended pledges of fealty over actually subduing these alien lands'[9]. Till then, the South had never yielded to invaders from the northern empires. But that was cold comfort considering that Thamizhagam never had a moment's peace from internal squabbles and aggression from across its borders by neighbouring kingdoms.

Tamil legend has it that the Chera, Pandya and Chola were brothers from Korkai, near the mouth of the Tamiraparani river[10], who separated later, the Pandya deciding to stay back and the other two leaving home to try their fortunes elsewhere. The sibling bond notwithstanding, their offsprings, the Pandyas, Cholas, and the Cheras had equal passion for love and war, enacted in five different eco-cultural regions. These five regions of the Tamil country, called the *aintinai*, developed a distinct, and often deadly variety of poetic imagery exulting in an act of love accompanied by an act of war. The hilly region, *kurinji*, excelled in poems on the diad of 'pre-nuptial love and cattle raiding'. The poets of the dry lands, *palai*, matched the mood of the landscape with their soulful lyrics on 'long separation of lovers and the laying waste of the countryside'. Those in the woodlands, *mullai*, specialised in the 'brief parting of lovers and on raiding expeditions'. The bards of the cultivated plains, *marudam*, predictably indulged in 'post-nuptial love, the wiles of courtesans and on siege'. Finally, the coast, *neythal*, boasted of poets who settled to singing the painful 'parting of fishermen's wives from their lords and on pitched battle'[11]. On the whole, the Tamil people had a penchant for different types of aggression and war which kept them happily engaged with each other, supplemented by invaders from across the Krishna and Tungabhadra in the north and down south from Lanka, who stepped into their landscapes now and then with evil intentions.

Coming back to tracing the origins of the Cholas, there is further mention about the Chola country around the first century of the first millennium in the *Periplus Maris Erythraei*, a very valuable handbook written by a Greek merchant and a little later by Pliny the Elder, a Roman author. But, indisputably, the Cholas had a much earlier origin considering that right from the 6th century BCE there was a thriving commerce between coastal Thamizhagam and Western countries as well as countries in the east such as China, Malaya and Cambodia. Archaeological excavations have irrefutably established the existence of towns and ports such as Madurai, Uraiyur and Puhar from at least the middle of the first millennium BCE[12] giving Tamil civilisation an equal footing with the second urbanisation of the North. From very early days, the relationship between the Cholas and Lanka had a baffling mix of respect and repugnance. The Mahavamsa account of the intercourse between the Chola country and the island of Lanka while 'sufficiently authentic and precise'[13] is also very illuminating. The chronicle has a lot to say about the relation between the Damilas and the natives of the island. In the middle of the 2nd century BCE, King Elara[14] from the Chola country came to the island and overpowered the local king Asela and ruled for forty four years 'with even justice towards friend and foe on occasions of disputes at law'[15]. King Elara was so impartial to the high and low when it came to dispensing justice, that 'he sentenced his only son to death for having unwittingly caused the death of a young calf by driving the wheel of his chariot over his neck'[16]. But all this did not deter the Lankan king Dutthagamani, who wanted to restore political unity in the island and reinstate the Buddhist doctrine, to wage war and kill Elara outside the walls of Anuradhapura, which city Rajaraja would later reclaim as his Lankan capital. On the spot where Elara's body had fallen, the Lankan king 'built a monument and ordained worship'[17]. This love and hate relationship between the kingdoms would continue for centuries later.

By the time the new lineage of Cholas of the Vijayalaya line appeared in the ninth century, like a phoenix rising from its Sangam era ashes, they had gathered impressive credentials to claim ownership of the Kaveri basin. The

Cholas set about stretching their history to earlier times than was believed till then, but nothing can prepare us for the fantastic history that Rajaraja's son Rajendra I recorded the origins of the Cholas[18] in the Thiruvalangadu copper plates[19] carrying the royal seal. The *prashasti*[20] of the Chola family conveyed by the Sanskrit portion[21] of the copper plate contains 271 lines of the most exquisite Puranic pedigree that any king would aspire for. The genealogy starts in verse 4 from no less an ancestor as the 'Sun and Manu, the latter of whom was produced from the Sun by concentration of mind'[22]. 'These were rooted in the epic-Puranic traditions of the Suryavamsa (solar lineage)[23] and Chandravamsa (lunar lineage). Then follows Manu's son Ikshvaku. The next few verses 'supply names of kings who ruled in the Krita, Treta and the Dvapara ages and as such can hardly be of any interest to the student of history, excepting perhaps the eponymous name Chola and the titles Rajakesarivarman and Parakesarin of the Treta age'[24].

Fig. 4 — Royal seal of the Chola Dynasty

Having established the origin of the Chola Empire to some unbelievably ancient point in time not less than 4 million years ago, the *prashasti* comes down to the Chola rulers of the Kali age. The first king mentioned is Perunatkilli who, born in this same family, was ostensibly highly learned. Next comes the most famous of the Sangam[25] kings, Kalikala, who renovated the town of Kanchi with gold and established his fame by constructing flood-embankments for the river Kaveri. The poet explains the name Kalikala as 'the god of Death (*Kala*)' either to the *Kali* epoch itself or to the more probable elephants (*kari*) of his enemies. It is worth mentioning here that the usual Tamil tradition of relating Karikala (rather than Kalikala) to the 'the burnt-leg' was derived from an accident which happened to the king while he was yet a boy[26]. But our poet of the weighty Thiruvalangadu plates was either ignorant of this or purposely ignored the earlier tradition. In that family was born Kochengannan, whose former birth as a spider and deep devotion to Siva are described in verse. The story of Kochengannan finds place in the *Periyapuranam*[27] under the name Kochengatchola-Nayanar. He is reputed to have been equally good at wielding the sword and muttering psalms, for he constructed a number of Siva temples in the Chola country while finding the time and energy to defeat the Chera king at Kalumalam.

Up to this point, the Kings of the first list belong to a very ancient mythical past and those of the second list starting from Kochengannan can be traced to the more tangible Sangam period, around the first millennium CE or earlier. There is no authentic information on many of the kings for 'of these several names in these legendary lists, which are by no means identical with one another, only two or three names appear to be historical. Karikala, Kochenganan and probably also Killi may be identified with the kings of the same name of whom we hear in the Tamil literature of the Sangam age'[28]. Karikalan and Kochenganan definitely stand out prominently and 'their memory is cherished in song and legend by a loving posterity'[29] for ostensibly very good reasons. In the great battle of Venni, Karikala handed out a crushing defeat to the Pandyas and Cheras, which Rajaraja would repeat even more emphatically a thousand years later. The war confederacy of the Pandyas and Cheras would haunt the Cholas again when they try to regain their kingdom later after centuries of oblivion.

This mythical ancestry tracing of their descent from the sun acquired more names as the Chola Empire expanded. The Anbil plates mention fifteen names before Vijayalya, the founder of the imperial line of Cholas. The Thiruvalangadu plates swell the list to forty-four and the Kanyakumari list runs up to fifty-two. But no two lists agree though some names are common between them[30]. The Kanyakumari inscriptions provide a quaint story of how the eponymous Chola landed in the South. The Chola was in pursuit of a Rakshasa, who had assumed the form of an antelope. After putting an end to the demon, the Chola chanced upon the great river Kaveri and found that it 'carried the very ambrosia, which the *devas* had churned with great effort out of the ocean'. After bathing in the river, he looked around for some Brahmanas, apparently to bestow gifts on them, but finding none, summoned them from Aryavarta and settled them down. He then cleared the forest, planted betel leaves, areca trees, fruit trees, and laid out gardens. Finally he gave the river Kaveri a status even higher than the Ganga by declaring that 'people bathe in the river Ganga and do penance in order to obtain *svarga*; but a bath in the Kaveri and penance on her bank would take those who do them to regions higher than svarga'[31]. If we put aside the obvious implausibility of this legend, then what stands out is the eagerness of the new lineage of Cholas to earn themselves the respectability of the orthodox North by importing its Brahmanas while at the same time giving the river Kaveri an edge over her more established cousin, the Ganga.

Beginning from the middle of the 9th century to the end of the 12th century, the Cholas gradually rose to an imperial position and ultimately dominated the entire region of South India between the Tungabhadra and Kanyakumari, including parts of Lanka and the entire Maldives. There is no clear evidence to trace the connections between the early Cholas of the Sangam period and the later Cholas who literally rose from obscurity in the 9th century, save for a few scattered claims to the lineage. The early Cholas had lost their pre-eminence during the Kalabhra[32] period between the 3rd and 6th centuries and had literally been reduced to feudatories of the more powerful Pandya and Pallava kingdoms. It is from this desperate position that we come across their first attempts to establish an empire which expanded into the largest empire that the South had ever seen.

During this period of roughly two and half centuries, the Cholas were constantly at war with their neighbours. In the northern part of their empire, it was the Western Chalukyas who were the major threat. It was with the help of the Eastern Chalukyas that the Cholas kept their borders intact. But the prolonged hostility between the two powers took its toll and feudatory powers such as the Pandyas and Hoysalas took advantage of the situation driving the empire to collapse.

The goddess of fortune smiled on the Chola Empire starting with the capture of Thanjavur from the Mutharaiyar chieftains around 850 CE by Vijayalaya Chola and kept at it for another four centuries. Vijayalaya established Uraiyur, near present day Tiruchirapally, as his power centre right in the middle of the Kaveri basin. 'With Vijayalaya commences a regular genealogy of the Cholas whose capital was Thanjavur'[33]. The new line of Cholas claimed an unbroken history from the Sangam age but 'barring the names of a few kings and some common legends, e.g., that of Manu sentencing his son to death as he had by an accident crushed a calf to death under his chariot-wheel, and the story of Sibi rescuing a dove from the pursuit of a vulture by offering it his own flesh—there is nothing to indicate the relation in which the Cholas of the Vijayalaya line stood to those of an earlier time mentioned in early Tamil literature'[34]. As we go on, we will be coming across several instances of careful image building exercises of the Chola dynasty that can only make one gape with wonder. Vijayalaya was still not free from the clutches of bigger powers and was content to function as a feudatory of the Pallavas but the death knell started ringing furiously for his adversaries with his advent. From here on, the Cholas played the Pallavas, who ruled north of the Kaveri river, against the Pandyas, who controlled the south of the river until they could exhaust both of them and establish their own independent regime.

Vijayalaya's son, Aditya I, defeated the Pallava king Aparajita – his former lord – in battle and took possession of his country, Tondaimandalam, the region around present day Chennai. But that was before he won a battle for the Pallava king at Thirupurambiyam, near Kumbakonam, somewhere around 879 CE. This battle was the next turning point in the history of South India and one that would put the region firmly under the grip of the Cholas. In the battle, the Cholas and the Gangas helped the Pallava king Aparajita to defeat the Pandya king Varaguna, but while the 'Pandyas never recovered from this staggering blow', it did no good to the Pallavas either. The latter 'though victory remained with them in the battle, owed it more to their allies than to their own strength'[35] which was a pity. Ostensibly, the Pallavas by then were suffering from severe war fatigue, having fought incessant wars on two fronts with the Pandyas and the Chalukyas. Aditya 'soon discovered his advantage and commanded the strength and energy to pursue it'. Added to the advantage was that his possible competitor, the Ganga monarch, Prithvipathi I had also perished in the battle. By all accounts, the Pallava king was so gratified that he had let Aditya 'to keep what his father had taken from the Muttaraiyars'[36] and also topped this with some new territory. But this only whetted Aditya's appetite for more until he decided to do away with their long-term ally, Aparajita, when he was seated on an elephant. Aditya who ascended the Chola throne around 870 CE, when he was still a subordinate ally of the Pallavas, emerged a king in his own right during the 36 years of his reign and there was no stopping the Chola juggernaut from then on. At the time of the battle we had heard of earlier, 'the Cholas held a small principality including Thanjavur and Uraiyur, but within twenty five years, their power became formidable', thanks to Aditya, 'the remarkable warrior and able diplomat'[37].

It was Aditya, like all repentant conquerors, who built a row of large temples of Siva, 'as if it were banners of his own victories, lofty and unacquainted with collapse, was built of stone on the two banks of the Kaveri from the Sahya mountain, inhabited by the lordly elephants whose cheeks dripped with (their) temple juice incessantly flowing, even up to the ocean which has the moon playing on the folds of its big restless waves'[38].

The Gangas, who were potential competitors to the Cholas, now accepted the latter's suzerainty with Prithvipathi II, the son of the slain Ganga king, presenting a silver vessel to the temple at Thakkolam, situated within the Chola realm[39]. Aditya reportedly married both a Pallava and a Rashtrakuta princess, the daughter of Krishna II[40], in pursuit of an elusive peace, since his grandson later had to wage war against the Rashtrakuta king Krishna III. There was never a loyal ally nor a stubborn adversary for the Cholas.

Aditya's son Parantaka I was a committed devotee of Siva, as all his successors would be later, but no less a warrior. Perhaps the entire Chola clan drew warlike inspiration from the fearsome dancing god, clothed in tiger skin with snakes coiled around his throat and arms. When Aditya died, Parantaka raised a shrine over his sepulchre, establishing a Linga on it, a Saivite adaptation of the Buddhist practice of erecting memorial stupas'[41]. From the time of Vijayalaya, the Cholas remained ardent saivites and 'were not slow to acquire for themselves a pedigree'. Vijayalaya built a Durga temple at Thanjavur, and Aditya built a number of temples for Siva, but the biggest effort to acquire a flawless pedigree would be Rajaraja's.

As soon as Parantaka sat on the throne, the Rashtrakutas led by Krishna II, who were lying quiet for a while after consummating a matrimonial alliance with Aditya, were back at the doors of the Chola kingdom with their war elephants. Parantaka repulsed them successfully and then drove the Pandya king right into the sea (the Bay of Bengal evidently) and carried his conquests even into Lanka across the ocean, though there are other reports that it is the Pandya and Lanka armies which invaded Chola territory and were defeated[42]. This explains the titles *maduraikonda* (one who conquered Madurai) and *maduraiyum-ezhamum-konda* (one who conquered Madurai and Lanka) often found added to the name of Parantaka in inscriptions, though he never brought Lanka under his control, as Rajaraja would later. Since Madurai and Lanka were raided by a succession of Chola kings, these titles came in handy for all of them. Some historians believe that Parantaka 'built the golden hall called Dabhrasabha (at Chidambaram) and thereby excelled Kubera, the friend of Siva'[43] but other sources such as the Leyden plates[44], state that he only covered the hall with gold! In either case, the gold came from the coffers of an adversary. He ruled over forty-eight years, among the longest of the Chola reigns, but the end of his reign could have been more peaceful. The Rashtrakutas, who could never stomach their earlier defeats, were back again in big force, this time with Krishna III at the head of the invasion. A bloody battle ensued in which Parantaka's eldest son, Rajaditya, was killed. Parantaka himself did not survive much longer and a pall of gloom settled on the Chola Empire for over three decades until Rajaraja restored the lost territories.

It is said that Rajaditya defeated king Krishnaraja in battle, even when death took him away from the battlefield, and he went predictably to heaven. The reference here is evidently to the battle of Thakkolam in which the Rashtrakuta king Krishna III and his Ganga feudatory Butuga jointly defeated and killed Rajaditya who was fighting from the back of an elephant. The summary way in which Rajaditya had been disposed of by the author of the Thiruvalangadu plates show that probably he did not succeed to the throne, although the Leyden plates explicitly state that after the death of Parantaka, Rajaditya "ruled" the kingdom. Either way, Rajaditya barely had enough time to savour his throne.

Rajaditya's brother, Gandaraditya ascended to the throne next. He produced a son who went by the name of Madhurantaka, who founded a town after his own name on the northern bank of the river Kaveri. The next king who ascended the throne, is Arindama (Arinjaya), the third son of Parantaka. His rule was evidently neither much to talk about nor long. From the Melpadi inscription[45], we learn that Rajaraja I erected the Siva temple called Arinjesvara (the modern Cholesvara) as a *pallippadai* (tomb-shrine) to his grandfather Arinjaya who was also known as *arrur-tunjinadeva* (the lord who slept at Arrur). Arrur, where Arinjaya appears to have died must be distinct from Tondaiman-Arrur, where Aditya I is believed to have died. The Cholas manifestly had a hard time subduing their enemies.

The next to ascend the throne was Sundara Chola Parantaka II whose fame rose to great heights. He initially enjoyed astounding victories thanks to his trustworthy allies, the Western Gangas, the Kodumbalur chiefs and the Cheras. The conquest of Madurai won him the title of 'maduraikonda', as it did for his predecessors. He achieved a phenomenal victory when he defeated the combined forces of the Pandyas and the king of Lanka at the battle of Vellur an alliance that had haunted the Cholas earlier and would continue to haunt them. One of the glorious deeds he committed was at a place called Chevura where he fought a vicious battle and caused 'rivers of blood to flow'[46]. But his fortunes changed in later years, when, at the battle of Thakkolam in 949, the army of Krishna III, the Rashtrakuta king, handed him a resounding defeat. Both Kanchipuram and Thanjavur, the power centres of the Cholas slipped out of their hands, but their resolve never weakened.

Arulmozhivarman (later named Rajaraja) was born to Sundara Chola. But for Rajaraja the path to the throne was strewn with the proverbial thorns. After the death of Sundara Chola, his wife Vanavan-Mahadevi is stated to have committed sati, but that is not certain. His son Aditya Karikala the crown prince, killed the Pandya king Vira-Pandya—the long-time elusive enemy of the Cholas—in a deadly battle, brought his head to his capital, and hung it on a spike. This set the precedent for more horror stories later.

Many kings of this period in the South seem to have excelled at cutting off the heads of their foes and have promptly added the phrase 'talaikonda' (having cut off the head) to their already long titles. But, purportedly, there is a kinder way to look at this since 'it appears, however, that the true meaning of the phrase is that the vanquished king had to acknowledge his defeat by humbling himself before the conqueror in a particular manner as it were, by placing his head at the disposal of the conqueror'. Inscriptions which describe the same event as *avan mudi mel vaittu* assuagingly indicate that the 'process "taking the head" consisted in the vanquished king bowing and touching with his head the feet of the conqueror seated in an open darbar'. This seems to be plausible considering that a few centuries later Krishna Deva Raya, after defeating Adil Shah of Bijapur, demanded that as the price of peace the vanquished should visit his darbar and kiss his foot[47].

This is further confirmed by the fact that among the practices of the Chola times, 'the king from Gangai-konda Cholapuram (the capital constructed by Rajendra, the son of Rajaraja) mounted his elephant by placing his foot on the head of his feudatory'[48]. In effect, the vanquished king either left his writhing head in the battle or his battered honour.

Before we move on, we need to backtrack a little and have a closer look at Sundara Chola's reign. It was during his time that the Cholas made a remarkable recovery from the earlier Rashtrakuta invasions. Their fealty status was a distant memory now, but, after all the frenzied fighting in the South, the alliance of the Pandya and Lanka was still intact. It is inferred that he died in the golden palace of Kanchipuram in the north of his empire while directing the war front affairs, earning the title of *pon malgaiyil tunjina deva* (the lord who slept at the golden palace). He was a man of letters and encouraged both Tamil and Sanskrit. 'A highly poetic eulogium of his reign, in the commentary of *Virasozhiyam*, bears witness to his patronage of letters. His last days were clouded by a domestic tragedy, to put it mildly. The king ordered the confiscation and sale of properties of some people for treason and murder of Aditya Karikala'[49]. The first record of this murder appeared during Rajaraja's reign which meant that it was suppressed during the entire reign of Uttama Chola, Rajaraja's uncle, with 'Sundara Chola himself having died of a broken heart soon after the murder (of his son) or having the natural course of justice obstructed by a powerful conspiracy'[50]. Soman, Ravidasan and Parameswaran, who were high ranked Brahmana officials in the army were accused of the murder. It can be inferred that Uttama coveted the throne and made it clear that the throne was his by right and that his cousin (Sundara Chola) and his children were usurpers. This argument did have its weight since, after the death of Gandaraditya, the throne belonged to his direct son, Uttama, but the latter being too young was denied the throne. Instead Gandaraditya's brothers ruled after him. The fact that Rajaraja agreed to wait for his turn and let his uncle, who allegedly masterminded Aditya's murder, rule, raises doubts about a deep palace intrigue, which even the monarch Sundara Chola dare not investigate.

The Leyden plates cover up this issue and report that that Madhurantaka (later named Uttama Chola), the son of Gandaraditya, succeeded straightway after the death of Aditya Karikala. Perhaps we have to give credence to the information furnished in the Thiruvalangadu plates and accept that while by right the succession was Rajaraja's, he voluntarily permitted his uncle Madhurantaka to rule the kingdom, on the understanding that he would himself he chosen for the office of the heir-apparent. Madhurantaka ruled the kingdom virtuously as a pious devotee of Siva, something unexpected of a murderous king. After Madurantaka, Arulmozhivarman (Rajaraja) was installed in the administration of the kingdom amidst the rejoicings of his people. His *digvijaya* or the conquest of the four quarters and the *tulabhara* i.e., 'weighing oneself against gold' were promptly organised[51]. Once in power, his chariots of war flaunting the tiger pennants criss-crossed the southern portion of the subcontinent until, by the end of his rule, his realm 'had grown to be an extensive and well-knit empire efficiently organised and administered, rich in resources, possessed of a powerful standing army, well-tried and equal to the greatest enterprises'[52].

Rajaraja gave himself grandiose titles such as *raja-rajadhiraja* (king of kings), and *ulagalanda perumal* (the great one who measured the earth), as most emperors did before him, and no one seemed to mind. A more modest interpretation of the second title would 'apply to the king who is known to have ordered a great land survey for revenue purposes'. A conceited meaning would be to compare the king 'to the god Vishnu who, according to a famous ancient myth, encompassed the universe with his three strides'[53]. The king's claim to Kshatriya status is reflected in his 'title of Kshatriya-shikamani (crest jewel of the Kshatriyas)'[54].

Notwithstanding his great authority and the mythical lineage, Rajaraja was a product of titanic changes in the South. His formidable military conquests and administrative genius rested on certain conditions maturing in the economic base of the region. But there is very little written record of his personality. 'No eyewitness has rendered to Rajaraja the service which Nuniz and Paes did to Krishna Deva Raya. There is not even a well-attested statue or a painting of this king that has come down to us. All that we know of his reign, however, and that is not little, attests his potent personality and the firm grasp of his intellect which allowed nothing to escape its vigilance and applied itself with as much vigour to the minutest details as to the sublimest ambitions of statecraft'[55].

His charities to temples were legendary, as was the valour of his army who brought the entire South under the suzerainty of the great monarch. Both in warfare and in peacetime administration he had no equal. He was so successful in keeping the turbulent spirits of his enemies and feudatories under check that the Chola Empire expanded to horizons never before reached. Is it any wonder that he is considered as the greatest of all Chola rulers given the fact that he restored Chola supremacy in the Kaveri basin after several centuries? He laid the foundation for the rule of his son, Rajendra I, under whom the empire stretched to its farthest and carried its flag beyond the seas.

In his reign, powerful productive forces were unleashed to take the empire to new heights in art, architecture, religion, literature, administration, statecraft, military and naval might. Was it a period of harmony between these productive forces and the imperial state, or was it a period of contention? Could his rule be termed as progressive imperialism, or a monarchy restricting the fullest growth of the new forces? These are questions that we will be grappling with as we go ahead with the narrative.

The commissioning of Nambiyandar Nambi to compile the *Tirumurai* and the erection of the Brihadeeswara temple with the world's tallest *vimana* (temple tower) were highlights of his rule. Were these simple acts of devotion or the acts of a sublime intellect to create a unified empire and loyal subjects around the temple as the heartbeat of the empire?

His empire building was extremely ambitious and no less ruthless. In addition to tracing his origin from the Sun god to the earthly Vijayalaya, 'eulogies in his inscriptions tell us that after defeating the allied forces of the Pandya, Kerala and Sri Lanka, he occupied the Pandyan country, the northern part of Sri Lanka, and the southern parts of Karnataka, and sent his army further north to Kalinga'[56]. The Solamarttanda–chaturvedimangalam inscription modestly describes that 'added to the usual list of his conquest, were the "Twelve thousand islands of the sea" by which name the Maldives are said to have been known in ancient times. This naval victory seems to be the last of Rajaraja's achievements, which proved to be the forerunner of still greater conquests of his son in later times'[57]. Other inscriptions admit with unrestrained glee that he destroyed the town of Madurai, conquered the haughty kings of Kollam, Koliadesam and Kodungolur and that the kings of the sea waited on him. 'In China, the names of the three envoys sent by Rajaraja I and Rajendra I are recorded in the official annals of the Song dynasty'[58]. It does not require a genius to conjecture that the attacks of the father-son duo on the Maldive islands, Sri Lanka and the Malay Peninsula 'was meant to get hegemony in the East-West maritime trade that rapidly developed from the ninth century when the Abbasids in the West and the Tang dynasty in the East were flourishing'[59]. So, here was an imperial empire in the making in the South as early as the ninth century. After all, the kings of the sea did wait on Rajaraja! However, military might may not have been the only factor for 'this expansion of the Chola overlordship under Rajaraja and Rajendra from their core domain in the Kaveri basin to the entire Tamil plain and its adjacent upland, it was not achieved nor was it maintained by military means alone'. Exemplary moral behaviour may have also contributed to this. 'Chola kings… were exemplars of medieval South Indian kingship and models of appropriate rulership for chiefs of the macro region; it was less the might of the Chola rulers than it was their moral appropriateness that provided the basis of Chola rule over the Coramandel plain'.

The 1000th anniversary celebrations of the Thanjavur temple was an occasion to dig up good and bad things about the emperor. The temple itself was an imperial temple, closely connected with the ruling dynasty, exemplified by the fact that 'it was also known as Raja-rajeshwara temple after the king!'[60] While his grants and gifts to temples have astounded many, it is a fact that during the reign of the Cholas, lands of the oppressed were systemically appropriated and the booty from war spoils were used to fund temple construction. Sanskrit and Vedic traditions were in vogue during his reign, while at the same time the *Agama* traditions of temple construction and puja were favoured, and Tamil hymns elevated to the position of the Vedas of the south.

The emperor contributed to the growth of Tamil by popularising the *Devaram*[61], the sacred Tamil hymns of the Saivite *bhakti* saints. Whether caste inequities widened during his reign or whether the sprouting of urban centres destroyed age-old kinship and caste ties requires much study.

Rajaraja encouraged the system of *thevaradiyars*[62], by providing a monthly salary and provided living amenities for 400 temple women, 240 musicians and 50 *othuvars* to sing the *Devaram* daily in temples. This has come under criticism from present day commentators, but unjustly so, as we will see in the final chapter.

Thanks to hundreds of stone inscriptions belonging to the period we have a well-informed account of Rajaraja's life and exploits. 'The illustrious Rajaraja I, under whom the South Indian monarchy attained a sweep and splendour till then unknown, conceived the idea of prefixing to his inscriptions a set historical introduction recounting in an ornate and poetic style of Tamil, the main achievements of his reign and kept up-to-date by additions made to it from time to time'[63]. But earlier kings and chiefs left the writing of the *prashasti* to the 'fancy of the poet-composer'. Rajaraja put an end to this fancy poetry writing and introduced historical documentation. He ordered the writing to be in a set form and in the language of the people. He 'initiated a practice which, as it was kept up by his successors, not only satisfied the boundless vanity of his race of kings, but furnishes to the historian a formal record of exceptional value of the transactions of each reign'[64]. Nevertheless, the inscriptions do have pronouncements to falter kings, which do not always reflect reality, and which need a keen eye.

Many of the inscriptions are records of gifts and of no real value in understanding the period under study. But records of larger gifts, particularly from the ruling circles, throw light on prevailing taxes, privileges, administrative protocols and policy towards a particular region or community of people. Of immense value are the stone inscriptions on the walls of the Thanjavur temple built by Rajaraja. They provide details of the temple economy and administration. 'Quite a number of other fairly long inscriptions give interesting information about the constitution and functions of village assemblies, the part played by craft and trade guilds in the economic and artistic life of the country, the courses of study and the numbers of pupils and teachers in important educational centres, and so on'[65].

Long inscriptions on stone or copper follow a certain pattern. The opening verses invoke either one or more deities of the ruler's choice. This is followed by a preamble called the *prashasti* in Sanskrit or *meykeerthi* in Tamil, which is a short eulogy of the ruler. Then comes a detailed description of the gift and to which institution it was made followed by various conditionalities for the enjoyment of the gift. Finally, the inscription ends with a fairly fearsome warning directed at those who would in any way obstruct or thwart the gift.

A typical *meykeerthi* recording the accomplishments of Rajaraja reads like this:

Hail! Prosperity! In the 21st year of (the reign of) the illustrious Ko-Raja-Rajakesarivarman, alias the illustrious Rajaraja-deva, who, while both the goddess of fortune and the great goddess of the earth, who had become his exclusive property, gave him pleasure, was pleased to destroy the ships at Kandalur and conquered by his army, which was victorious in great battles, Vengai-nadu, Gangapadi, Nolambapadi, Tadigaipadi, Kudamalainadu, Kollam, Kalingam and Ilamandalam, which is famed in the eight directions; who,-while his beauty was increasing, and while he was resplendent (to such an extent) that he was always worthy to be worshipped,-deprived the Seriyas of their splendour,-and (in words) in the twenty-first year of Soran Arumori, who possesses the river Ponni, whose waters are full of waves[66].

Fig. 5 ~ A typical inscription from Brihadeeswara Temple in Thanjavur

The point made here is that there is no dearth of information about the reign of Rajaraja Chola. But since media and communication are the monopoly of ruling classes at any given time, one has to sift fact from fiction. This is easier said than done. Referring to contemporary documentation created by friends and foes of the Chola Empire provides a fairly realistic assessment of Rajaraja. We often come across legends and myths, impossible deeds and fantastic victories in these sources. There are also rival claims about the size of the army, the brutality of conquests, the size of booty plundered, and the number of cities torched. We will be referring to many of these issues later in the narrative. Professedly, the characterisation of his rule is not one of black and white, but many shades of grey.

It is with these controversies and questions that we enter the main narrative.

2

KINGS OF THE SEA WAITED ON HIM

Rajaraja Chola was born in 947 CE into a world of greed, deceit and intrigue. But this did not unduly worry his parents, who believed that he was another 'Vishnu supporting on his two arms, long like the weapon, the glorious goddess, Sri Lakshmi, who closely embraced the whole of his body, and bearing on the palms of his hands, the *sankha* and *chakra* in the

Fig. 6 - Statue of Rajaraja on horseback

form of auspicious marks'[1]. Such endearing eccentricities about royal babies born with the insignia of Vishnu and destined to become emperors were not uncommon in the imagination of poets and parents of those times. The Naga-women of the kingdom reportedly danced on the occasion of the birth of this emperor for a very good reason because 'this king in all probability shall relieve our husband (*i.e.,* Adisesha) of the weight of the earth on his head'[2]. This was a tall call for the infant, who nevertheless took up this challenge with incredible humility and grew up into an ambitious king who would add many more such legends to his illustrious lineage.

Earlier, his grandfather Gandaraditya, 'who with his queen Sembiyan Mahadevi claims a bigger place in the domain of religion than politics'[3] had found more comfort in muttering psalms than in wielding the sword with the inevitable result that 'at his death the Chola kingdom had reduced to the size of a principality'. Taking advantage of his piousness, the Rashtrakuta king, Kannaradeva, and his Ganga feudatory, Buthuga II, had made deep inroads into the South, right upto Rameswaram. Gangaraditya's brother, Arinjaya, who succeeded him, had an extremely short stint clearing the way for Sundara Chola, his son, to step into the portals of power. Sundara Chola, promptly declared Aditya Karikala, his eldest son as yuvaraja, smelling some sort of future trouble from Gangaraditya's son. This particular gentleman, Uttama Chola, had initially renounced worldly pleasures and had turned a devout Saivite, much to the delight of his pious parents. But at some point, when the fragrance of palace pleasures had wafted into his nostrils, his piousness gave way to unmitigated ambition.

In a sparsely documented palace intrigue, in an action too dreadful to contemplate, Aditya was killed, just when he was ready to take his cup, and a truce established by Sundara Chola according to whose terms Uttama Chola entered the royal chamber and occupied the throne for years to come. Apparently, Rajaraja did not want the throne as long as his paternal uncle was 'fond of his country'. Rajaraja was promptly appointed heir-apparent, while Uttama Chola 'bore the burden of the earth'[4]. Sundara Chola had tried to regain the land lost by his uncle, Gangaraditya, to Kannaradeva.

Earlier, before his uncle decided to do away with him, Aditya Karikala had killed Vira Pandya in the South and mounted his head over a spike while his father Sundara Chola had taken his forces to the North to regain lost territory. The old man died at his golden palace in Kanchipuram, while still directing his campaigns. By the time Uttama Chola came to power, the bulk of Tondaimandalam (northern Tamil Nadu) had been recovered from the Rashtrakutas for the Chola Empire. Not much is known of Uttama's conquests, if any, but the Rashtrakutas had given place to Taila II Chalukya 'who claims a victory against Uttama Chola'[5]. Be that as it may, the 'murder of Aditya Karikala remained unavenged throughout the 16 years in which Uttama Chola ruled'. It is almost certain that Sundara Chola 'died of a broken heart soon after the murder (of his son Aditya) or after having found the natural course of justice obstructed by a powerful conspiracy'[6].

The fact that even Rajaraja, in spite of his popularity and the divine insignia on his palms, had to turn a blind eye and a deaf ear to this 'powerful conspiracy' indicates that he may not have been unhappy at all with the strange truce with his uncle. This would explain why he was loath, as the next yuvaraja, to punish the murderers of his elder sibling. Aditya had certainly not been a pushover. He had won his laurels very early as a yuvaraja in the wars against the Pandyas and Rashtrakutas. His murder would have certainly caused huge resentment among the people and the administration, if not besmirching the carefully built Chola reputation. An enigmatic obituary to the fallen prince read 'Aditya disappeared owing to his desire to see heaven. Though his subjects, with a view to dispel the blinding darkness caused by the powerful Kali (Sin), entreated Arulmozhivarman (later Rajaraja), but he, versed in the dharma of the Kshatriya, did not desire the kingdom for himself inwardly as long as his paternal uncle coveted his own (i.e., Arulmozhivarman's) country'[7]. Uttama Chola had to choose the hard life of coming to power and retaining it at a critical time, or perhaps a hard life had been chosen for him. His reign lasted only 15 years from 970 to 985 CE, when he died early probably consumed by guilt.

Rajaraja's anointment, at the age of 38, after his uncle finally released him from the agreement with his death, not only turned the fortunes of the Cholas for the better but took their empire towards its peak. His entry into kingship was avowedly breath-taking when 'the ends of the quarters heavily roared with the tumultuous sounds of the war-drums, rows of bells and bugles, kettle drums, tambourines and conches'[8] Though the king was weighed in gold (*tulabhara*) as custom demanded, he remained '*a-tula* (unequalled)'. Events after that confirmed that Rajaraja was set upon writing his initials in bold across the pages of history.

From the time he seated himself on the diamond studded, tiger emblemmed throne in 985 till the end of his reign in 1014 and right up to the 13th century, the Cholas were the undisputed rulers of South India. A strategist par excellence, Rajaraja decisively destroyed the alliance between the Pandyas, Cheras and the ruler of Ezham,[9] or Lanka. A victory over this deadly triumvirate had consistently eluded his predecessors. At the battle of Khandaloor he subdued the Cheras. He then launched a devastating attack on the Pandyas and a successful naval expedition to Lanka, which resulted in the destruction of Anuradhapura and the setting up of a Chola capital at Polonnaruwa. The decisive victory forced Mahinda V, the king of Ezham, to scamper into the hills in the south-east of the island. The Western Chaulukyas and the Rashtrakutas in the north met a similar grisly fate under the wrath of the Chola army. The Maldives were captured and became a jewel on the crown of the Cholas.

Each one of these victories left his adversaries quaking in fear while serving him as a stepping stone to the next. A closer look at how they were crafted is important to understand the imperial vision of this king, who had waited for his turn patiently while his uncle ruled. Quite early in his reign, as early as in the fourth year, Rajaraja Chola launched a massive military campaign into southern Kerala. The conquest was so triumphant that he earned the title *mummudi Chola devar*, the ruler of all three kingdoms of the South. In addition, this conquest also bestowed on him the title *kandhaloor salai kalamarutta*. This title has been consistently repeated in the various inscriptions of Rajaraja, his son Rajendra I and his successors. The fact that this victory has been rehashed many times points to its importance both in the military and ideological spheres[10].

Though there is evidence that this battle took place in the fourth year of the reign of Rajaraja, it is only in inscriptions dated around the eighth year that we find mention of Kandhaloor Salai[11]. The Pandya-Chera-Lanka alliance had been harassing the Chola kings for over a century now. The latter were undeniably unforgiving towards this alliance, for there are frequent gleeful references to the conquest of the Chera king and the Pandyas in Malainadu, i.e., the West Coast of South India. Kandhaloor-Salai, which is confirmed to belong to the Chera territory, was probably held by the Pandyas when it was attacked by Rajaraja[12].

One interpretation is that the phrase 'kandhaloor salai kalamarutta' indicates the destruction of ships at the port of Kandhaloor in Venadu. The word, salai, is understood here as a roadstead or harbour. However, another interpretation is that the word means an 'institution of learning' in the sense that is prevalent even today in Tamil Nadu. It has been suggested that salai and kalam may also respectively mean a 'feeding house' and 'eating plate'.. It was a higher institution of learning and catered to advanced Vedic students[13] who studied not only Vedic texts and logic but also other secular subjects. The subjects taught may also have included martial arts, and other forms of training[14]. This brings up the question whether the phrase salai kalamarutta means the destruction of a port with its ships or the destruction of a higher institution of learning, something a conqueror would desist from.

A more kindly but improbable interpretation of the 'destruction' presents the confrontation as a polemical contest between the King and the learned men of the salai, 'an idiom of conflict and conquest'[15] resulting in the King winning the debate and claiming the ideological surrender of the students. One would assuredly welcome such a non-violent confrontation in the political sphere as well, in addition to ideological, where the war would be carried out in words and defeated warriors 'would be permitted to continue their rule, but on condition that they recognised the supremacy of the Cholas'[16]. But this royal decency seems very unlikely to have been committed in this instance, considering that immediately following this victory Rajaraja set upon a marauding war against the Pandyas and Mahinda, setting fire to his capital Anuradhapura and ravaging it in the process.

Kandhaloor Salai belonged to the *Ay* chief, who was a vassal of the Pandya King in the mid ninth century. It is possible that the Salai came under the control of the Chera Perumal King, Bhaskara Ravi Varman Tiruvadi (978-1036). Since the Perumals were allied with Pandyas, the battle at Kandhaloor Salai could very well be the first decisive step of Rajaraja to break this annoying alliance. There is now a broad consensus that the phrase *kandhaloor salai kalamarutta* means 'who destroyed the fleet in the roadstead of Kandhaloor'. A Chola stone inscription unearthed from a village near Thiruvannamalai in Tamil Nadu in 2009 supports the theory that a naval engagement did indeed take place at Kandhaloor in 988 at the cost of many ships and an institution thrown in as well. All things considered, the Chera king got off easy with his own head intact.

Why would the beheading of a few teachers and pupils be trumpeted many times in the *meykeerthis* of not only Rajaraja but the Chola kings who succeeded him? The only possible explanation is that it was a significant victory worth gloating over since the battle broke the age-old nexus between the Chera Perumals and the Pandyas. It destroyed the ships of the Chera kingdom, a pre-condition for the naval attack on Lanka, which followed soon. It was also a foresightful act to bring the flourishing maritime trade from the west coast under the control of the Chola Empire. 'From an early time until perhaps the fourteenth century, the sea presented an opportunity for South Indians to trade and to pillage'[17]. Entrepôts on the Coramandel coast in the east and the Malabar Coast in the west were dotted with international ports such as Puhar, Korkai, and Musiri. These ports exported wares manufactured in the southern peninsula and imported goods from Egypt, Rome, Arabia, Africa, China and the South-East. During the period of urbanisation, maritime trade multiplied. South

Indian merchants commanded fleets of ships capable of long-distance trips. Often, they required mercenaries or official patrols to protect them from rapacious pirates and from the attacks of their greedy competitors. Given the control over the fertile Kaveri basin and international access through the vast seacoast and innumerable ports, the kings of the South were rarely motivated to cross the Vindhyas in search of territory and wealth. These were the basic considerations which got Rajaraja moving towards breaking the alliance between the Cheras, Lanka and the Pandyas, 'in order to break the monopoly of trade held by these kingdoms with west Asia'. The Arabs had established themselves as middleman traders in the west coast and had even 'integrated into local society in the Malabar and Konkan'. The Cholas were only too aware of the potential Arab competition when they set their sights on trade with south-east Asia. The Maldives were also annexed by Rajaraja precisely for being a 'staging point in the Arab trade'. The destruction of Anuradhapura and the setting up of Polonnaruwa is also presumably an indirect attack on a key link in the Arab trade network[18].

The Chola threat to the regime of Bhaskara Ravi Varman had other interesting offshoots. The threat had motivated the Chera King to grant titles and privileges to Joseph Rabban, a foreign merchant prince. The grant was, in a rare show of unity, 'approved by the war council of six feudatories of the King and the Commander of the Eastern forces'. In effect, the grant sealed a strong alliance between the Chera and the Jews, who had come centuries earlier to the Malabar Coast as traders, and now became a part of the Kerala polity, even adopting the matrilineal system of the region. The basis of the alliance, not surprisingly, was the fact that the 'Jews possessed a number of ships equipped with sailors and warriors to defend themselves against pirates'. When the Chola fleet sunk the Chera ships at Kandhaloor, Ravi Varman had no option but to bind the Jews to his kingdom through the gift of titles and privileges, a gift which seldom fails to earn a reciprocation of loyalty. A Chola invasion against Kollam in 998-99 could have hastened this alliance, with the Jews already showing some mettle in the war. In exchange, tax concessions and trade privileges would have been expected, but what finally turned out was much more than that. However hard it may be to believe, the foreigners were bestowed with nothing less than seventy-two aristocratic privileges, essentially admitting this 'foreigner with a different ethnicity and religious culture into the ranks of the native aristocracy at the highest level', amounting to 'the final phase of integration for this exotic group of adventurers'[19]. What all this amounts to is that there were inherent weaknesses in the Chera Perumals which could be exploited by the resurging Chola dynasty. A permanent Council of Brahmana Ministers called the shots in the Chera palace, unlike their eastern neighbour. In addition, the 'absence of a big home territory, army and administrative staff ... and the relative independence of district governors in conferring titles alienating property'[20] hampered the Perumals from becoming a dominant force in the region.

Rajaraja took up the Lanka expedition next with the modest expectation that 'the eight quarters might praise him'[21 22]. In the game of thrones in the southern peninsula, the kings of Lanka traditionally played the joker in determining the outcome of battles. Their alignment with the Pandya, Chera, Chola and Pallava kings was purely for self-preservation. No specific cultural or religious ties influenced them. When the Cholas were a vassal state, the relationship with Lanka was decided by their overlords. But from the time they broke out of their feudatory status, they took a very serious view of the alliance of the Lanka kings with the Pandyas and Cheras. When Rajaraja ascended the throne, the expansion of the empire and the securing of sea routes gained enormous politico-military significance, as never before. Lanka was an area that deserved meddling.

Crossing the ocean had never been a deterrence, but until the middle of the 10th century, military forays of the South Indian kingdoms into Lanka had been ad-hoc. After subduing the enemy, the armed forces usually retreated to the mainland with their loot and plunder. However, Rajaraja's invasion of Lanka had none of the irresoluteness or the brevity of his predecessors. It was extremely aggressive and rested on the long-term strategy of establishing the supremacy of Chola power over international sea routes. Lanka was subjected to ruthless plunder and destruction of major political and religious centres. A fortified centre was established at Polonnaruwa from which the rest of the island could be controlled[23].

A sword remains strong only when it is constantly tempered and Rajaraja wanted to keep it that way. The invasion of Lanka by Rajaraja excelled even that of Rama depicted by the 'picturesque account'[24]

> *Rama built, with the aid of the monkeys, a causeway across the sea and then slew with great difficulty the king of Lanka by means of sharp-edged arrows. But Rama was excelled by this (king) whose powerful army crossed the ocean by ships and burnt up the kingdom of Lanka.*

This naval expedition took place during the reign of Mahinda V who had been ruling from 981. Mahinda V, the king of Lanka, was driven out of his kingdom, sardonically by a rebellion among mercenaries he hired from his Chera and Pandya allies. This was an unexpected windfall which Rajaraja seized with glee and in one fell swoop got rid of his adversary, not by cutting off his head but by making sure that he stayed away in the forests. The Chola invasion brought death and destruction to the beautiful island kingdom. 'Anuradhapura, the capital of Ceylon for over 1000 years, was finally destroyed by the armies of Rajaraja'[25]. All that the gods had given to the ancient beautiful city seemed to have been snatched by a cruel hand in one destructive sweep. Northern Lanka became a province in the Chola Empire and became mummudi-sola-mandalam. To control the turbulent province of Rohana, the Cholas created a new capital in the strategically located Polonnaruwa, formerly a military outpost. It is not only improbable, but a manifest certainty, that many Buddhist monasteries were destroyed during the sacking of Anuradhapura. Adding to their insult and misery, Rajaraja ordered the building of Siva temples in the Chola style[26] in the conquered territories. Mahinda's defeat took a heavy toll and a long wait for the local rulers to take the island back into their hands. The perverse pride of the Cholas to see treachery play havoc with their enemies knew no bounds.

The complete subjugation of the island, however, happened twelve years later, somewhere in 1017 CE, under Rajendra I. In his expedition, this dashing monarch, captured the 'the crown of the kings of Lanka, the exceedingly beautiful crowns of their queens, the fine crown and the garland of Indra which the Pandya had previously deposited with them and the whole of Ilamandalam (the island) on the transparent sea'[27]. The Lankan king 'having been shorn of his queen, son and other belongings' gave up any pretence of further war and 'sought the two feet of Rajendra'. The Mahavamsa, without mincing matters, confirms all this and adds more gory details in that the Chola monarch 'violently destroyed here and there all the monasteries; like blood-sucking yakkhas, they took all the treasures of Lanka for themselves'. Apparently, the Chola monarchs did to Lanka what the Delhi Sultanate dynasties would do later to the temples of the Deccan and the South. Chola entrenchment in northern Lanka lasted about three-quarters of a century, from roughly 993 (the date of Rajaraja's first invasion) to 1070. At this point in time, Vijayabahu I recaptured the north and expelled the Chola forces restoring sovereignty to the hands of local royalty.

The conquest of northern Lanka was not just a military incursion for the emperor on a rampage. In his 29th year of reign, in 1014, Rajaraja made a grant of several villages in Lanka to the temple he built in Thanjavur. The previous owners and ryots were declared, in most cases, to have been replaced. This implies that the original holdings were altered and those holders who were prepared to accept the emperor's proposals were included. The subjugation of Lanka was complete[28]. But all said and done, the Lanka expedition would have been the most perilous for the ambitious king, with the danger of being cut off from his capital by the Pandyas and Cheras regrouping themselves, looming large in his war strategy. Lanka was far away from the capital and supplies for the invading army from that distance required a neutral, if not a friendly, buffer zone.

It is not certain whether the Pandyas were vanquished before or after the Lanka victory, but with Rajaraja seizing the king Amarabhujanga, the rule of 'dissolute kings, whose rule was secretly mischievous being much afraid of him at heart, wished to hide (themselves) somewhere (just like serpents with sliding crooked bodies)'[29] was ended. Even the moon could not protect the Pandyas, as its Chandravanshi protégés 'became the white parasol of this (king Rajaraja) who was intent upon conquering that (southern) quarter'[30]. With this conquest, Rajaraja added yet another title 'pandya kulashani' (Thunderbolt to the Race of the Pandyas), and the Pandya country came to be known as 'Rajaraja Mandalam'. A few years earlier, the Pandyas, Cheras and Lanka were kingdoms in their own right, now they were reduced to mere provinces in a greater realm, but not quite. Long after the Chola conquest of these areas, the Pandya and Chera kings retained their capacity 'for making trouble for their suzerain in the face of powerful viceroys'. Whether this indicates the 'mild character of Chola imperialism' or the difficulty faced by the Chola emperors to retain control over their distant and powerful fealties is a question to be researched. Rajendra I, his son Rajadhiraja and the latter's brother Rajendra II seem to have been busy in securing their empire's borders constantly.

Expeditions against the Pandyas and Cheras were not one-off forays for the mighty emperor. Not content with sinking ships, and torching cities, Rajaraja turned his attention to the north of Kerala and cast his acquisitive eyes on the hilly Kudamalainadu (Coorg), a stronghold of the Pandyas. The southern campaigns must have stretched Rajaraja's resources to the last gold coin in his war booty, but he did not pause. He was damned if he would give his northern enemies any hope of spending peaceful nights in their harems.

To be fair though, the expeditions were not just impelled by a wish for more loot and plunder. In the Thanjavur delta irrigated by five rivers and their numerous tributaries, 'by the latter half of the tenth century, density of land occupation should have reached a high level'[31]. Sale and alienation, gifts, inheritance and dowry had rendered unoccupied lands for induction of new tenants scarce. As an extreme measure, in villages provided as land grants to Brahmanas, the non-Brahmanas were forced to sell their land

and become cultivating tenants. Such was the scarcity that Kundavai, the elder sister of the Emperor, had to buy a paltry 1.5 acres from a village to be dedicated to a temple just outside Thanjavur. In another instance, one of the many queens of the Emperor, Ulagamahadeviyar, had to buy some temple land at Thiruvayyaru to build another shrine in her name. The royalty themselves were forced to purchase land only in small parcels. In real terms, the 'expansion of the empire could have mitigated this situation in more ways than one'[32]. The employment of farmers, shepherds and weavers during the off-season in expeditions solved the problem of remunerative employment through raids. As soon as new territory was annexed to the Empire, 'mercantile militia[33], merchants, priests, Brahmanas and *Vellalars*'[34] migrated in waves to the conquered river basins. Cultivation was extended, settlements spread out and temple establishments set up, palaces built, and new administrative regions created.

The next highlight of the conquest was the storming of the fortress of Udagai, ensconced amidst the verdant forests of the Western Ghats, sometime before the year 1008. This storming may not have happened in the first attack and must have taken several forays. Rajaraja must have savoured the victory with immense satisfaction for he was 'always depriving the Seriyas (Pandyas) of their splendour'[35]. It is perhaps this particular victory that made Rajaraja add the title of 'Mummadi Chola' (the Chola king who wears three crowns of the Chera, Chola and Pandya) to his already impressive resume. The title did little to calm the fears of his adversaries in the north. But it took many heads and a long wait before he could cross the hills of Coorg. It appears that an envoy sent by Rajaraja was insulted by the chief of Kudamalainadu and all hell broke loose. The later day poet Ottakuttar says that Rajaraja crossed 'eighteen forests'[36] to avenge his envoy and set fire to Udagai, which act had become an addictive habit of the emperor by now. Other accounts describe a more drastic picture of the king cutting off the heads of eighteen princes in retaliation. The war booty from the 'land of Parasurama' (Kerala) must have been substantial since there are several references of Rajaraja donating idols and other stuff large-heartedly to temples in the core area of his empire[37]. As the emperor's army advanced, temples in the Chola country acquired new towers and gifts.

Once Rajaraja had prevailed upon all the eight directions south of the Kaveri, he turned his covetous attention to the north. This emperor just did not believe in half measures. In the north lay the realm of many formidable enemies of the king, but his decisiveness, his thirst for conflict and his supreme self-confidence in expanding his empire prodded him forward. The high standards of valour set by his precedents must have been poured into his ears from when he was in his mother's womb. Around 998, he annexed the regions of Gangapadi, Nolambapadi and Tadigaipadi (present day Karnataka) to his fast expanding empire and the even faster swelling of his treasury. While the Nolambas, who were feudatories of Gangas, were reportedly extinguished, the reference was only to their power and not their physical presence, since in later years several Nolamba subordinates served the emperor in his army providing grist to the mill of suspicion that they 'turned against their Ganga overlords and paid off old scores by taking the side of the Cholas openly'[38]. Apparently, the attack on the Nolambas was actually a deathblow to the Gangas and delivered the Ganga country into the firm grip of the Cholas for more than a century. The easy success was possible because of the disappearance of the Rashtrakutas, a formidable power earlier in alliance with the Gangas in about 973. So, with one fell stroke, Rajaraja had broken the disquieting alliance of these great powers in the north-west. The districts of Tumkur, Chitradurga, much of today's Bangalore, Kolar and Bellary districts and even parts of Salem and North Arcot fell into the orbit of the Chola Empire. More importantly, with anti-Chola alliances regularly ending up with something like a dinosaurian extinction, it confirmed the fact that Rajaraja had not attracted too much hostility too soon.

The Western Chalukyas, in contrast to being chastened by the sordid fate of other kingdoms around them, were by no means indifferent to Rajaraja's expansionary wars. The Chola emperor had sized up his opponent in the north-west with the same hostile suspicion though. No provocation for a war was required and none given, for there was enough past baggage to start one. Back in 973, the ruler of Vengi, Dhanarnava, had met a gory end at the sword tip of Telugu Choda chief, Jata Choda Bhima who ruled Vengi from 973 to 1000. Rajaraja got onto the wrong side of Bhima when he gave shelter to Dhanarnava's offsprings, Shaktivarman I and Vimaladitya. In fact, Rajaraja went so far as to give his daughter Kundavai in marriage to Vimaladitya, the younger of the brothers. The king was firming up alliances through wedlock, a time-tested method. The matrimonial alliance could not be construed as an excess of Chola gallantry towards a hapless kingdom, but many decades later, there was cause to regret this chivalrous impulse among the main descendants of the Cholas, and a cause to rejoice for their northern branch. Much later when the grandsons of Rajaraja were overwhelmed in 'desperate conflicts of which they saw no end', the Chalukya-Chola king Rajendra came to occupy the imperial Chola throne, 'ensuring a continuous and active life for the empire of Rajaraja'[39]. Bhima invaded Tondaimandalam, the northern part of Rajaraja's empire in a fit of rage and was defeated and imprisoned promptly. Rajaraja went ahead with his game plan and appointed the elder brother Shaktivarman I to the Vengi throne under his tutelage.

Much as it would appear to be a diplomatic coup, Rajaraja's 'intercession in Vengi affairs was the direct and natural result of the political development of the early years of his reign, rather than of any diplomatic design to dissociate the Eastern Chalukyas from their Western cousins'[40]. The Eastern Chalukyas 'had become an old and decrepit race' after three centuries of self-destructive wars with the Rashtrakutas and were on the verge of hara-kiri when Rajaraja came to their succour through 'a position of respected though a subordinate alliance'[41], if that were at all possible.

If Rajaraja had made the mistake of thinking that his enemies would have learnt their lesson, he was in for a rude awakening when the Western Chalukyas decided to take him on again. They had emerged under Taila II from centuries of subordination to the Rashtrakutas and were all set to improve their fortunes now. But the wave of opportunities on which

Rajaraja rode eluded Satyasraya (997-1008), son of Taila II and the present Chalukyan king. While Rajaraja's enemies were weakening, Satyasraya's kept harassing him so much that 'they failed to do more than just keep their ancestral territory, the Rattapadi, the seven and a half lakh country intact'[42]. The sun was ascending on the Chola Empire while it was dipping behind war clouds for the Chalukyas, who were well past their prime. To reiterate, the history of the declining years of the Chalukyan dynasty amply demonstrate that 'far from their being sought out by Rajaraja as valuable political allies, they (Eastern Chalukyas) owed their position to the great monarch'[43].

Saktivarman ruled Vengi from 999 CE for 12 years after which his younger brother and the emperor's son-in-law, Vimaladitya, was installed on the throne in 1011. In the intervening years, Rajaraja had to come to the rescue of his protégés against the ambitious Western Chalukya warrior, Satyasraya, on many occassions. As mentioned before, Satyasraya was beleaguered on several fronts by the Cholas, Paramaras, Chedis and the Chalukyas of Gujarat. Victories and defeats followed one another closely but the doughty King never gave up. Unable to swallow his bloated pride when his eastern brethren landed in the lap of the Cholas, in a fit of rage, Satyasraya invaded Vengi in 1006. In one last defiant snap to save the pride of the Western Chalukyas, his general Bayalanambi reduced some of the enemy forts to dust and established himself in Chebrolu in Guntur district. Satyasraya's attack must have dismayed the Chola emperor to no small extent, considering that he was just settling down after a wearying campaign lasting years, to build the best administrative apparatus that the South had ever seen. Rajaraja retaliated swiftly and sent his trusted warrior son Rajendra to attack the Western Chalukyas with a massive army in 1007. Rajendra proved that it was certainly not the age for frail princes. The 900,000 strong Chola army advanced as far as Donur in Bijapur district and with the frenzy of a rampant elephant 'plundered the whole country, killed women, children and Brahmanas, caught hold of girls and destroyed their caste'[44]. The description was neither unjust nor inaccurate. No doubt, there were worse slaughters organised by the Chola kings, but not many of this scale. Had Satyasraya recognised this earlier, he may not have troubled himself to worry about his eastern cousins. Though he retaliated valiantly, Rajendra is reported to have captured a good part of the Raichur doab and sacked Manyakheta. Simultaneously, an army advanced from Vengi and captured the fortress of Kulpak, 60 kms northwest of Hyderabad. Satyasraya succeeded in preventing the Cholas from crossing the Tungabhadra, but the two-pronged attack was more than he had bargained for. He paid for his insolence when finally, he watched from across the river, with a sallow face, the Cholas walk away with a large booty. Adding insult to the Chalukyan pride, the Cholas gloated that 'being produced from Taila (his father whose name translated into 'oil'), this (slipping away) was natural to him'[45]. This degree of personal animosity was not surprising considering that a few centuries earlier, the Chalukyans had gloated over the burning of Kanchi and the Pallavas, who bore the brunt, in turn had scorched Badami, their capital. The all too familiar history of scorching cities among the kingdoms in the South notwithstanding, the memory of the cries of the Chalukyan women would have haunted Rajendra as his army trudged back with the war booty on the long road back to Thanjavur.

From the moment that he set out with his mammoth army to conquer the whole of the Southern peninsula, Rajaraja had done all that he could to live up to the promise of building the largest empire that the people of Tamil country had ever seen. At the end of the campaigns in the north-west, the Chola Empire had practically annexed all the territory that had ever been held by the Gangas and Nolambas in Mysore and nearly the whole of Bellary district so that 'Tungabhadra became the boundary between the two empires'[46].

Towards the closing years of his reign, Rajaraja conquered and annexed the 'old islands of the sea numbering 12,000', the Maldives. The conquest of Maldives is a demonstration of the naval might of the Cholas, which Rajendra would exploit to spread the empire to parts of south-east Asia in the years to come. The destruction of the naval dockyard at Kandhaloor and crossing the ocean to establish a capital in northern Lanka were all a part of the grand design of Rajaraja to conquer the seas.

A later account of these campaigns, not surprisingly, announced rather matter-of-factly that "Rajaraja destroyed the town of Madurai, conquered the haughty kings of Kollam, Kolla-desam and Kodungolur, and the kings of the sea (kadal-arasar) waited on him"[47].

3

RISE OF CITIES AND THE EXPANDING WORLD OF MERCHANTS

When Gaius Petronius Arbiter, a Roman courtier under Nero, chided fashionable Roman ladies for exposing their charms much too immodestly by clothing themselves in the 'webs of woven wind'[1], referring to the fine muslins imported from India, it wasn't the lone complaint of a paranoid protectionist. Pliny the Elder was more vehement when he remarked 'this is the price we pay for our luxuries and our women'. Their agitation was well-founded. Indian cities reportedly drained the Roman Empire annually to the extent of 55 million sesterces—around half a million pounds—sending in return goods which were sold there at a hundred times their value in India. By the time of Augustus, 120 ships were setting sail every year from Myos Hormos[2] to Indian ports. This meant that as far back as the first century of the Common Era, Indian cities and ports were powerhouses of world trade. The Periplus of the Erithraen Sea talks about south Indian ports such as Musiri, Korkai, Kaveripattinam, Kodumanal and Arikkamedu. Poets eulogised 'Musiri to which come the well-rigged ships of the Yavanas, (then a term for the Romans and which later also included the Greeks) bringing gold and taking away spices in exchange'[3]. The air in these ports was redolent of vibrant cosmopolitanism, more variegated than anywhere else in the subcontinent. Since the Indian ports exported much more to Rome than they imported, trade was almost one-sided. Roman gold coins were hoarded in the cities, if not melted, building a huge external balance. Not surprisingly, sometime in the fourth century, there was a dip in Indo-Roman trade. Ostensibly by that time, Rome's treasury was a big empty hole, after having been "robbed" of all gold. Trade with Southeast Asia too declined, leading to 'the crisis of the *Kaliyuga*"[4]. A long period of de-urbanisation had set in between the third and sixth centuries in north India. Long-distance maritime trade with Rome and Southeast Asia declined along with a general paucity of coins, particularly the Roman variety. Merchants and artisans went through a rough patch so much so that travellers like Fa Hsien and Hsuan Tsang bemoaned the desertion of towns in the Indian subcontinent, especially Buddhist centres, in their foreign accounts of this time. Besides a dip in foreign trade, the crisis was also orchestrated by 'migration of artists and Brahmanas from towns, localisation of crafts in rural areas and the obliteration of distinction between town and country'[5]. The disruption of social relationships ossified occupational groups into castes. The hypothesis of urban decline in the north has to be taken with more than a pinch of salt for while certain urban centres declined, others continued to flourish, and some new ones emerged[6]. The ports of the early Cholas had been busy in this emptying of the Roman treasury but then they had almost disappeared for several centuries until Vijayalaya re-established their line and Rajaraja more than offset the prestige lost in the earlier centuries. From all accounts, the external balance continued to pile up during the reign of Rajaraja, and this time it was not just the Roman coffers which were getting depleted.

The crisis of *Kaliyuga*, had not touched the southern cities, presumably because it was a region 'where the brahmanical social order of the varna system had taken no roots'[7] at least in the early centuries of the first millennium. Tamil society mercifully escaped the 'social upheaval located in the crisis of the *Kaliyuga*'[8]. There is no evidence in the region of evil days falling on artisans and Brahmanas or of Brahmanas migrating from towns to rural areas. In fact, 'it was a period of re-urbanisation for some of the early historical urban centres like Kanchipuram' confirming that 'the hypothesis of urban decay has no validity whatsoever for this region'[9]. Under the Pallava-Pandya rulers, who preceded the Chola Empire, new integrating forces such as land grants and temples, 'led to the extension of agricultural activities and a more intensive organisation of production geared to support large populations'. By the end of the 9th century, clusters of such settlements 'emerged as the foci of urban growth'[10]. Cities such as Kanchipuram and Madurai had a respectably long historical past at least from 300 BCE. From all accounts, they were bristling with energy, the city looms excelling in their fine quality of the textiles comparable to the 'slough of the snake and to a cloud of steam' and yet 'these muslins carried much fine floral work and were of different colours'. Though the domestic market was large, foreign trade also flourished, draining the gold away from foreign lands. Salt and pepper merchants moved about with their families in trains of carts; armed with a spare axle to negotiate the rough terrain. The bazaar in the big cities was a busy place with colourful banners hoisted over the shops, their coffers filled with plenty of gold, and overflowing taverns. The thriving maritime trade found reflection in poets comparing an elephant running amok to a storm-tossed ship in their lyrics and stories did not tire of referring to shipwrecks. Salt, dried fish, and processed tamarind were conveyed in boats through inland waterways or along the coast. Foreign ships came laden with horses in the company of bristly Arab merchants. Several ports dotted the eastern and western coast of South India. Large boats which carried white salt and returned laden with paddy, when anchored in the harbour, resembled a row of horses tethered in the palace stable. Great ships sailed straight into the harbour of Puhar without slacking sail, if accounts are to be believed. Puhar, the greatest of ports on the eastern coast, at the mouth of the Kaveri, received war-horses that came by sea, bags of black pepper brought overland by car, gems and gold from the northern mountain, sandal and agil woods from the western mountains, pearls from the southern and coral of the eastern sea, the produce of the Ganges basin and the Kaveri valley, food stuffs from Lanka and luxuries from Kadaram besides other rare and precious products. Undeniably it was a cosmopolitan city where people from different countries speaking various languages lived in demarcated quarters, presumably amicably, and contributed to the vast and increasing wealth and prosperity of the elite, some of it tricking down to the lower strata of society. If poets and epics are to be believed, its merchants were not greedy cheats, but honest dealers who were content with a modest profit, feared wrong, spoke the truth, and gave the same consideration to the interests of their customers as to their own, breaking down all rules of the free market. The ports were even more numerous on the west coast than on the east thanks to the luxuries preferred by Roman women. Pearls, gems and precious stones were traded in abundance through boats and large ships, generating a lot of demand for the timber and ship building industry[11].

Now, more than a millennium ahead of that period, agriculture had expanded enormously, and bourgeoning trade and crafts had connected these cities more securely to the hinterland in the Tamil country, as well as with the coastal ports. Cities started playing multiple roles, as 'political centres, centres of manufacturing and trade, and as sacred or ceremonial centres'[12] as we approach the period of Rajaraja.

The Kaveri delta had been the most important resource base for kingdoms from ancient times, but particularly from the 7th century onwards, about three centuries before Rajaraja, the control of this region determined the dominant power in the South. The delta had attracted conquerors from the north and south offering them wealth and power. While the Cholas were still serving as feudatories, paying tributes, mortgaging their honour and waiting to emerge from obscurity, the Pallavas of Kanchipuram and the Pandyas of Madurai, their masters, were flexing their muscles and launching wars over control of the region. The rivers of the Arisilaru, flowing near Kumbhakonam, never lost their reddish hue for centuries. The Pandyas, led by Rajasimha, teamed up with their sidekick Cholas and besieged the Pallava Nandivarman II at a place called Nandipuram in 745. Nandivarman must have had a tough time breaking the siege, since it was one of a 'number of battles which his general Udayachandra had to wage to stabilise the position of his master'[13]. This 'stabilising the position of his master' actually meant that the general had to rescue his master several times from enemy prisons. The next great battle for the control of Nandipuram was fought by Nandivarman III (846-69) where 'six armies'[14] fell in a mighty onslaught. The Cholas sided with the Pandyas or the Pallavas, depending on which way the wind of success blew, but uncomfortably as subordinates all the way. The battle at Tiruppurambiyam, in the late ninth century, finally liberated the Cholas from their servility. Aditya Chola I (871-907) took advantage of the weakening of the Pandyas and Pallavas, like a hyena dining on the corpses of larger predators, fighting to the death 'for the Pandyas never recovered from this staggering blow, and the Pallavas, though victory remained with them in the battle, owed it more to their allies than to their own strength'[15]. It was Aditya who really 'threw off the Pallava yoke, and soon established Chola power up to Tondaima*nadu* near Kalahasti (near Chennai)'[16]. In the South he extended the kingdom up to Pudukottai, but not beyond. Aditya is also reputed to have conquered the Kongu country in the west and is said to have brought gold to enrich the Chidambaram temple.

Aditya I happened to be the son of Vijayalaya, the first of the Imperial line of Cholas, built over the ruined fortunes of the Pandyas and Pallavas. Before the son's fatal exploits at the battlefield, the father had already grabbed Thanjavur, a few kilometres away from Kumbhakonam. The Tiruvalangadu plates 'quaintly affirm that Vijayalaya caught hold of Thanjavur for his pleasure as if the city were his lawful spouse'[17]. No celestial omens appeared on the horizon, but the victory changed the fate of South India forever. Vijayalaya started the imperial journey of the Cholas around 850 but only after vanquishing the Muttaraiyar's, the fellow hyena. Like the Cholas, the Muttaraiyars could not hunt on their own and had to feed on the leftovers of the Pandyas and Pallavas. They 'played a clever game and were ready to change their allegiance to suit their interests'[18]. But, in the bloody Arisilaru battle, they put their bet on the losing side, the Pandyas. Vijayalaya, who sided with the Pallavas, grabbed Thanjavur from the Muttaraiyars, while the latter were still licking their wounds. The Pallavas technically won the battle but lost the war for 'little could the Pallava ruler have suspected that in thus employing the Chola subordinate, he was, as the Indian saying has it, training his tiger-cub to a taste for blood'. Before Vijayalaya the Cholas were just intermediaries in the battlefield, trudging behind their masters. But the cub soon spawned an ambitious line of tigers who demanded increasingly more blood until they had established 'one of the most splendid empires known to Indian History'. In its heyday, in the 11th century, the Chola empire would grow into one of the half-dozen greatest powers on Earth at that time and control about half a million square miles - more than five times the size of Britain[19]. What made this stupendous achievement possible was the rise of the cities and the growth of productive forces.

The capture of Kudandai (present day Kumbhakonam) and Thanjavur were crucial for establishing such an empire for they were the growth engines of the Southern economy. Under the imperial Cholas, the Kudandai complex covered a larger area than the present-day city and it had twin cities, Kudamukku and Pazhayarai. It contained four *nadus*, agrarian administrative units, within it. Major economic activity was centred round the Nageshwara temple, which the royal family reconstructed from its modest existence. The temple records 'endowments made in the form of land, cows, sheep, gold and money'[20]. Apart from the royal family, these endowments were made from Chola officials of high rank, local merchants, traders from distant lands like Kerala, and large *Vellala* landowners from various parts of the empire. Closely associated with the temple were Brahmanas, shepherds, members of the *Kaikkolar* weaver community and others. The temple coffers were filled with gold lumps and Chola gold coins, the *kazhanju*. The quantities involved were staggering for those times. There is a record of an assembly in the city raising gold through sale of land to meet the hefty demand of Paranataka I of 3000 *kazhanju* of gold (roughly 15.6 kg) to fund his Pandya wars[21]. The city was an important hub on the trade grid of the South, 'a centre of betel nut and areca nut cultivation' as well as a preferred source for metal work and textiles. The city even boasted of a Chola mint. The twin cities 'were knitted to their rural and coastal hinterlands through intricate ties'[22].

Rajaraja had enough victories under his belt for a lifetime now, allowing him to concentrate on administering the cities and expanding trade. The temple in the cities played the role of employer, landowner, consumer of goods and services and more importantly as a banker. But not all economic activity emanated from or around the temple. The cities were extensively linked with the hinterland, markets, ports and overseas trade posts through a maze of trade networks. The urban economy and trade were controlled by the corporate assemblies of merchants in the cities, the *nagarams*, with its members called the *nagarattar*. 'The *nagaram* was the link in a hierarchy of markets, linking the villages to the market town, which was linked to higher order centres like the *managarams* (big cities) and port towns'[23]. It collected taxes and functioned as the city government.

The *nagarams* pulsed with economic activity, if we are to believe the poets and inscriptions. The *nagaram* had the 'kadai, the shops, angadi, the markets or bazaars, and the perangadi, the big market in the inner city, the wholesale market'[24]. Streets and main roads crisscrossed the city. The *nagaram* had its social hierarchy as much as the rest of Chola society. Its membership was broad-based, consisting of merchants, Vellala landowners, Sankarapadi oil merchants, Saliyar weavers and fishermen, and the lower order artisans like carpenters, masons, goldsmiths and leather workers'[25]. But control of the corporate body rested with the top layer who had capital to invest and royal patronage to hang on. The existence of *nagarams* for different occupations increased specialisation in marketing. Craftsmen used advanced techniques for production. The earlier cumbersome hand oil mills were promptly replaced with bullock-driven oil mills[26], improving production manifold. The textile weaving industry was given a facelift and textile looms mushroomed. The city quarters called the *kammanacheri*[27] where goldsmiths, coppersmiths, blacksmiths, carpenters and sculptors lived must have been a busy area. The members of the Vishwakarma *kula*, the *Kammalars*, as these craftsmen were called as a professional group, also had their own *jati* affiliations. The *Kammalars* were craftsmen, on a higher social plane than the artisans. 'While the maker of ploughs would exist in the village community with a certain degree of relative physical immobility, socio-economic security and comparatively static living standards, the *Kammalar* craftsmen who had moved out of the custom determined 'local' market would band together . . .

benefiting from the temple economy and an expanding clientele'. They were more mobile, had greater earning opportunities but also faced greater risks 'from the withdrawal of patronage or the decline of temple centres with the fall of dynasties'[28]. But that happened later with the fall of the Chola Empire. In Rajaraja's time, however, the ballooning demand for buildings, stone engravings, sculptures and frescos, not to mention coins and jewellery, provided ample opportunities for craftsmen to move up the caste ladder. One could almost draw a straight line from the professional elevation of craftsmen to their breaking of the Shudra shackle. The upward mobility of the craftsmen and their striving to break out of their low Shudra status in the varna system comes out sharply in the myth surrounding Vishwakarma.

According to this myth, it was not Brahma alone who created the universe; without Vishwakarma he could not have chiselled it into shape. The big bang happened when the five natural elements formed an enormous egg which exploded like thunder, creating the universe. Like his partner, Vishvakarma, the divine architect of the universe, was born with five heads; three of his faces were of three metals—gold, copper and iron—from which emerged the goldsmith, the copper smith and the blacksmith. The other two faces belonged to the stone smith and the carpenter. Vishvakarma then made giant tongs out of the power emanating from Brahma, the creator and Vishnu, the protector and joined the tongs with the nail symbolising the power of Rudra (Siva, the third of the divine trinity in his role as destroyer). This was how the first tool of the smiths with the divine power to create galaxies was fashioned[29]. So, craftsmen had their own Brahma in the form of Vishwakarma, and with this confidence they staked out their claim for the status of the Brahmanas, even wearing a thread in later centuries. Beyond doubt, Rajaraja's empire had set powerful forces at work, who had the audacity to claim an equal status in the caste hierarchy, only to lose it in modern times.

Metal casting and other crafts were part of the everyday vocabulary of the people to the extent that the seventh century *bhakti* poet Andal described her love for Krishna in these terms:

My beautiful lover, it is as if he has put clay around me
and poured molten metal into my heart[30]

However unromantic this may sound, Andaal, who had grown up in the heart of the metal casting region, was referring to the technique called *ghanam*, which craftsmen use to this day to manufacture bell metal lamps and temple bells[31]. Keeping craftsmen happy would have been motive enough for the Chola administration to plan the new cities with specific quarters for this most needed section of urban society.

Pazhayarai, the twin city of Kumbhakonam, served more as a residential stronghold for the imperial Cholas. 'Every Chola ruler, starting from Aditya I, not only used it as his residential stronghold, but also personally contributed to its development by erecting temples, ... and making rich endowments of land and gold'[32]. It was also a military centre, with army cantonments surrounding the palace area. In spite of the fact that the more successful Cholas like Rajaraja, 'chose Thanjavur for their monumental edifices and rich benefactions', the city never ceased to function as an administrative centre. Rajaraja's father Sundara Chola called himself the king of Nandipuram, the other name for Pazhaiyarai[33]. The importance of Pazhayarai and the adjoining region can be seen from the fact that Rajaraja drew a large number of employees from these areas to take care of the Thanjavur temple, the iconic centre of the Chola Empire. Such employees included 400 temple women, and 'male temple servants, *viz.,* dancing-masters, musicians, drummers, singers, accountants, parasol-bearers, lamp-lighters, watermen, potters, washer men, barbers, astrologers, tailors, a brazier, carpenters, a goldsmith, and others'[34]. The incentive to move into Thanjavur would have been irresistible since 'each person received one or more shares, each of which consisted of the produce of one *veli* of land (26,755 sqm), which was calculated at 100 *kalam* of paddy'[35]. It was boom time for the cities.

Kanchipuram, the capital of the Pallavas, until the Cholas decimated them and appropriated the city, continued to survive as a *managaram*, thanks to its status as a manufacturing and export centre. It should not be surprising

63

that the city had a large population of about 48,000 in the eleventh century considering that 'the large number of streets would indicate how populous the city was and how the weavers, oil-mongers, cloth merchants and the *Nanadesis* with trans-regional trade affiliations had thronged in the city'[36]. Two classes of silk weavers, the *Pattusali*, had set up shop in the four quarters of the city. They had close connections with the temple, managing its accounts, and perhaps using the endowment money as capital for their manufactures, or at the minimum helping themselves to preferential loans from the temple corpus. The merchants were the wealth managers of temple funds, not just in Kanchipuram but in other cities as well, and the bigger the temple corpus, the bigger the operations of the merchants.

Superficially it might appear that the rise of the cities was allegedly fuelled by 'the increasing power of the Chola state, the increasing popularity of the Vaishnava and Shaiva *bhakti*, and the emergence of the temple as a prominent religious institution in the urban landscape'. But this is perhaps mixing up cause and effect since temples and religion were just the superstructure of a bourgeoning economy, though the temples did create a demand for goods and services of their own. It is the 'upward mobility of groups of peasants and artisans' and 'the freedom provided by cities to ideas and actions'[37] that are more likely reasons for the rapid spread of the movement. The emergence of temples as power centres must have affected the regular gifts that Brahmanas were hitherto accustomed to receiving. Each temple generously employed Brahmanas, as they did from other castes, but 'in the late Pallava and early Chola periods, there was a significant shift of royal patronage from gifts to Brahmanas towards gifts to temples'[38] but that did not mean that *brahmadeya*[39] villages, which sprung up from Pallava times, stopped flourishing. These villages were exempted from taxes and the Brahmana donees were given the right to collect taxes and cess from the occupants. Building and patronising temples by royalty was an age-old phenomenon, but the Cholas took up this task with more than a flourish. 'The magnificent temples at Thanjavur and GangaikondaCholapuram were architectural proclamations of the close connection between the political and religious domains'[40].

Thanjavur, the new administrative capital of Rajaraja (for he retained the royal palace at Pazhayarai), was located in the south-western edge of the rich Kaveri delta region, on the southern bank of the Vadavaru river. A settlement had existed at the same location in pre-Chola times, but a phenomenal transformation catapulted the city into a major royal and temple city, the most powerful and prestigious city south of the Godavari in those times[41]. Considering its central location in the Kaveri basin and on the trade network, the Cholas were willing to sacrifice the legitimacy they would have acquired easily had they continued to keep the ancient and historic city of Uraiyur, the centre of the Sangam era Cholas, as their capital. The city of Thanjavur expanded around the imposing Brihadeeswara temple at its core, with its tall *vimana* and gopurams forming the city's skyline. The area around the temple formed the downtown with multi-storeyed mansions housing the city's political and priestly elites. The outer circle housed the next most powerful class, the rich merchants. The city boasted of four angadis, the markets, catering a variety of goods to different strata and having different opening and closing hours. The temple generated considerable demand for milk, ghee and flowers, as well as services of 'priests, temple women, musicians, washermen and watchmen'[42].

The temple at the centre of the city was a cultural and artistic emporium. Special performances and festivals commemorating royal birthdays and festivals (which were never in short supply) kept the temple grounds crowded and busy throughout the year. Donations poured in not only from the royal family but from high-ranking officers, wealthy merchants, and big landlords. Regular contributions came in from surrounding villages and colonised territories, not to speak of sudden spurts of income from the spoils and loot from war. Revenue accruing from as many as 40 villages in Cholamandalam, the core area of the state, and another 16 villages in conquered territories such as Karnataka and Lanka flowed into the temple's coffers[43]. The temple was a massive corporate entity even by today's standards, employing around 600 people. Elaborate arrangements were made by the king for the provision and maintenance of services with '67 lamps being lit

Fig. 7 - The 13-storeyed Sri Vimana (tower) of the Brihadeeswara Temple

Fig. 8 - Sri Vimana of Brihadeeswara Temple — Outer wall detail

Fig. 9 - Decorative elements on the outer wall of the Sri Vimana of Brihadeeswara Temple

every day, of at least 145 watchmen being on the payroll, about 369 places giving or receiving resources to it'[44]. But the city drew its fibre not only from the temple but from its myriad connections with manufacturing and trade networks. The Chinese documentor Zhao Rukuo[45] described the city even more grandiosely. According to his effusive description, the city had seven-fold walls each seven feet high and the city itself measured 6.6 km long and 3.9 km wide, quite large for those times. Each wall was about 100 paces apart, the four outer walls built of bricks, the next two of mud and the innermost of wood. The outer walls were surrounded by streams and the main people's quarters were within the first three walls from the outer edge. Ministers occupied the space inside the fourth wall and the princes, the fifth. The sixth wall enclosed Buddhist monasteries and the seventh wall comprised the royal palace with a huge array of four hundred rooms[46]. The temple was left out of the description and the presence of 100 Buddhist monks near the centre sounds fanciful but probable.

The city was a microcosm of the empire's best and worst. Traders and artisans flocked from all corners of the empire and from beyond. People speaking several tongues walked its streets and bylanes. The city sucked up the empire's resources and talents like a sponge – its money, artisans, craftsmen, traders and musicians. Conventional religious sects battled with the heterodox ones for recognition and patronage. The city started with multi-storeyed mansions at the centre and ended up with despicable hovels at the periphery. It was a city of appalling contrasts. Yet to say this would be to overlook the finest collection of stone and brass sculptures, the stunningly colourful festivals, the grandness of the emperor's palaces the fine rhythm of the grand temple's othuvars when they recited the hymns, and the dance and drama extravaganzas which must have put Indra's pageants to shame.

Two cities outside the Kaveri delta—Kanchipuram in the north and Madurai in the South—continued to be patronised by Rajaraja, even though they were capitals of captured territories. Kanchipuram was the erstwhile capital of the Pallavas and Madurai, the erstwhile capital of the Pandyas. When the Cholas were feudatories of these two powers before they set up their imperial regime, the Pallavas and Pandyas alternately dominated the Kaveri delta from their respective capitals. When the subordinate power trounced its masters, the relationship between the cities and the centre turned opposite. Thanjavur, in the heart of the Kaveri delta, cast an imperious eye at the capitals of the two erstwhile kingdoms and the long arm of the tax officials reached out to them. But these cities never lost their importance. Kanchipuram continued to grow as a prominent centre of weaving and commerce. It was connected to the port of Mamallapuram from where it traded with the Romans and later with Arabs, Persians and the South-east. During Rajaraja's reign its hinterland continued to expand through expansion of agriculture and the growing web of trade. It maintained its tradition of 'cultural significance and was an important centre of Buddhism, Jainism, Vishnuism and Shaivism'[47].

Weaving communities, the *Saliyar* and the *Kaikkolar*, had existed for several centuries and were encouraged to expand their manufacturing centres during the Chola period. The *Kaikkolars* were also an elite reserve army sought after during wars. The fact that they had well-demarcated quarters in all the cities and that too around the temple square is proof that they were part of the power structure, the owners of larger establishments having close connections with the royal family and figuring among the top contributors to the temple treasury and towards building maintenance, provision for perpetual lamps, installation of images and celebration of festivals. The muslins and chints of South India had an international market which valued the variety of vegetable dyes such as red safflower, indigo and madder used in production. Both vertical and horizontal looms were being deployed and the patterned loom might have come into existence at the time of Rajaraja signifying a great advance in technique and style. The smaller weaving establishments sold their produce at local markets and fairs. Inter-regional and international trade were controlled by the ubiquitous and powerful guilds. Taxes from the weaving industry must have been one of the biggest income streams for the empire going by the different types of taxes on looms, cotton, yarn and on the dyers. For the same reason it also had royal patronage with the state announcing tax concessions and remissions to attract weavers to new settlements[48]. The richer sections of weavers were money lenders as well. They managed donations provided by the royal family for festival celebrations at temples in their city. They were also members of the temple trusts, managing the temple corpus and accounting for incomes and expenditures, which must have given them access to cheap funds for their enterprises. In return for their "services" to the temple they enjoyed tax concessions, making a killing overall. In a trenchant account, Uttama Chola appointed *pattasalins* (leaders of the weaver's guild) as the managers of the Uragam Vishnu temple and deposited 200 *kalanju* of gold on perpetual interest of 30 *kalanju* for one year, to be paid in monthly instalments to meet expenses of lamp-holders for the festival and the flag-hoisters. This reflects the high social status of the upper crust of the weaving community and the royal patronage extended to them[49]. In effect, the less utilitarian aspects of the Chola policy on taxation were only too visible in the close connections established between the rural centre and the craft and trade guilds.

The eastern coast of South India was peppered with small and large port towns. Mamallapuram, near Chennai, was the chief port of the Pallavas, linking external markets to the manufactures of Kanchipuram and the northern hinterland. To the north of the port city were Mayilarpil, Kovalam and Tiruvadandai. Kaveripattinam (Puhar), to the south of Mamallapuram, enjoyed its heydays during the first few centuries of the first millennium and was still an active port at the time of Rajaraja but playing second fiddle to Nagapattinam, further south. Kollam, on the western coast, controlled the trade with the western markets, the precise motivation for Rajaraja to give it top priority in his shopping list of conquests. A guild of foreign merchants going by the name of *Anjuvannam*[50] played an active role in the economic activity of the port, and there are evidences of agreements between the city merchant guild, the Manigramam[51], foreign traders and the king regarding a number of trade related issues such as taxes, provision of warehouses and the protection of merchants and their wares. By all accounts, ports and market towns of South India were the hubs of a flourishing transit trade as well as direct trade with areas as far flung as South-east Asia, China, Arabia, Persia and Africa. Ships laden with 'rice, pulses, sesame, salt, pepper, oil, cloth, betel leaf, areca nut, and metals'[52] plied the seas.

Protected mercantile towns, called *erivirappattanam*, mushroomed during the Chola period. They were some sort of Special Economic Zones of the empire, described as 'inland ports'[53] and believed to have been set up in remote and inhospitable areas. It is very likely that they were warehousing centres on trade routes used by itinerant merchants. These centres were protected by royal sanction and where such sanction was not forthcoming, the merchants took upon the responsibility of defending their lives and warehouses with their own troops. The term '*erivira*' could actually mean 'mercenaries with spears'. These merchants belonged to one particular contingent of the merchant guilds whose caravans moved into hostile territory with armed protection. Not all of the pattanas were in inhospitable locations, though. The Erivirapattana in Tirunelveli district was part of a large urban settlement where the entire temple, its treasury and temple servants had been placed under the protection of the Chola army, after the Pandya country was conquered[54]. Apparently, the social and semi-military system of Erivirapattana 'strikingly recalls our East India Company. The '*vira valanjiyar*', as the merchants were styled in Tamil, signifies 'valiant merchants' – the predecessors of our 'gentlemen adventurers'[55] of the colonial period, though of a home-grown variety.

As we had seen earlier, the conquests of Rajaraja in Kerala and Lanka were 'more than looting expeditions and aimed at controlling important trade centres'. The Lankan expedition established Rajaraja's control over the Gulf of Mannar, which was not only 'an important entrepôt of maritime trade'[56] but a centre for pearl fisheries as well. Rajaraja promoted contacts, from across the Bay of Bengal, with South-east Asia which expanded further under his son Rajendra. There is a record of the King of Srivijaya (South Sumatra) and Kadaram (modern Kedah in Malaysia) patronising the building of a Buddhist monastery at Nagapattinam. The Srivijayan King from the Sailendra dynasty, Maravijayttungavarman, built the Chudamani Vihara in the port town, in some kind of a joint venture with the Chola state. But the relationship seemed to have turned sour soon during Rajendra's reign. The most likely reason was that the Chola navy saw an opportunity to establish its dominance over the seas of South-east Asia, when the Khmer (Cambodian) king Suryavarman requested aid from the Cholas against their Tambralinga (a kingdom in the Malay Peninsula) rivals. Notwithstanding the fact that the Tambralinga king was allied with Srivijaya, Rajendra went to war and decimated his rivals[57]. An alternative viewpoint could be that the Srivijaya Empire stepped out of their turf and started harassing the Chola ships sailing to China and the Far East forcing Rajendra to intervene with his Navy.

The dynamics of South Asian trade shows that 'trade overtures or agreements acquired some form of legitimacy through religious donations to temples and viharas'. In the case of the Nagapattinam Vihara, the camaraderie between the Chola and the kingdom of Srivijaya, which the Vihara was supposed to represent, did not last long. But 'Chola rulers made liberal endowments in the 11th century... and the persistence of Buddhist influence in Nagapattinam – particularly the Theravada influence – may be attributed to the trade relationships of South-east Asian countries with the Coramandel coast'[58] improving vastly. Through Srivijaya, first China and later Burma and Sri Lanka were involved in this activity. Rajaraja need not have troubled himself to build the Vihara considering that in a few decades his son would launch a ferocious war on Srivijaya, but then there is a thin line between diplomacy and war.

In the second half of the ninth century China was racked by internal political troubles which rendered it unsafe for foreign traders 'who now returned to the Malay Peninsula and Sumatra, whither the Chinese ships had to go for purchase of foreign goods'. But by the end of the tenth century, the political situation in China had become normal and the Song government was eager to give a fillip to foreign trade. Trade was made a government monopoly and missions were sent abroad by the emperor 'with credentials under the imperial seal and provisions of gold and piece-goods' to induce foreign traders to come to China. The Cholas, as the emerging maritime power, were only too eager to take advantage of this opportunity. Their envoys, or rather what was recorded as an embassy, 'took with them very valuable presents, but they were only ranked with those of a vassal state in Eastern Turkestan'. Perhaps the distance of the Chola Empire, or the 'novelty of the direct connection now started' or mere arrogance prevented the Chinese to give adequate respect to the 'position and importance' attained by the Cholas. The Chola embassy left towards the close of Rajaraja's rule and took over three years, 1150 days precisely[59], to reach China in 2015, after completing odd jobs on the way. Rajaraja was not alive when it returned to convey the lukewarm attitude of the Chinese. If the embassy had returned a few months earlier, the emperor's curiosity about the huge Song Empire would have been satiated. The embassy had travelled to China with gifts of pearls 844 kgs of pearls, sixty elephant tusks and nearly 40 kgs of frankincense, enough to impress any monarch. The Chinese interpreters let the emperor know that 'they (the embassy) wished to evince the respect of a nation for (Chinese) civilisation'. But the pearls, unaccountably, failed to impress the emperor even as Rajaraja had allegedly admitted in his missive that 'to present the products of my country is like ants and crickets being attracted to mutton, and to pay tribute and serve Your Majesty is like the sun-flower and giant hyssop being drawn towards the sun'. And quite predictably 'they were ordered by Imperial Decree to remain in waiting at the side of the gate of the palace'. A redeeming incident was that 'it happened to be the Emperor's birthday and the envoys had a fine opportunity to witness the congratulations in the sacred Enclosure'. Chinese accounts, while admitting that the southern kingdoms never paid tribute to their country, give an unflattering account of what Rajaraja wrote to the Song emperor, in which while observing that 'your goodness protected even the feeble reed and your trust extended to the fish in the deep water'[60], he avows that 'I presume to consider that as your subject I am a small being like a mosquito and a humble creature like a papier mache dog, having been living for generations in a barbarous town'[61]. There is reason to look at these peremptory accounts with mistrust. If it had been the intention of Rajaraja to get into the Chinese emperor's good books as a mosquito and papier mache dog, his embassy would have directly sailed to Guangzhou to offer fealty to the emperor. But instead, the embassy of 52 persons visited all major ports on the way, and almost as a last item in the shopping list, dropped sails on Chinese shores. But the Chinese Emperor must have soon realised his mistake since trade continued to grow under Rajendra. It is anybody's guess that Rajendra's expedition against Srivijaya, 'rendered communication with the Southern seas and the Empire of China more easy and more regular'[62]. In an ill-conceived move, driven by the calculation that 'it would be more lucrative for local traders if the China-India trade had to terminate in Srivijaya', the kingdom tried to impose itself as a middleman in the trade. But the hand twisting of the Chola merchants raised the wrath of Rajendra, who promptly sent his navy and brought the region under his control. Srivijaya could have had its mercantile interests in mind, but so did the Chola Emperor. In this case, 'military power decided the issue'[63]. The Straits of Malacca came under Chola purview and South Indian shipping and commerce started to have a field day in the region. By the 13th century a colony of Tamil merchants, 'perhaps members of a guild' had settled in Quanzhou in Fujian province in China. Several images and artefacts were found here along with a bilingual Tamil-Chinese inscription. Hordes of Chinese coins have been discovered in the Pattukottai taluk of Thanjavur district to vouch for the flourishing Indo-China trade. Emboldened by the expanding trade and a huge Navy to defend it, the Cholas continued to happily meddle in the affairs of the South-eastern states well into the twelfth century.

There is evidence that powerful guilds controlled the trade with South-east Asia. Corporate organisations of merchants called *samaya*, which means an organisation created through agreement or contract, were prominent in the tenth century. They were governed by a code of conduct — a code that must have insisted on transparency among traders but conveniently allowed the use of force to capture trade routes using the free market theory. One such powerful guild was the *ayyavole*, known as *ainnurruvar* (the Five Hundred) in the Tamil country. It was originally established in Aihole in Karnataka and 'soon became the largest supra-regional association of merchants' unlike trade associations in China which were a state monopoly at that time. The '*manigramam* was another important merchant guild located in the Tamil country' which operated independently but later got subordinated to the Aiyyavole in the 13th century. The *manigramam* was not just a local organisation but an international one, 'having a base at Takuapa in Thailand' among others. This had been established earlier under the Pallavas, and inscriptions suggest the existence of an 'autonomous coastal settlement here'. An interesting aspect was that the 'guilds were based on occupation and economic interest and membership cut across lines of caste and religion'. These large merchant guilds had direct links with specialist craft associations such as that of weavers. Yet another association of foreign merchants was the *anjuvannam*, referred to earlier, which was initially involved in trade activities on the Kerala coast and 'later fanned out to other areas'[64]. Interestingly, this is a group of Jewish traders, who began their commercial activities in the eighth and ninth centuries and spread to other coastal areas of South India by the time Rajaraja consolidated the Chola Empire. Evidently, it had wide connections with the local merchants and the Five Hundred, 'a symbiotic relationship fostered by trade interests'[65]. Unequivocally, 'the *nagaram* organisation and specialisation in the marketing of specific commodities thus proved to be a major factor in the urbanisation' that fuelled the expansion of the Chola Empire. The simultaneous appearance of a large number of diverse occupational groups, other than agriculture in such centres, resulted in the expansion of cities, with separate quarters for merchants, artisans and weavers. This led to a 'highly complex social stratification' which is 'another notable feature of this urbanisation', and 'its connection with the emergence of specialised crafts and artisan groups is undeniable'[66].

'Horse trading was yet another specialised occupation and was entirely controlled by merchants from Malaimandalam'[67] in Kerala. Arab trade in horses was conducted mainly through the western ports and the Cholas depended on Kerala merchants to procure and transport them to Tamil areas. This encouraged settlements of merchants from Kerala in the heart of the Chola country and in the Pudukottai region.

Regions such as modern Pudukottai and the Salem-Coimbatore belt stimulated urbanisation through their strategic location on trade routes. The Pudukottai region acted as the buffer region between the Chola and Pandya heartlands and just as the Arisilaru river in the north, saw streams of blood flow in the frequent wars until the Cholas established decisive control. To make doubly sure that the trade route from the northern parts of the empire to Lanka was always open and Madurai, the erstwhile capital of the Pandyas, was firmly in his grip, Rajaraja engineered matrimonial ties with the Irukkuvel chiefs of Kodumbalur, a *nagaram* of considerable size in the region. Rajaraja resorted to such alliances on more than one occasion in the interest of keeping the capital cities under his control. He married his daughter to the Chalukyan prince Vimaladitya to retain control over Vengi. Marital alliances with the Chera, Pandya and Ganga royal families were also encouraged. The ancient port of Korkai near Tuticorin was the chief port of the Pandyas from ancient times, known for its pearl fisheries and documented by Ptolemy and the Periplus in the early centuries of the first millennium. When the Chola army cut across Pandyan territory and subdued both their allies, the Cheras and Lankans, both the port of Korkai and the capital city of Madurai fell into their accommodating hands.

Rajaraja's coins have their own story to tell. Several thousand of them have been recovered, in spite of the fact that they had 'mostly disappeared in the goldsmith's crucible'[68], thanks to being a recognised currency for about six centuries from the tenth to the sixteenth. The Cholas boasted of using coins right from the late centuries of the first millennium BCE. They were made of copper, square in shape, bearing on the one side the figure of a standing tiger with an uplifted tail and on the other side fish, elephant or other symbols. Above the tiger is shown the sun, symbolic of the solar race of the Cholas. The tiger with it roaring countenance, lifted paw and upturned tail is specially referred to as the royal crest of the Cholas in Sangam literature. Praising the valour of the Chola King Nalamkilli, the poet Kovur Kizhar ecstatically describes that when he captures the opponent's forts, as a rule, he imprinted his crest of the roaring tiger. In the ancient port of Kaveripattinam itself, the wooden doors of forts were marked with the tiger, the royal crest[69].

At the time of Rajaraja, two types were in circulation, largely. The first type has the bow-tiger-fish emblem stamped on both sides with the legend 'Sri Raja Raja' written in nagari characters. The second type shows a standing man on the obverse, presumably the king himself, and a seated figure on the reverse with the same legend as the first one. Both of them were ostensibly available in plenty in gold, silver and copper, going by the huge hoards discovered. The style of the coins are actually a take-off from the Kushan coins, which in turn copied the Romans. There were variations. Rajaraja introduced slight variations for different territories, such as the coin with the fish emblem circulating in the Pandyan country, a small consolation for the conquered territories[70]. The Cholas flaunted gold and silver coins, compared to the earlier Pallavas who had to be content with lead and copper coins. The money economy thrived, and the increased prosperity and economic development were unmistakable, though limited to elite sections of the cities. Gold coins, called the *kazhanju* and *kasu*[71] were used for gifts to nobles and temples, and the occasional poet and prostitute. Wages to agricultural workers and temple staff were paid in paddy[72]. But for all practical purposes, while the '*nagarams* and itinerant trade brought money into more frequent use', monetisation was on a low key, with paddy being the overall basis of an exchange system[73].

The rise of the cities, specialisation in crafts and trade, and the merchant guilds were crucial to the expansion of the Chola Empire, which 'in some ways, was the most significant of the dozen or so empires which rose and fell during India's long, tumultuous history'. The empire survived some 460 years, longer than any of them. 'The Choza was also the only Asian empire (bar the Japanese) to have indulged, albeit briefly, in overseas expansion. It conquered Sri Lanka, the Andaman and Nicobar islands and, temporarily, parts of south- east Asia - the islands of Sumatra, Java and Bali, and the southern part of the Malay peninsula'[74].

Fig. 10 - Coins of Uttama Chola

4

POWER TO SHARE

After raining death and destruction on his foes in all the eight directions, Rajaraja held sway over the whole of South India including the Telugu, Karnataka and Kerala countries, though there is a 'paucity of Chola records outside the Tamil country proper'[75]. He had ample time serving as a yuvaraja under his uncle Uttama Chola to plan his future military campaigns to perfection and an administrative apparatus that would be required to retain the vast territory and wealth his numerous conquests would bequeath him. The resultant Chola state was a model for centuries to come and an instrument that commanded respect at home and abroad. Jealousies swirled around the royal family and internecine rivalries surfaced now and then but the monarch, ostensibly, maintained a fine balance to keep his subjects happy and the aspirations of the newly emerging urban elite and wily feudatories under check. He was only too aware that quarrels can drag the first imperial state of South India down an endless tunnel. Towards his later years, though, wars were not a preferred option. Why waste energy on wars when enemies could be bought and matrimonial alliances with adversaries consummated?

In spite of the availability of thousands of inscriptions, copper plates and literary evidence, the state of Rajaraja Cholan is a complex and sometimes confusing kaleidoscope of institutions, politics, society and religion. A popular view that prevails even today is of a state where 'much greater things were accomplished by corporate and voluntary effort, a greater sense of social harmony prevailed, and a consciousness of active citizenship was more widespread'[76]. Others viewed it quite the opposite way, as a 'state of plunder and piety'[77] where sky high temples were built and maintained from the spoils of war and loot. For all practical purposes, however, South India seems to have left behind tribal chieftains and small principalities of the earlier centuries during the 'Byzantine royalty of Rajaraja and his successors with its numerous palaces, officials and ceremonials and its majestic display of the concentrated resources of an extensive empire'[78]. This view has been criticised as a pre-conception of historians contrary to evidence which led them to believe that the Chola state is a great unitary state under a powerful king 'whose will was worked through an elaborate bureaucratic apparatus assisted by a powerful military establishment'[79]. But this scepticism has become feebler as new data on the empire surfaced over the decades. Several levels of state organisation are evident from inscriptions – from the central royal administration to corporate assemblies of towns and villages and to a proliferation of trade and craft guilds, which we had a glimpse of in the earlier chapter. One cannot easily dismiss the view that the townships in the Chola Empire offer a 'remarkable parallel' to that of the 'cities of Gaul in the Roman Empire as can be seen from the description of the latter by Faustel de Coulanges'[80]. The *nagarams* and the *managarams* owned their public property, received donations and bequests, directly administered this property, regulated land rights, lent out their money on interest and gathered octrois and an abundance of taxes. They had to obey all the orders of the imperial government, a commitment they were more than willing to give in exchange for autonomy in certain internal affairs. But the city was a complete organism and had a life of its own so much so that if 'it was not a free state; it was at any rate a state'[81]. There could be some exaggeration here. It appears at first glance that there is a glaring contradiction between a powerful central state governing a large area on the one hand and autonomous cities which were almost free states, on the other. But as we shall see, the Chola state was a powerful central state, capable of managing its entire realm, but shared its power with village assemblies, corporate bodies of towns and merchant guilds, not to speak of feudatories and high officials.

The existence of the self-administered peasant localities, the *nadu*, could lead one to believe that the state consisted of several independent segments which recognised a 'sacred ruler whose overlordship is of a moral sort and is expressed in an essentially ritual idiom'[82]. In simple words, this implied that Rajaraja was essentially driving an empire whose parts were scarcely under his control and that he was a ritual king rather than an emperor on whom the 'kings of the sea waited'. The description of the Chola state as some sort of a 'ritual' wonder certainly 'ignores the basis of enduring power and military success achieved by the Cholas'[83].

There was a time, several centuries ago, when the 'Crowned King' of the Chola land, shared with two other crowned heads, a 'land studded with petty principalities held by a somewhat turbulent, but not uncultured, aristocracy'. But after they subdued the other two crowned heads, using methods, fair and foul, and after driving back the Rashtrakutas, the 'Chola monarchy embraced the whole of Southern India'. At the time of Rajaraja, the 'Chola state ceases to be a small state and grows to imperial dimensions'. Starting from very humble beginnings, the king has now apparently graduated to the title of 'Emperor', that is *chakravartigal*[84]. Not till much later, after the conquests of the South and North, do inscriptions upgrade him to 'Emperor of the Three Worlds'[85]. From his reign starts the prefacing of stone inscriptions with an account of the exploits of the king in set form. To cap it all, the Thanjavur temple which Rajaraja built 'rose in the proportion and technique of its architecture as much above any other temple.'[86]

Many accounts portray the Chola palace as a centre throbbing with gaiety and vivaciousness. The royal household oozed of opulence. There were 'numerous servants of various descriptions including body-guards of sorts'. Women seemed to have had control over much of the palace with bathroom and kitchen establishments totally under their supervision. The palace servants, who enjoyed 'fair competence in return for generally very light work' were organised into *velams* and had their quarters right near the palace.

According to a Chinese historiographer, the Cholas followed a very weird custom at state banquets, at least in the later Chola regimes, where 'the king and four court officials first prostrate themselves at the foot of the throne and then play music and dance together. They do not drink wine but do eat meat. Their custom is to wear clothing made of cotton. They also eat bread. For serving food to the tables and entertaining guests, the king employs over ten thousand courtesans who serve in rotating daily shifts of three thousand'[87]. Apparently, each important member of the royal family had his or her own 'entourage of personal attendants'. Going by the inscriptions, the kings, his queens and their numerous relatives erected temples, endowed them on a liberal scale and spent considerable sums of money on the reclamation of land, promotion of irrigation works, maintenance of schools and hospitals. All this, evidently, led to a profuse display of 'loving regard and affection which generally actuated the feelings of the people towards their rulers of various grades'. One would look at with suspicion the official propaganda that 'much that was collected from people by way of numerous taxes… was returned to them in the form of charitable endowments'[88]. This could very well be a fairy tale that the ruling circles promoted to convince their subjects of their benevolence. But it seems to have worked, as it does even today. Not wishing to be left behind, this practice, of charitable endowments, was generally followed by the 'official nobility, the merchants and other well-to-do classes of society'.

By the time of Rajaraja, Vedic rituals almost lost their backing from the royal family. Emphasis, manifestly, shifted to 'dana, gift, in preference to yagna, sacrifice'[89] leaving out many gift loving Brahmanas in the cold. Innovative methods of gifts for the rich to gather religious merit such as the *tulabhara*[90] and *hiranyagarba*[91] were introduced. The temple and the matha, flourishing on such gifts together with the creation of *brahmadeya* villages through royal land grants to Brahmanas, worked out to be an excellent combination to establish and prolong the Chola rule. The Jain pallis and the Buddhist viharas also had their fair share of this royal benevolence.

Seemingly, the cult of *Deva-raja*, the God-king, seeped into Chola territory from the Indian archipelago and the Indo-Chinese peninsula where the idea had perhaps originated. Several temples and often the chief icons in them were named after the ruling king who established them. Rajaraja built the Arinjigai-Iswara temple at Melpadi to commemorate Arinjaya, his grandfather, who died fighting in the battle at Arrur. An image of Sundara Chola was set up at the Thanjavur temple and arrangements were made by his daughter Kundavai, Rajaraja's elder sister, for its worship. Kundavai herself, not to be left behind, endowed a statue of herself in the same temple. In what we witness, the identity of the king and god had merged to such an extent that there are instances of 'construction of sepulchral temples over the remains of kings and princes'[92]. Reminiscent of the Pharaohs, renovations of some temples in later times, unearthed human bones under the sanctum sanctorum[93]. It is a fact that in the early centuries of the Tamil civilisation, power was not considered 'something summoned from another world' such as the celestial gods of the Rig Veda; 'it was immanent in the things one comes into contact with every day'. So, when new gods were imported from North India, as we shall see in more detail in the next chapter, the king and god were called using similar terms. The temple and the palace had an uncanny resemblance to each other. The 'deity was treated like a king, being awakened in the morning with auspicious music, getting married, and receiving many of the same ceremonies as the human king'[94]. The king and the deity, indulged in frequent promenades around the city streets, in splendid processions, to give their respective subjects and devotees, an audience. The deity enjoyed 'occasional excursions outside the temple for bathing, enjoying the hunt, or resting in his garden, accompanied by an entourage'[95], and most importantly his consort. Musicians, singers, and dancers accompanied the deity in procession. In one instance, Kundavai ordered that thirty-two temple women, the Acharya, drummer and the musicians of the Siva temple she had built in Darapuram in South Arcot district, to participate both in Siva's hunting festival and in the festival procession of the Vishnu temple of the same village, in a demonstrative show of the royal families identity with both Saivism and Vaishnavism[96].

From all accounts, Rajaraja had an impressive army boasting about seventy regiments with 'a corporate life of its own and even free to endow benefactions or build temples in its own name'[97]. In fact, it is from such civil transactions that we come to know more about the army rather than from the war front. These transactions could have happened in between wars and could have also been the upshot of a successful campaign with a part of the war booty landing in the temple treasury. There are references to the elephant corps, cavalry, infantry and the dreaded troops of the *Kaikkolar*, the soldier turned weavers. In addition, there were bowmen, swordsmen and regiments of the *Velaikkarar*, who might have been a volunteer force[98]. But other sources refer to them as the most loyal and dependable forces of the king, and the finest swords in the Chola realm. The conquests of Rajaraja are real enough to dismiss the notion that 'these conquests neither presupposed nor required a vast, standing army'. It doesn't seem logical and effective that he relied on 'military power possessed by numerous chiefs and itinerant merchant groups'[99]. To rely on conscripts from ranks of the last king he had slain, their loyalties uncertain, would have been a foolhardy move for the emperor. The army had set up local garrisons and cantonments (called *kadagams*) across the Chola country and taken over the temple maintenance of the city. An inscription about a military regiment called the Mundrukai-Mahasenai (the Great Army with Three Arms) found in Thirunelveli district talks about the exploits of the regiment in defeating the Kannara, subduing the Gangeya, destroying Vizhinjam on the sea, taking the hill country of Malai*nadu*, routing the fleet at Salai, putting to fight the Chalukyas, capturing Vanavasi and dismantling the fortress of Vatapi[100]. It is not improbable that being an elite regiment in the army, it could have been involved in all the major campaigns of the emperor. Many of the military leaders (senapatis) surprisingly had Brahmana roots. The evidence of garrisons and regiments certainly makes it clear that 'they were not a mere rabble beaten up for particular occasions with no training in the military arts and no taste for the field'[101]. But, importantly, the army was not cut off from the civil population as is the case today. There are many instances of the army interesting itself in civil affairs and making charitable endowments to temples and protecting them. The *Kaikkolar* must have been the regularly paid royal troops and the Nattupadai, the popular militia. The inimitable Zhao Rukuo, the Chinese historian, whose description of the royal palace had already amused us earlier has this to say about the Chola army:

'It fights wars with the various other states of India. The government has 60,000 war elephants, each seven or eight feet in height. In battle, the elephant carries warriors in a house on its back. These warriors use arrows at long range and spears at close range. When the army wins a battle, even the elephants are given titles to recognize their merit. The people of this country are impetuous and unafraid of death. They will even duel with swords in front of the king, fighting to the death without regrets'[102].

This has to be taken with a pinch of salt since Zhao Rukuo never left Chinese shores and based his narrative on travelogues of Chinese merchants. Neither should we dismiss this altogether as a fancy story. In spite of meagre details, 'the many military expeditions... suggest an effective army organisation' supported by 'periodical levies of troops from the chieftains'[103].

The notion that plunder and piety were close siblings of the reign of Rajaraja cannot be dismissed completely. Leave alone their enemies, the Chalukyas, the Cholas themselves have carved on stone how they had created an 'intolerable burden for many generations to the people on either side of the Tungabhadra by the bitterness of warfare'[104]. Poetic exaggerations of fair play and chivalry totally avoided mentioning these wars where 'wanton injury was inflicted on non-combatant populations, and women subjected to cruel disgrace and mutilation', though a later composition, the *Kalingattuparani*, brings out the horror of the Kalinga war in fascinating details. The destruction of Jaina bastis by Rajendra under the command of

Rajaraja, was not a malicious accusation by a defeated enemy but a 'grim business of fire and sword'. The royal family and war commanders had no scruples about admitting that a huge amount of booty fell into their hands from foreign conquests. The construction and maintenance of the mammoth Thanjavur temple, renovation of other temples throughout the Chola country, building of educational institutions and hospitals were often 'only the bestowal of plundered wealth on public institutions', a phenomenon that that people are not a stranger to even today. An inscription on the north wall of the central shrine of the Thanjavur temple lists not less than 148 items of silver seized by Rajaraja from his Pandya and Chera conquests[105]. Donations to temples from the war booty would have made a curious fellowship of mercenaries and priests in the transfer. Likewise, revenue from many villages from captured territories in Lanka, Tondai*nadu* and Malai*nadu* were assigned to the maintenance of the Thanjavur temple[106].

Many questions have been raised about the authenticity of the Srivijaya conquests and the existence of a navy at the time of Rajaraja. Some have scoffed at basing the existence of a Chola navy upon 'a few questionable references to numberless ships' in Chola inscriptions and upon the 'mysterious adventures of Rajendra I in Malayan waters'[107]. Even more ridiculed is the concept of a 'greater India' and Hindu colonisation of South-east Asia. But there are too many maritime activities which could not have been accomplished with just dugouts and canoes. South Indian colonies had sprouted in the Malay Archipelago and Indochina from as early as the Sangam period. The embarrassment caused to the Embassy sent by Rajaraja to China cannot discount the existence of large ships to make the long journey. Tamil inscriptions at Takuapa prove the existence of a South Indian mercantile corporation, the *manigramam* as early as the ninth century. The conquest of the northern part of Lanka, Khandaloor and Vizhinjam would have required at least a modest fleet. Considering that the Periplus could not have been totally off the mark in commenting on the active maritime activities of the Coramandel coast, 'the existence of a well-ordered fleet comprising ships and boats of different grades must be admitted'[108]. The Arab merchant Sulaiman while making several trips between the Persian Gulf and China in the 9th century had said about Maldives that they 'built ships and houses and executed all other works with a consummate art'[109]. A century later, Rajaraja could have arrived at the same opinion and launched a campaign to capture Maldives to take advantage of this 'consummate art' and build himself a navy. Certainly, the Embassy to the kingdoms of Indochina showed that Rajaraja's regime was not a self-obsessed one; it was definitely open to the influence of the outside world just as its bustling ports.

That the Chola state was a monarchy is never in doubt. There is no evidence that Rajaraja consulted his council of ministers, if it existed at all. Considering his fairly long and smooth reign, the ministers were either kept away from the corridors of power or they lacked a taste for intrigues. A labyrinthine and powerful officialdom assisted the king in administrative tasks, 'controlling, supervising and regulating an existing order' to which the King added occasional details. There was no legislative power in the modern sense, or any control over executive actions by legislative bodies, pretending to be independent as we see now. The legislation was more in the nature of declarations, *vyavasthas*, which were local laws in broad conformity with the established dharma of the times. Public opinion when it was in consonance with established dharma did matter and a regime which violated dharma was in danger of facing the wrath of the people and its allies. Unlike the situation today where local civil and criminal disputes manage to climb up to the highest level of adjudication, the society of that time 'did not commit to the care of government anything more than the tasks of police and justice'[110]. So, while the King had a right over his subjects' lives, his sword rarely came out of its scabbard while maintaining law. Local corporate bodies in the villages, towns and trading centres generally took charge of the essentials of social regulation, with of course the most influential and wealthy having their final say. But royal mandates expressed through a system of royal inscriptions in the various localities of the vast empire had to be observed by local social groups on issues such as land transfers and imposition of taxes.

It is quite possible that the 'superior executive strength' of the Chola state created 'a highly organised and thoroughly efficient bureaucracy'. This is evident in the creation of an administrative hierarchy which regulated public life and mopped up a huge amount of taxes. However, much needs to be investigated about the 'nice balance struck between centralised control and local initiative' which supposedly ensured that the problem of 'the man versus the state never arose'[111]. Though the officers went by the generic name of *adigarigal*, they were categorised into *perundanam*[112], higher grade, and the *sirudanam*, the lower grade, officers[113]. The division was so unbending and ingrained into the psyche of the Chola establishment that even other officers, the *karumigal*, and the servants, the *panimakkal*, and even divisions of the army stood divided on these lines. Not only the King but even the feudatories such as Pazhuvettaraiyar Kandanmaravan endorsed such a grading. Higher officers certainly received lucrative entitlements besides the gold and silver looted from enemy treasuries. Officials being remunerated with land (often grabbed from peasants) according to their status was quite common. The income from this land, one part in cash and the other part in kind was the *jivita*, some sort of a regular pension, for the officer. The ownership of land itself was left in the hands of the poor peasant, who after paying off the officer's dues, would have had very little to survive on. The officer was free to transfer or sell his rights over the dues from the peasant's meagre income to others as he may wish, making the entitlement a transferable right to loot.

Subject to taxes and the frequent dipping into the peasants' income through cash and kind transfers, not all self-governing villages would have been a very happy place to live. A number of such subsistence villages formed the *nadu*, the larger ones calling themselves valanadu. Above the valandu was the manadalam, the proving proper, the largest administrative division. There were about eight or nine such provinces, including Lanka, at the end of Rajaraja's reign, which meant that they were much bigger than the present districts of Tamil Nadu. The names were changed so frequently when a new occupant sat on the Chola throne – not an uncommon phenomenon even today — that 'Chola geography came to suffer as much from the plague of homonyms as the kings themselves'[114]. The kings had their own confidantes. Sundara Chola, Rajaraja's father, showed his 'affection' for his 'noble minister' Anirudha brahmadiraja, a Vaishnava Brahmana from Anbil, by a generous perpetual grant of 10 velis of land (about 20 acres). Rajaraja ordered a grant of the Anaimangalam village to the Chudamani-varma vihara in Nagapattinam, for the joint venture project with Srivijaya, an act that many in the higher corridors of power would have viewed askance.

The high values of dharma, often formidable and imposing set by his predecessors, delineated the perimeter within which Rajaraja dispensed justice to his subjects. The ideas of the politically subversive epic *Silappadhikaram* were still the norm in the Chola Empire even if several centuries had rolled by after the Pandyan king, 'in his anxiety to be reconciled to the queen'[115], cut off the head of the innocent Kovalan, the hero of the epic, under the false presumption that he had stolen the queen's anklets. Justice was immediately and unequivocally served. The Pandyan king died of remorse and his capital, Madurai, was burnt to ashes, with all its people presumably for having tolerated such an unjust king. In the epic, the Chola king is an exemplary ruler, but Madurai the capital of the Pandyan king 'is steeped in pleasures'[116] to such an extent 'that even sages turned into young men; As they pursued these women..'[117]. But it is the Chera king Senguttuvan, who defines kingship that would rankle all future kings of the South as they sat on their throne to dispense justice. According to the Chera king rajadharma entails:

To forswear tyranny and ensure the welfare

Of his subjects is the king's duty. Born

Of a noble line, suffering is his lot. His throne

Is not to be envied[118].

The later epic Manimekalai, presents the idea even more forcefully and palpabaly:

If the king swerved from the rule of law,

The planets would step out of line.

If the planets stepped out of line,

The rains would fail. If the rains failed,

Life on earth would cease. It would be true

To say: 'One who rules the world as a king

Should look upon every life as his own'[119].

The legend of Manuneedhi Cholan, often quoted by authors of the time of Rajaraja, has it that the king hung a giant bell in front of his courtroom for anyone needing justice to ring. And one fine day, he was drawn out to his palace door by a cow who decided to give the bell a try after her calf had been killed under the wheels of his swaggering son's chariot. In order to provide justice to the cow, the king gave a death sentence to his own son which so impressed Lord Siva that both son and calf were brought back to life. The legend has often served as a metaphor for fairness and justice in the Tamil psyche and no Chola king worth his salt had forgotten to swear by this predecessor.

Tamil literature of the period such as *Kalingattuparani*, of which we will see more in a later chapter and *Vikrama Cholan Ula*, also eulogise a Sibi Chakravarthy, whose legend was already popularised by the Mahabharata and the Buddhist Jataka tales. In his Chola incarnate, he was called Sembiyan and many Chola kings too took his name. The *devas* wanting to test his sense of justice and compassion turned themselves into a hawk and pigeon and forced the king to take a stand. If he wished to save the pigeon, then he was depriving the hawk of its food. So, he better decide what is justice. Sibi offered his own flesh in compensation which pleased the *devas* so much that he was restored to his original self with all his flesh intact.

These legends and their logic must have influenced the decisions of rulers at the highest level. In day-to-day situations, there is reason to believe that 'justice, like legislation, was very largely a matter of local concern'.

Most disputes were settled by the village assemblies and the urban guilds. An imaginative story by Sekkizhar, who compiled the hagiography of the sixty-three nayanars, the Saivite *bhakti* saints, gives us a colourful account of judicial procedures. When the young Sundaramurthy, a Saivite saint, decides to enter wedlock, Siva appears from nowhere on the eve of his marriage as an old Brahmana and gives Sundarar the shock of his life by producing a document in which his grandfather had signed a deed of perpetual bondage on behalf of himself and his descendants. The plaintiff takes the case to the *Sabha* after Sundarar tears the document to pieces. The judges initially raise an objection that a Brahmana cannot be enslaved under any conditions. They relent when they hear that Siva has the original document and what was torn was just a copy. The age of the document and signature are established as genuine by the record office which has facsimiles of the grandfather's writing and signature. The judges have no choice but to pronounce that Sundarar has lost his case to the old Brahmana sage. In this creative enlargement of the holy lives of the Saiva saints, 'Sekkizhar drew upon his intimate knowledge of contemporary life to lend colour and verisimilitude to his narration'. So, the trial scene described a century later than Rajaraja's time could still be 'treated as a fair specimen of the daily occurrence in the numberless villages of the Chola kingdom'. The disputants state their own case and are thankfully rid of advocates. The conviction with which the disputants put forward their pleas, the personal knowledge of the judges, the presence of evidence are all crucial to arrive at a judgement. The presence of record rooms have been confirmed by other inscriptions. The only anomalous outcome is that a 'document can override custom however well established' or that a specific agreement can supersede public opinion and accepted morality. 'But we need not press on this inference'[120] since the plaintiff ultimately reveals himself as god and gets away with any dispute over his residency in the locality.

There was no distinction between criminal and civil offences in the empire and cases were dealt with in village courts or at the next higher level, to the officer of the king's government in the administrative setup of the *nadu*. 'There was a great deal of rough natural justice dispensed through extra-judicial channels', something which we sorely miss today. Village and higher-level committees barred persons convicted of theft, adultery and forgery – again an unlikely practice today. Those persons who had ridden a donkey, ostensibly for committing a crime, were also barred from public life. Surprisingly, capital punishment was reserved only for treason. Even offences such as manslaughter and murder were punished with fines as lenient as maintaining a perpetual lamp burning in the nearest temple, or endowing sheep, or paying a fine. Rioting and incendiarism also attracted fines. Offences against the king and his relatives were dealt with more severely, but even here, the killers of Rajaraja's brother Aditya Karikala got away with just the confiscation of their properties. But it is difficult to imagine that inscriptions tell the whole story. Such leniency is in great contrast to the way Chola military forces treated people in captured territories. However, the Chinese writer, whom we had seen earlier reported that 'heinous crimes are punished with decapitation or by being trampled to death by an elephant' which had long been favourite punishments adopted by Indian kings.

There is strong reason to believe that 'under the Cholas the villages of Southern India were full of vigour and strength'[121]. But this applied to only a section of the population since village assemblies had as its members only the propertied and educated adult males. Large village assemblies appointed several committees, the *variyams*. Work done in the *variyams* was voluntary. A number of other corporate structures existed at the higher level of the *nadu* and the nagaram.

Not very different from today's villages of Tamil Nadu, the rural populace eked out their living under the mountainous burden of 'a hierarchy of rights and statuses'[122] which created social and spatial segregation, with the ritually impure, the *paraiyars*, living on the outskirts. This was true of both the Brahmana elite dominated *brahmadeya* villages and the non-Brahmana elite dominated *urs*. The cultivating Vellalars slogged under a few dominating landowners of the same caste, as tenants. The Vellalars were classified as Shudras, but the 'tag did not carry with it the connotations of a lowly social status and discrimination'. In some respects, the landowning Vellalars wielded as much social clout as their Brahmana counterparts. Potters and blacksmiths, who belonged to different *jatis*, owned small plots of land and provided services for the village, in exchange for a social status just above the *paraiyars*. Royal land grants and progress of agricultural technology saw to it that 'economically powerful and locally influential landlords' emerged under royal patronage. The landed elites of the larger villages organised in urs and *sabhas* seemingly had considerable clout in the affairs of the Chola state and managed tax collections and regular supply of commodities to the urban centres. However, 'in emphasising the peasantry as the prime social, economic, political and cultural element in South Indian history' many historians 'ended up sidelining kings, chieftains, merchants and other urban groups'[123]. The rural elites, caught up in their caste antagonisms, helplessly saw power, slowly and surely, drifting away towards the rapidly growing political centres, manufacturing hubs, trading ports and ceremonial centres. With the urban centres under the control of Buddhism and Jainism in the early centuries of the first millennia, the Brahmanas might have initially rejoiced getting land grants and becoming the dominant power in the *brahmadeya* villages starting from the time of the Pallavas. The Chola kings made a decisive departure and made their gifts more to religious institutions and not just to individual Brahmanas, severely undermining their influence in the urban centres. But on the other hand, to claim that the villages were full of 'vigour and strength' does not seem to be such a defensively feeble argument considering that the economy was on the upswing and villages benefited from an unprecedented spurt in demand for all its products and services from the fast expanding towns and cities. For centuries later, the advance in canal and tank irrigation achieved in Chola times would ensure that the Kaveri belt remained the rice bowl of the South with inscriptions revealing 'striking similarities with the general patterns of irrigation prevalent in the Kaveri delta today'. The type of irrigation used depended on 'which type of technology was best suited to a particular terrian' with the village and town assemblies stepping in to maintain tanks and farmers 'granted sowing rights over adjacent plots of land in return for taking the responsibility of dredging tanks'[124].

The *nagarams*, production and exchange centres, increasingly flexed their muscles and reached out to markets at the inter-regional and international levels. The gold rush from Rome had stopped but new markets from Africa to China kept the production hubs of the Chola region bustling. Some of the *nagarams* were given *taniyur* status, 'which made them independent and free of the jurisdiction of the *nadu* they were located in'[125]. The members called the *nagarattar*, at least the well-heeled sections, owned and managed land in the city as well as the nearby agricultural region, extending their authority over the countryside. The *nagarams* emerged as an influential layer in the social order, and lavished their gifts, mostly in gold and silver, on temples and institutions. There also emerged corporate organisations 'associated with specialised groups' such as producers of textiles, ghee, oil and spices. Oil and seafaring merchants had their own guilds.

Crafts underwent significant improvement in techniques attracting larger investments and operations. The hand operated oil mills gave way to bullock-driven ones and textile looms mushroomed.

Perhaps the growing clout of these urban elites resulted in a gradual shift of royal patronage from land grants to individual or a group of Brahmanas or other rural groups, and to the temples. This combined with donations from the well-to-do merchants, on whom the smell of money would have clung like perfume, resulted in magnificent temple complexes in or near urban centres. The urban elites extended their religious and political control over the empire, quite certainly at the expense of the rural elites.

The layout of a city and its segregation into quarters reveals the class differentiation within the city. In Thanjavur, which was both a royal centre and a temple city, the temple was situated in the centre and dominated its life. The royal palace and quarters of the political and administrative elite were located around the temple. The priestly elites lived nearby, but this did not obviously include all Brahmanas. Other urban groups such as merchants formed the next outer layer of the city's inner core. A set of goods and service providers mushroomed around the temple complex. Milk, ghee, oil and flower producers must have lived in quarters quite near the temple to make frequent visits possible. Sanitation workers, washermen, janitors, temple dancers, musicians and security guards lived in residential areas in the outer periphery of the temple.

The building of the Brihadeeswara temple in Thanjavur itself indicates the presence of an organised workforce, masons, stone sculptors, and financial managers who manged the donations. From inscriptions we learn that more than 600 employees were commissioned from nearby villages and towns to take care of the daily chores at the temple. Farmers and cattle owners living in nearby villages supplied the temple requirements. In fact, through royal fiats, revenue and services to the temple were ensured from even far away villages, even though such services and contributions could have been much less voluntary than was the case with the elite sections of the empire. In any case, such unusually generous offers to temple employees from the emperor would not have gone unchallenged by the administration. But the splurging of the royal treasury in this grand endeavour received the profuse support of his grand aunt and elder sister, both of whom were besotted with the temple in equal measure.

Taking another example, the Kudamukku-Pazhaiyarai complex operated in a similar fashion, with Kudamukku representing the religious centre and Pazhaiyarai, the royal complex. Kudamukku was an important trade junction. Betel nut and areca nut cultivators lived nearby. Metal and textile craft centres operated in the city. There is even some evidence of a mint located in the city. Other *nagarams* and *managarams*, the big cities such as Kanchipuram and Madurai and ports such as Mamallapuram, were also organised on the same lines.

All this confirms the close ties between the cities and countryside and the urban population being differentiated into the royal family, political and administrative elites, the priest elite, wealthy merchants and traders who must have had control over the production centres, artisans and craftsmen, service providers for the temple and administration, and a rural community with its own division of labour, surrounding the city. The rapid expansion of urban complexes, trade centres, and ports also point to the growing clout of the urban elites over the rural populace. This is further evident from the fact that royal decrees were issued to ensure regular revenue, goods and services from villages around Thamizhagam and even from foreign lands such as Ezham. Even among the craftsmen and artisans, those who had migrated to the towns and cities were not near as bad as their country cousins who wallowed in poverty.

'Merchants banded together in powerful guilds' but among them were the *nandesis*, 'the most celebrated of these guilds'. These corporations were already well established at the time of Vijayalaya and must have gained more muscle during the peak of the Chola regime. Many myths surrounded their origins and they 'comprised many sub-divisions born to wanderers over many countries'. No country boundaries could stop them and through 'land and water routes they penetrated into the regions of the six continents'. They seem to have preferred trade in high margin goods such as 'superior elephants, well-bred horses, precious stones of all sorts, spices, perfumes and drugs'. Like the monopolies of today, they were 'a powerful autonomous corporation of merchants whose activities apparently took little or no account of political boundaries'. Their international character must have earned them a respected and privileged position wherever they went. In the Chola country they had their own mercenary army, 'doubtless for the protection of the merchandise in their warehouses and in transit'. This show of might would have created sleepless nights for Rajaraja for when the situation demanded 'they also concerned themselves in the details of the local administration in the places where they settled'. They were some sort of a transnational corporation with change in regimes and the 'vicissitudes of war and peace' hardly bothering them[126].

It appears that not all the merchant guilds were under the close vigilance of the Chola state but a more indulgent explanation can be that 'the state was not eager to interfere in their transactions, and would not do so except on invitation'. On the other hand, the state could not give an effective military backing to its merchants engaged in all foreign trade, something which the European states would indulge in abundantly later. Rajendra's war with Srivijaya may be an exception if we accept the general view that 'neither the merchants nor the state in South India had any ideas of the possibility of economic imperialism'. The campaign could have been easily followed by 'colonisation of the coastal areas and an attempt to conquer the hinterland'. Ostensibly this did not happen leaving one to surmise that the objective of the Emperor was 'to protect Indian commercial interests'[127]. In spite of sending war ships to protect their merchants from pirates, who were both state or non-state actors, 'trade to them (the Cholas) was an end in itself; they were willing to carry on trade if conditions were favourable; it never occurred to them that foreign lands may be compelled to buy and sell at the point of the bayonet'[128].

Thanks to the economic development and the increasing demand for mobility in the caste system, 'an important innovation in societal organisation' emerged at the time of Rajaraja called the 'Right- and Left-Hand' divisions. This was a brilliant 'social division of all the non-Brahmana and non-Vellala groups and other tribal elements brought in as agricultural workers and menial service men'[129]. These divisions, from all accounts, were more prominent in areas where merchants assumed control and management of temples. As the demand for their services in agriculture, textiles and in temple-building and allied activities expanded, these groups ended up with more 'concessions and privileges'[130]. Considering that 'neither division finds mention among those groups named in the detailed Chola inscriptions dealing with matters requiring assent from local groups,'[131] they were relative and not rigid social structures. They were essentially supra-local coalitions of various castes across the region. The Left-Hand division, the *idangai*, generally represented the mercantile and craft occupations. The Right-Hand division, the *valangai*, was associated with those involved in agrarian activites. The core *idangai* spokespersons were the goldsmiths, silversmiths, blacksmiths, and skilled carpenters and stone cutters. Oil processors and weavers who were connected to the markets in urban places also rallied behind this division. Urbanisation must have certainly impelled the formation of these divisions. In the initial stages, for agricultural workers and mobile artisan-traders who strove for 'a measure of security and political leverage'[132] with respect to the landed gentry, rallying behind the *idangai* would have been a compelling option. In due course, the *idangai* which broadly represented the urban productive forces, could flex its muscles against the well-entrenched elite of the countryside. We would be looking at these divisions in some more detail in a later chapter.

'The omnipotence of the Chola state was exaggerated by earlier scholars', but it is impossible to 'ignore the basis of enduring power and military successes achieved by dynasties such as the Cholas'[133]. 'War and loot were certainly part and parcel of the politics' of the Chola state, but its formation and persistence certainly indicates that it was 'based on something more than sporadic looting expeditions'. An administrative structure and revenue infrastructure certainly existed since its long-term and sustained military success was 'ultimately based on the state's ability to mobilise and control people and resources'[134]. As the Chola Empire expanded, particularly at the time of Rajaraja and Rajendra, 'official titles especially at higher levels of administration' became the norm, Taxes were standardised, and chiefs gave way to 'high-status officers'[135].

With a huge empire at his command, Rajaraja would have definitely felt that sitting on a throne was a thousand times harder than winning one. Running the empire would have been nothing short of a nightmare, what with enemies all around—looted, maimed and driven to despair—looking for the opportune moment to invade his territory. But he was now a chastened king, the wildness in him tamed, and wisdom seeping into its place. Rajaraja would have had to accommodate various chieftains who helped the Cholas in their imperial quest, as much as the officials and chiefs of guilds, and he did this with aplomb.

With each victory, feudatories of enemy kings flocked to his banner. Some of the chiefs were from great houses 'which on occasion produced a warrior leader of such ability as to break the surface of obscurity'[136]. The Pazhuvettaraiyars from Tiruchirapally district were 'closely allied to the royal family from the days when Parantaka I, Rajaraja's great grandfather married a princess from the family, and apparently enjoyed full responsibility for administering an area around Pazhuvur[137]. Like the Chola monarchs and princes, the chief Kandan Maravan had high-ranking officers and nobles serving him. The Irukkuval chiefs of Kodumbalur, in Pudukottai district, 'prudently cast their lot with the Cholas and became the mainstay of Chola power, serving in Chola armies and intermarrying with the ruling family'[138]. Another important official was Madhurantakan, the son of Rajaraja's uncle and predecessor Uttama Chola, who took charge of temple affairs[139]. The Lata chieftains of North Arcot 'remitted, at the request of his queen, some taxes in favour of a Jain temple'. A descendant of the Ganga king of Kolar, built a temple at Tiruvallam, which came under his chieftainship. Chieftains were allowed to imitate the royal centre and build temples in their region, but Rajaraja saw to it that none of their towers reached even half the height of the Thanjavur temple. Temples had always been recipients of gifts and endowments, from the time they became a fashion in Pallava times, but now in the imperial empire of Rajaraja these flowed like a torrent. Such temples and temple endowments were plenty, prompted by motives not always related to ecstatic devotion. The Vaidumba family ruled around Cuddapah district. Likewise, the Banas, 'who shared the same fate as the Vaidumbas at the hands of Parantaka', served as officers.

Among the relatives, Vallavaraiyar Vandiadevar, who was married to Rajaraja's elder sister Kundavai, who 'was much respected and treated with great affection'[140] by the emperor, must have exercised considerable clout in the empire. The younger Kundavai, Rajaraja's daughter, was married to the Chalukya Vimaladitya who survived under the protection of the Chola Empire. Sembiyan Mahadevi, the queen of Gandaratiya, Rajaraja's grand-uncle, must have been a powerful lady for Rajaraja to build two memorials for her later in his regime.

The Changalavas and Kongalavas of Mysore and Coorg respectively were the northern vassals in the vast empire. Some of these chieftains were co-opted into the system as officers; others retained control over their homelands, albeit as feudatories. But these chieftains were only too aware of the sordid history of Rajaraja's ancestors stabbing their former masters to usurp power. Rajaraja might have wished that many of these chieftains and officers, who demanded a share of power, had been lost in the wars. As if confirming his worst nightmares, it was the rise of these chieftains a couple of centuries later that contributed to the decline of the dynasty. But that was at least a couple of centuries later. Notwithstanding the fact that chieftains would have been as tough as an old banyan root and as hard as the Thiruchi stone when it came to negotiating their share of power, Rajaraja handled them tactfully. Doubtlessly, in all the formative years of the Chola Empire, sharp knives must have followed the emperor, but none reached him as they did his brother, because he combined ruthlessness with diplomacy, authority with a share of power. More importantly he 'drew less on political authority and more on the institutions established at this time, together with the articulation of cultural forms'. It would not be an overstatement to say that 'in many spheres of cultural life' ... the standards established during this period came to dominate the pattern of living in the south, and to partially influence the patterns existing elsewhere in the peninsula'[141].

Monogamy was an option the kings of India forfeited long ago. Rajaraja had at least fifteen queens, confirmed from inscriptions recording gifts to temples and other institutions, an assured way to etch their names into posterity. Not all of them had the privilege to sit by his side on the Chola throne. The queen commanding the most respect was Loka-mahadevi and the royal couple have been captured in a sculpture performing a *tulabhara* and *hiranyagarbha* in a temple at Thiruvisalur. Vanavan-mahadevi who was the mother of the illustrious successor of Rajaraja, king Rajendra, seems to have taken a lesser place. Most, if not all, the marriages must have been political arrangements with feudatories and erstwhile opponents, for a place in his harem alone would not have been a decent compensation.

Death took him away in 1014, when the Chola Empire had already reached dizzying heights and his son Rajendra I had received excellent tutelage as the yuvaraja. Rajaraja died of natural causes and with the supreme belief that the Chola Empire would last forever and expand into new regions. The sigh of relief from his enemies did not last long for Rajendra took up the mantle from his father's firm hands.

5

DONORS, REBELS AND DEVIANTS

A post-Sangam literary work recalls a dancer called Nataka Ganika who was offered 1008 *kazhanju* of gold by the king, 1000 towards her professional fee as a dancer and a paltry 8 for spending a night with him, a strangely specific price. Assuredly, it was customary for the king witnessing a maiden performance of a dancing girl to long for her pleasure. This is not a one-off observation. In the epic *Silappadhikaram*, the Chola king Karikalan presents the danseuse Madhavi with 108 *kazhanju* of gold on her maiden performance and a garland of green leaves, which she sells for 1008 *kazhanjus* to the highest bidder Kovalan, the hero of the epic, to become his concubine. But it is not wise to rely on literary evidences alone when assessing the status of women in the post-Sangam period, particularly during the Chola period, since legal documents in the form of inscriptions have a weightier story to tell. On the aspects of proprietary rights and political-economic independence, the upper strata women of this period irrefutably scored more points over their sisters living a few centuries earlier. There are recorded testimonails of women's right to own and alienate property, sign documents and deeds, supervise administrative units, issue commands in their own name, and serve as administrative officers among the many responsibilities that they exercised[1].

Wives of kings and nobles were frequent donors to temples along with other female members of the royal family. As we had seen earlier, Sembian

Mahadevi, the grand aunt of Rajaraja herself enjoyed a saintly status and kept the stone inscribers busy with her numerous donations. She was a lavish patron of the sacred arts and 'contributed generous gifts of images, land and cash endowments towards the creation of twenty-one temples'[2].

Rajaraja's elder sister, Kundavai, also played an appreciably significant role in the empire's temporal and spiritual matters, significant in those times. Her endowment of 10,000 *kazhanjus* of gold to the Thanjavur temple is legendary[3]. She had her own palace in Pazhayarai[4] and had enough income to enter into land transactions[5]. Among the women of the Empire, her political and religious clout paled only in comparison to her grand-aunt, Sembiyan Mahadevi. 'Her great filial devotion is seen from the fact that she is credited with the making of metallic images of her parents and presenting them to the temple built by her brother at Thanjavur'[6]. Her religious devotion was matched equally by her philanthropy. In addition to raising many temples and making gifts, she has to her credit the construction of irrigation tanks named after her and her father respectively near Brahmadesam in the North Arcot district. She survived Rajaraja and after his death established a hospital at Thanjavur in the name of her father, for which she gifted land for the construction and for its maintenance in perpetuity.

Rajaraja's queen, Lokamahadevi, is also known to have generously funnelled money from her coffers for building temples. In fact, she even had powers to issue a royal charter. Precisely at the time that Rajaraja built the Thanjavur temple and named it Rajarajeswaram, this queen built another temple about 18 km away from Thanjavur, and named it Lokamahadevisvaram, with her royal charter inscribed on the temple walls, worded exactly as the order issued by Rajaraja at the main temple[7].

Records establish, though they belong to a period a few decades ahead of Rajaraja, that the queen exercised independent authority as an emperor, literally as the She-king, endowed with concurrent kingship powers along with her husband. The king's coronation also transferred powers automatically to the queen to issue royal orders and share the throne and the administration. That certainly is an assertive demonstration of gender equality, though limited to the royal family.

A class apart from such elite women of the ruling echelons were the class of temple courtesans, the *devaradiyars*, servants of the Gods, who 'made considerable benefactions to temples'[8] and in exchange had hereditary rights conferred on them in providing services and entertainment in temples and during festivals. Inscriptions rarely mention their profession but instead call them as 'devotee of God', 'daughter of God' and 'woman of the Temple'[9]. Reportedly, when his massive temple got done, Rajaraja transferred 400 Temple women from temples all around his territory to serve the Rajarajeswaram temple at the capital. This large contingent of *devradiyars* would have certainly added to the perception of grandeur, where the temple was concerned, but abasing the *devardiyars* as nautch girls would be a misnomer. It would be indeed 'squeamishness' on the present-day observer who judges the *devaradiyars* from present day 'notions of the hideous traffic in helpless women and girls that has grown in large modern cities'[10]. They were trained dancers and musicians, the better off providing amusement and intellectual companionship and the worse off serving as a 'temple-drudge' who 'when she consented to serve a passing stranger, still believed that she was performing an act of worship'[11]. Their social standing was not at all insignificant, considering the huge endowments made by them to temples and institutions. And here, Rajaraja must have cocked a snook at detractors who would have, without fail, opposed the regular salary and social status that were provided to these 'temple drudges'. From all accounts, the status of women could not have been much worse than what it was even a century back from today or even for that matter, in many pockets of the country today. Some of the *devaradiyars* were even allowed to marry and lead a normal life while still performing their duty. Beyond doubt, Temple women constituted a social category distinctly diferent from Palace women or from ordinary family women. At the same time, their social existence was not circumscribed for 'at no point during the Chola period do we find that the identity of the temple woman was defined by heredity or membership in a particular caste or community, by professional skill, or by ritual function'[12].

One of Rajaraja's inscriptions mention a striking aspect of his magnanimity when he gifted forty two cows to a temple while allowing six cows to be gifted by Varaguna, a servant maid, to make the required total of 48, to endow for the perpetual lamp. It is certainly an honour conferred on a servant maid[13].

From the Sangam period to the 11th century, the position of women went through a complex process making it difficult to have one final say on the issue. Early Sangam poetry reveals a tribal society, the slowly emerging state system commensurate with a rise in production and trade, and the general marginalisation of women as lovers, mothers and wives. Despite these limitations, different areas of the Tamil macroregion followed cultural practices which gave a better status to women. In the post-Sangam literary works, key actors such as the Jaina nun, Kavunti Adigal in the *Silappadhikaram* and the heroine of *Manimekalai*, a Buddhist nun, come out as foreceful proponents of the moral order propagated by these heterodox sects[14].

The high tide of the *bhakti* movement in the earlier centuries had thrown up many women saints, known for their compositions and revered as equal to male saints in temples. It was not terribly common to find saints, writers and poets among common women but not impossible either. However, women *bhakti* saints, of the non-royal variety, experienced devotion in a way fundamentally different from that of the male saints, with 'their female body directly impinging upon their identity as *bhaktins*'[15]. It was, undisputably, an uphill path for them to win the position of sainthood, in a society steeped with the idea that a woman's place is at home. While renouncing their social obligations, 'they did not join an alternative order or become nuns'[16]. Though their youth and beauty were a burden, and marriage and family life came in the way of their devotion, and they 'risked being labelled as rebels and deviants'[17] they made a significant impact on social life, such as the likes of Andaal, an Alwar in her own right – who impressed upon Lord Ranganatha to call for her to Srirangam in all her wedding finery, and Karaikal Ammaiyar – who considered herself as one of Siva's frightening but loyal ghouls. The *bhakti* movement gave some breathing space for women as much as the temples supported the *devaradiyars*, if one tends to view it from that angle. It is not a trifling matter that the 'dominant Brahmanical ritual world is attempted to be turned upside down, boundaries operating in the social world collapsed, and the shackles imposed by a rigidly hierarchical social order stretched'[18] by the *bhaki* movement whose impact lasted well into the 10th and 11th centuries.

A very interesting aspect, which to a certain extent bears witness to the status of women in society, is whether in the realm of gods there is gender equality. During the earlier period in the Tamil region. Regional goddesses had their independent existence. The need to strengthen the Saivite iconography during the Chola period and the relentless advance of urbanisation and trade 'bring into the narrative certain stereotypes with regard to men and women that are magnified in the divine realm, reflecting the attitudes and expectations of early medieval society'[19]. For instance, in the integration of the regional goddess Korravai into the Puranic identities of Parvathi or Durga as the spouse of Siva, the Tamil saints had to balance continuity with the Sangam traditions with the Puranic influences. In the final analysis, however, 'although local goddesses in the classical tradition were transformed into divine spouses, in local cultic worship the goddesses remained independent and fiery, subservient to none'[20].

Inscriptional evidence about the involvement of women in crafts and arts is sparse, if not altogether missing. 'Unfortunately, going back into history we can only talk about craftsmen. The craftswomen were not visible'[21]. Evidently, they played only a subordinate role. 'The woman was not the potter, but she was the one who kneaded the clay, and helped set up the kiln. In metal crafting, she did the polishing and the final details of the ornamentation'[22]. In spinning, weaving, fishing and agriculture one can hazard a slightly more prominent role for women.

A host of societal factors impinge on the status of women in any particular society and no single axis of oppression or elevation would be capable of explaining all the nuances. In regard to the status of women, as with other marginalised groups, 'the rhetoric of a one-dimensional oppressive structure understood within the normative varṇa-jāti framework (semantically reduced as caste) is as reductive as the eulogizing of this structure as providing a pan-Indian social cohesion'[23]. In the final analysis, however, women did play a significant role during Rajaraja's regime and atleast some sections of them had certain legal rights. This, in spite of the fact, that the Chalukyan women who lost their men and honour to the marauding army of Rajendra would have a different tale to tell about the treatment meted out to women in that period.

6

THE DANCE OF SIVA

It would be blasphemous to say that Kings determine the fortunes of gods. But that is what the Chola kings did to perfection. When Vijayalaya captured Thanjavur, the heart of the Kaveri delta, and unfurled the Chola flag with the tiger as its emblem, the Silver Age of South Indian Saivism and Vaishnavism commenced. Vijayalya's son, Aditya I, who in a battle pounced upon his Pallava overlord Aparajita when he was mounted on an elephant and slew him, made amends by covering the banks of the Kaveri, 'along its whole course from the mountain to the sea, with a number of lofty and impregnable temples built of stone and dedicated to Siva'[1]. His son Parantaka I, not to be left behind, continued the good work of his father and 'covered the roof of the Chidambaram temple with gold', perhaps in celebration of the victory over the Pandyan kingdom. His son Gandaraditya who, uncharacteristic of the Chola tradition, was more a saint than a warrior, and his equally religious queen continued to fund the renovation of stone temples. His nephew, Sundara Chola, was a faultless devotee of Siva. But none of the earlier emperors matched the scale and grandeur of the Thanjavur temple nor the brilliant Saivite iconography that Rajaraja developed to hold his empire together. The temple and the city could be easily counted among the marvels of the 11th century. Forever, it put paid to the accusation that the Cholas had usurped Thanjavur through treachery.

Under the Cholas, temples and *mathas* adapted and expanded themselves 'which attracted the imagination of the populace and the benefactions of the rich'[2], to the extent that towards the close of Chola rule, their ascendancy over the Buddhist vihara and the Jain palli was complete and irreversible. The Saivite and Vaishnavite cults succeeded in closing their ranks, and absorbing all forms of theistic belief into their orthodox fold, in such an ingenious manner that the 'heretical' sects 'who denied the sanctity of the Veda and questioned the existence of the Deity' were totally outclassed. But, ironically, in this fight against the 'heretical' sects, the *bhakti* movement, which originated in the South as a movement of secularisation and social reform, became a handy tool to serve the imperial need of the Cholas to establish a striking iconography for the consolidation of their empire. It was no fault of the movement itself. Royal power always kept a tab on popular movements 'for reasons of political expediency' and the *bhakti* movement which guaranteed a 'network of loyalty'[3] was too scrumptious to be ignored.

Earlier, Sankara and Kumarila, in the eighth and ninth centuries, had taken the battle against 'heresy' well ahead by making sure that Vedic thought 'absorbed many of the distinctive features of the speculative system and the practical organisation of the latter day Buddhism'[4]. While Sankara was censored for this as a Buddhist in disguise, the damage done to Buddhism in the South was fatal. But long before Sankara and Kumarila, the Saivite Nayanmars and the Vaishnavite Alwars had appeared on the scene. Particularly between the sixth and ninth centuries, they traversed the length and breadth of the entire Tamil country many times over and won over the hearts and souls of the people. Their devotional verses were filled with ideas of social reform and notwithstanding the religious shell within which they operated, their thoughts were progressive, transmitted through emotional poetry. The choice of Siva and Vishnu as the icons of the *Bhakti* movement by the saints worked wonders, but the credit for promoting these deities to the top rungs of the Vedic pantheon belonged to empires which thrived several centuries before Rajaraja.

The promotion of the Saivite and Vaishnavite cults is closely intertwined with the period of consolidation of the Brahmanical ideology which started around 300 BCE leading to 'increasing popularity of temple-based sectarian cults'[5]. The Puranas, religious sculpture and architecture, sectarian symbols on coins, and royal prashastis proclaiming the sectarian affiliation of kings were all part of this trend. The earlier popular Vedic gods were pushed around to make way for Siva and Vishnu. A number of gods representing natural phenomena were worshipped during Vedic times, such as Indra the war and weather god, Surya, the sun god, Agni, the fire god, Varuna the guardian of the cosmic order, Yama the lord of the dead, and the fearsome Rudra among others. Even in the early Buddhist scriptures, Indra and Brahma reigned as the supreme gods. Early Sangam literature in the South, and the epic *Silappadhikaram* mention Indra as an important god who commanded festivals in his name. The various solar deities were merged into the Sun God, Surya, who had a few temples built for him in the early centuries of the Common Era. Around the fourth century CE, the reshuffling of gods started. The popularity of Brahma, the four- faced god, waned around the time of the Gupta Empire[6]. Other lesser gods such as Varuna, Yama and Soma lost much of their prestige with the passage of time. The war god Skanda, became very popular in the South as Kumara, Kartikeya, Subhramanya and Muruga. He was originally a non-Vedic god who was incorporated into the Saivite pantheon as the son of Siva and Parvati. Ganesa or Ganapati (chief of the ganas, Siva's attendants), and his most popular South Indian form Pillaiyar, became another son of Siva and Parvati. Hanuman, the monkey god, is much revered in the north while many in the South believe him to be a god of a southern tribe relegated as monkeys and slaves by invaders from the North.

By the 2nd century BCE, according to inscriptions on the Besnagar column, 'the cult of Vasudeva was receiving the support of the ruling classes'[7] and was even being promoted as the Indian version of the Greek god, Heracles. Soon after, Vishnu was identified with Vasudeva. Narayana, 'a god of obscure origin mentioned in the Brahmana literature'[8] was identified with Vishnu and Krishna, the author of the Bhagavat Gita. In fact, the ideas of a supreme God, Narayana, and the various *avatars* of Vishnu was central to the Pancharatra (five nights) movement in the late first millennium BCE.

The movement later merged with the Bhagavata tradition and contributed to the development of Vaishnavism.

The Gupta kings called themselves bhagavatas, devotees of god, named themselves after the gods, and assiduously developed a religious icon for their rule. They etched the figures of Lakshmi, the consort of Vishnu, and Varaha – the avatar of Vishnu as a boar – on their coins, and 'made mythology a state concern, enlisting particularly Vishnu and his heroic incarnations for their politics'[9]. They promoted Vishnu as the supreme god and made believe their subjects that it is Vishnu who sponsored the Gupta Empire. A little later Krishna emerged as a god in his own right with his paraphernalia of legends and cults. Temples were built for these gods; icons were sculptured, and Vedic myths were codified into puranas. By the fifth century, Vishnu, Siva, their family members and incarnations and secondary adjuncts were well established and associated with this or that dynasty.

Over many centuries, other popular divinities were associated with Vishnu – a divinity in the form of a boar, a pastoral flute-playing divinity, the Brahmanic hero Parashurama, and Rama, the hero of Ramayana[10]. The cult of the Boar incarnation was important in some parts of India in the times of the Gupta Empire. Rama might have been a chief who lived in the 7th or 8th centuries BCE and 'had no divine attributes'[11] in the earlier versions of the Ramayana. Though his incarnation was earlier than Krishna's, the avatar of Rama became popular only at the start of the medieval period. By the 11th century, the ten avatars of Vishnu had been incorporated by Vaishnavism[12].

Within Vaishnavism, 'the divine cowherd' of the Yadava clan, Krishna, gained immense popularity and 'emerged as a major focus of devotional worship'. Many legends describing Krishna's exploits during his younger days are available in the Harivamsa, a part of Mahabharata. The Bhagavata Purana, which seems to have been composed just before the time of Rajaraja in South India contains the Krishna-charita which gives a fantastic account of his exploits and his pranks with the gopis (cowherd girls). An avatar who is a formidable opponent to his enemies and who is at the same time capable of amorous relationships and lustful pranks would have been irresistible to devotees compared to the mundane Vedic and Buddhist forms of worship. The relationship between Krishna and the gopis can be actually viewed as a metaphor, illustrating the relationship between the devotee and god assuming interesting and titillating dimensions[13].

The meteoric rise of Siva is no less spectacular. Siva emerged from the Vedic god Rudra with a sprinkling of the whims of a local fertility deity from Harappan times, added to his personality. Unlike Vishnu, Siva is enigmatic. While the former sleeps in the primeval ocean in the comfortable embrace of the thousand headed Adisesha, Siva 'lurks in horrible places such as battlefields, burning grounds and crossroads'. He is adorned with a garland of skulls and surrounded by ghouls and evil spirits, the fearsome Ganas. Vishnu is the protector, but Siva is death and time (Mahakala), the destroyer. He is the patron deity of ascetics, and sports matted hair, coiling snakes around his neck and arms and a smear of ashes on his forehead and body. He sits in deep meditation at the Kailasa Mountain but can break into enthralling dance when time demands. 'He is not only the god of mystical stillness, but also the Lord of the Dance (Nataraja)'[14]. No less than 108 dance moods have been attributed to him, 'some calm and gentle, others fierce, orgiastic and terrible'. He is most famous for the tandava, 'in which the angry god, surrounded by his drunken attendants (ganas), beats out a wild rhythm which destroys the world at the end of the cosmic cycle'. In his other form, the Dakshinamurthy (South facing God), the universal teacher, is more relaxed 'with one foot on the ground and the other on the throne on which he sits, and with one hand raised in a gesture of explanation. But the phallic emblem, the *linga*, as old as Mohenjo Daro itself, became the form in which he was worshipped most. As Pasupati, the Lord of Beasts, he is a four-armed god with one hand in an attitude of blessing, the second one, as though bestowing a boon, an axe in the third, and a small deer springing from the fingers of the fourth'[15]. Skanda (Murugan) and Ganesha were associated with Siva.

The consort of Siva became a goddess in her own right, and this again needs to be understood in a historical context. Mother goddesses were around all the time, but after the decline of the Harappan civilisation, up to the Gupta period, they were not of much use to the ruling classes. It is then that they emerged from obscurity to a position of importance, 'when feminine divinities, theoretically connected with the gods as their spouses, were once more worshipped by the upper classes'[16]. Goddess Sakti had been a shadowy figure as the consort of Siva earlier, but rose to a position of importance and began to be worshipped in special temples. In her benevolent aspect she was worshipped as Parvati, daughter of the mountain, or simply the mother, Amman, in the Tamil country. In her grim aspect, she took on the names of Durga, inaccessible, and Kali, the black one, among others. Sometime later, the Tamil war goddess Kottravai, 'who danced among the slain on the battlefield and ate their flesh', had an independent origin, probably from as early as 300 BCE, being mentioned in the *Pattupattu*, the Ten Idylls. She later merged with Kali and gave up her original vehicle of the blackbuck for the lion of Durga and Mahishasuramardini, the killer of the bull-headed demon, Mahishasur. When Vijayalaya laid the foundation of the great Chola lineage, he also thought fit to promote goddess Durga in the iconic form of Nishumbhasudani, the slayer of the demon Nishumba, as the tutelary deity of the empire.

The fortunes of gods, in the final analysis, very much depended on the ruling classes who required a popular deity to rally around the subjects and vest their rule with divine sanction. Vishnu, Siva and Vasudeva became popular gods at a much later period in Indian theology. Various local cults were assimilated into the character of the two trends of Vaishnavism and Saivism over several centuries. When the seers of the *Bhakti* movement appeared on the scene around the sixth century, their choice of an icon was not very taxing, since there were only two.

The *Agamas*, the authoritative texts of the Saivite movement, are supposed to have been dictated by Siva himself. They are believed to have been composed between the years 400 and 800 in the Tamil speaking region. Though they recognise Vedic principles of *jnana* (knowledge), they give importance to *bhakti*, the devotional and often ecstatic relationship between god and his devotees. The *Agamas* categorically recognise Siva bhakti as superior to the performance of Vedic sacrifices. Tamil Saivite mantras precede the Vedic mantras in religious rituals at the home and in temples even today.

The capital city of Thanjavur 'was both a ceremonial and political centre'. Most other cities in the Chola region were temple cities but nowhere did the temple become 'at once a product and symbol of socio-cultural milieu' of the Chola period as it did in this city. As a political centre, the city represented 'a state which evolved through a steady process of integrating different pre-existing politico-cultural zones' such as the Pallava, Pandya, Chera and Lanka regions. The promotion of the Saivite cult and its propagation through the institution of the temple was crucial in the emergence of royal-ceremonial centres and 'to the political visibility of the Chola monarchy'[17]. The Cholas instituted grants for ritual singing of bhakti hymns as well as the development of architecture, sculpture, painting, music and dance all contributing to the brilliant iconography of the Chola Empire. Under Rajaraja, among his most sensational endeavours, Nambiyandar Nambi recovered damaged palm manuscripts of Saivite hymns from the vaults of the Chidambaram temple, and compiled them into the Saivite canon, *Devaram*. It would not require a great strain on the intellect to account for the fact that members of the royal family were included in the hallowed list of the sixty-three Nayanmars who represented the Saivite canon. Kochchenganan, among the early Chola kings of the Sangam period and Gandaraditya, Rajaraja's grand uncle were among them. The Thanjavur Brihadeeswara temple was different from other Saivite temples, not only because of its size, but because it was created deliberately as a temple-cum-royal centre, unlike other stone temples in the Chola region which sprung up in towns and on trade routes.

The capture of Thanjavur, at the heart of the Kaveri delta, by Vijayalaya from the Mutharaiyar chieftains was a superb feat which turned the fortunes of the Cholas in the right direction. The development of this city into the premier city of South India and erecting the stupendous Rajarajeswaram temple[18] satisfied 'Chola political needs, ideological forces and the protection of the core resource base'[19]. The temple was given a cosmic symbolism by calling it the 'Dakshinameru', the southern Meru as the axis of the universe, and the deity by association became the 'Dakshinameruvitankar'. It was not only a centre of territorial authority of the Cholas, it was also a centre on earthly space symbolising the 'order which pertained to the other world structure'[20]. The main shrine was consecrated along with the shrines of the eight quarters, the ashtadikpalas, Vedic gods such as Indra, Agni, Yama and Vayu, who were situated at cardinal points around the central sanctum of Siva. The Rajeswara Nataka, a play on the monarch, was regularly performed in the temple complex, and so were festivals to commemorate the birth asterisms of the royal family.

For Rajaraja, the 63-metre-high central tower, the *vimana*, of the Thanjavur temple and its more than 5000 sq.m of built up stone structures served as a metaphor for the grandeur of the empire. The taller the temple tower, the more awe that the emperor struck on friends and foes alike. But moments like these also revealed another side of Rajaraja – a lover of art and architecture and the finer facets of life. The main shrine of Dakshinameru, standing in the centre of the huge courtyard, was symbolically the cosmic axis of the universe, or atleast of the vast Chola Empire. Structural innovations ensured the 'architectural stability, balance and aesthetic impact'[21] of the temple and went a long way in demonstrating the zest and energy of the sprawling empire. Though Chola architectural style borrowed many of the 'forms and features from Pallava, Pandya and even Chalukyan temples', they towered above their predecessors in style, scale and ingenious innovations such as the *devakosthas*, the brilliant niches all along the temple walls. It will not be far from truth to conclude that the Thanjavur temple 'marked the most creative period in Chola art and in South Indian iconography'[22]. It was easily the richest temple of the time. By the twenty ninth year of his reign, the emperor had presented a vast amount of gold, ornaments, jewels and vessels, 'much of it from the booty that fell to him as a result of his wars'[23]. The quantity of gold, by conservative estimates, amounted to about 221 kgms. Jewels added upto another 27 kgs. And this was just the king's contribution. Villages contributed annually 116,000 kalams of paddy, equivalent to nearly 17,000 tons, to the temple. All this would have been more than sufficient to gratify the incredulous eyes of chieftains and vassals. Every other temple in the empire, big or small, played the same role in the neighbourhood, as that of the Great temple in the capital city, the difference being only one of degree.

The temple sculptors introduced even more iconographic forms of Siva than traditionally inherited, in a double-tiered *vimana* wall with a double row of niches. The Tripurantaka form[24], which we will see in more detail later, deserves special mention. Some historians believe that this was Rajaraja's personal deity whose 'unique iconographic symbology was used to restore to his lineage the honour and dignity damaged by their defeat by the Rashtrakutas at Takkolam'[25]. If so, this was a brilliant and conscious assimilation by the emperor of his divine and royal roles. From the more strategic attempt to create an all-powerful icon, the choice of Tripurantaka was a superb act. This form of Siva rides on a chariot driven by Brahma and while bending forward in warrior-like fashion, lets loose the fatal arrow with Agni as its fiery head, Vishnu as its shaft and propelled along by Vayu as the feathered plume. In the standoff between the Saivite and Vaishnavite sects, this legend came in handy for the former to deride Vishnu who took the form of Mayamohin, an alias for Buddha, who corrupts the demons with anti-Vedic doctrines[26]. It was the brainchild of a man who was confident that he was indeed the human manifestation of the Lord of Dance. By using this myth and the iconographic form in the temple's sculptures and frescoes in a dominant form, 'Rajaraja achieved his aim of consolidating Saivism and subordinating other faiths'[27] but not to the extent of antagonising them. The Saivite Nayanmars were given pride of place in the temple niches. Rajaraja made special arrangements for the regular singing of the Saivite hymns, the *pathigams*, in all the Siva temples in the Chola country.

The Thanjavur temple served as the political iconography of Rajaraja, representing the significant efforts at centralisation of power through various measures such as revenue surveys, assessments, redefining the *nadus*, encouraging the growth of *nagarams*, and setting up of an efficient revenue department and a systematic tax structure. The temple received revenues not only from the core Chola territory but also from captured areas. The corporate bodies of villages and *nagarams* around the temple managed and used gold deposits and contributions to the temple as capital for their enterprises and paid interest in the form of consumables and services for the temple. The enormous booty from the coffers of the Cheras, Pandyas, Lanka and Chalukyas was turned into ornaments for the temple deities. The centralised power of the Cholas was on full display. Even royal ancestors were deified as in the case of Kundavai, setting up an image of her father Sundara Chola, called *pon maligai ttunjina devar* – the monarch who slept (died) at the golden palace – with that of his queen's by the side.

The painted figures of Rajaraja with his guru Karuvur Devar in one of the chambers in the temple and sculpted figures near the panel representing Dakshinamurthy preaching the 'highest knowledge' to the wisest sages, is a clever attempt by the builder of the temple to project himself as an ardent devotee of Siva. 'Dakshinamurthy is a uniquely south Indian icon' required to 'counter the influence of the Sramanic teachers who were known to preach and proselytize'[28]. Another panel shows the eight-armed Bhairava, another form of Siva, who cut off one of Brahma's head for his reprehensible acts towards his own daughter, driving one more nail on the coffin of Brahma's past glory. The panel which shows Sundara ascending to Kailasa on an elephant, after his wedding is rudely stopped by Siva, as we had seen earlier, also speaks of Siva's greatness. The accurate portrayal of numerous icons, some of them bringing out the complex attitudes and themes in legends, talk about 'a high state of efficiency attained in the art of casting metals and a more or less constant and profitable employment for the skilled artisans'[29].

The establishment of the Saivite iconography was closely followed by the monarch 'acquiring a near total identity with divinity, compared to the cult of *devaraja* in Kambuja, the medieval kingdom of south-east Asia'[30]. To drive this point 'the paraphernalia of the Chola temple mirrored the royal court' and the 'royal and temple servants were identically perceived and had similar duties'. The equally minute and complete fabrication of the ornaments and jewels that decked the prosperous gods 'testifies the superior excellence reached in the art of the goldsmith'. In short, the temple was all rolled into one – the landholder, employer, consumer of goods and services, while also filling in as a bank, school, museum, hospital and theatre. Though loot and plunder accounted for its prosperity, it nevertheless served as a nucleus gathering around itself all that was best in art, music, poetry and technology. Close monitoring by high ranking officers and the king himself ensured that temple management staff with sticky fingers were kept away from the business side of its affairs.

The choice of Saivism for creating the iconography of the Chola state had many irresistible compulsions but Vaishnavism was not left by the wayside at all. In fact, the 'line of Vijayalaya may be said to commence the Silver Age of South Indian Saivism and Vaishnavism' with Rajaraja's reign easily being the peak. For it is certain that 'the sacred hymns of the Nayanmars and Alwars were arranged in canonical form sometime in the eleventh century'[31]. When Nambiyandar Nambi, the author who arranged the Saiva canon 'substantially in the form in which we now find it', found the long lost manuscripts of the hymns of nayanars in the dingy vaults of the Chidambaram temple, Rajaraja must have fallen on his knees and thanked his stars. Nambi must have had a lot of difficulty in compiling the hymns to satisfaction as many hymns later found in stone inscriptions were absent in the initial compilation. This in spite of state support, for nothing short of magic could have reversed the destruction by white ants of the bulk of the palm leaves containing the hymns. Thanks to the fact that the practice of reciting the hymns in temples 'had come into vogue long before the time of Rajaraja' and that they had 'attained the status of divine literature' long before Nambi set about the task of compiling and editing them must have saved the emperor a lot of trouble. From the reign of Parantaka, endowments were set up for the regular recitation of these hymns in temples accompanied by music.

As we observed before, the rise of Saivism did not exactly foist a step-motherly treatment on Vaishnavism. For instance, Aniruddha Brahmarayar, the chief minister of Rajaraja was a renowned Vaishnavite whose family could boast of a social-reformist tradition. It could not be a strange coincidence that Vaishnava hymnology had a similar history to that of Saivism, for the consolidation of the Chola Empire required the gathering together of hymns, myths and hagiography of saints to establish religious canons that can keep the centrifugal forces under check by providing a divine status to the king. Towards the beginning of the tenth century, perhaps a few decades earlier to the consolidation of the Saivite canon, Nathamuni performed the same magic on Vaishnava lyrics that Nambi would do almost a century later. The story behind the compilation of the Vaishnavite canon is even more cloaked in religious sentiment. Nathamuni happened to hear some visitors from Kurugur, the birthplace of the greatest Vaishnavite saint Nammalwar, recite some of his hymns. 'Captivated by the melody of the hymn and noticing that it comprised only ten out of thousand verses composed' by the saint, Nathamuni made haste to Kurugur to retrieve the remaining hymns. Try as he might, he could not summon the vision of Nammalwar using his yogic powers. It was after 'reciting 12,000 times the hymn of Madhurakavi'[32], the disciple of Nammalwar on his guru, that both of them appeared and 'imparted to him the knowledge of the four Prabandhas'[33]. It may be 'cruel and futile to dissect such fanciful tales' today but they served the Chola Empire well, building a great tradition of devotion and piety. Chola kings provided endowments to Vaishnava temples, though not on the scale enjoyed by the Saiva temples. But, for all practical purposes, enough and more had been done to bolster the bourgeoning popularity of the *bhakti* saints and their hymns.

A positive outcome was that these hymns sung in temples by local priests in the language of the people 'emphasises the rank assigned to them by the side of the Sanskritic Vedas', which remained the privilege of Brahmanas. The love-hate relationship between Sanskrit and Tamil continued to linger. At one level the bhakti sects 'focused on the local cult,

Fig. 11 - Child bhakti saint Sambandar

forms of worship and language' which kept Vedic rituals at bay. At another level, they popularised deities known to other areas of the subcontinent'[34] in an attempt to homogenise the pan-Indian puranas with the *sthala* puranas, the local temple histories, of the South. Evidently, people of the South shaped their lives to the world of Vedic customs, but they never let their guard down to allow too deep an intrusion by Sanskrit into their homes.

The hagiography of the Saivite saints that, 'more than a century later, found its classic poet in Sekkizhar', was already popular at this time and found representation in the iconography of the time. Sambandar the child-saint, for instance, is generally represented as a child 'holding the golden cymbals, *taalam*, that Siva himself gave him to keep his tender hands from getting sore while keeping time, *taala*, to the hymns'[35]. 'The artists took

119

hold of the essential elements of sambandar's life story and used them to formulate his portrait' but while doing so, made him look like the 'dancing child Krishna', 'blurring categories of the divine and saintly'[36]. His life had a miraculous and early ending when the adolescent saint was whisked away by Siva, who graciously allowed 'the bride and the entire wedding company'[37] to accompany the groom to Kailasa. In contrast, Appar, who spent a long life of over eighty years visiting temples, holds a hoe, the *uzhavar patai*, with which he cleared the temple courtyards of weeds and grass, 'an image appropriate ... both for the humble service, tondu, and the *Vellala* farmers' attachment to land'[38]. Quite different from Appar and Sambandar, Sundarar, the handsome saint, appears as 'a well-dressed, princely young man, often in the company of his wives'[39].

The battle against 'heresy' had been joined by the Nayanmars and Alwars well before Rajaraja, but their own differences simmered, interspersed now and then with tales of friendly cooperation. One such legend narrates an improbable but spiritually productive meeting between the Saivite Sambandar and the Alwar Thirumangai. Sambandar, who had taken up cudgels against Jainism, wanted to invite the Vaishnava, for whom Buddhists were a bugbear, to exchange notes on their experiences. But Sambandar came up against a wall, when Thirumangai refused to visit the former's hometown Shiyali because he 'would not set foot in a city which had no temple of Vishnu'[40]. Sambandar overcame this by enticing the Alwar with the news that there was an ancient image of Vishnu which was still being worshipped, though the temple had fallen on hard times. Thirumangai consented to visit the city and sang beautiful hymns which enthralled Sambandar and induced the rich donors of the city to undertake the renovation of Vishnu temples as well and to 'shed their hostility to the sister creed'. Though they had lived at different times, the legend of their cooperation served to stem the anti-Vedic tide. Rajaraja, while taking a fancy to the Saivite cult, kept the Vaishnavites also contented, unlike his later successors who let the division between the two sects spiral into 'relentless sectarian hostility'[41]. Not only that, Rajaraja 'patronised all persuasions in equal measure'. His sister built a temple each to Siva, Vishnu and Jaina at Rajarajapuram, now called Darapuram, with her gifts to all these shrines recorded in the same stone inscription. Several temples housed the Siva and Vishnu shrines side by side, though in the famous Chidambaram temple, Vishnu lies 'in front of Nataraja, absorbed in contemplation of the foot lifted in his dance and supplicating him for a view of the other foot as well'[42] putting Vaishnavites to considerable embarrassment. In any case, it was not a bad idea to encourage two religious canons, since different roads led to the same castle. From all accounts, Vaishnavites, Buddhists and Jains were not marked out for any targeted hostility by the regime, but the amity between the Vaishnava and Saivite seers at the time of Rajaraja should not be taken to mean that absolute peace and equality prevailed among the followers of the cults because 'nothing in the history of Indian society is more remarkable than its fatal capacity to combine intellectual tolerance with social exclusiveness'[43]. Though communal divisions were kept under check and philosophical schools respected, social differentiation and oppression would have likely exacerbated in Rajaraja's regime driven by the increasing chasm between the rich and the poor.

Whether it is a pursuit of tolerance or a fancy for eclecticism, the popular pantheon of gods included 'an assortment of all conceivable deities'[44]. Besides various forms of Siva, the icons presented to the Thanjavur temple by the royal family and other patrons included Ganapati, Subrahmanya, Vishnu and Surya. Images of Saivite saints, though they had lived only a few centuries back, were elevated into deities deserving regular worship. In fact, the Tiruvottriyur temple 'offered worship to all the sixty-three Saiva saints'. Many lesser gods, who were the more locally worshipped ones, such as forms of the Pidari and Settaiyar were included. They could usually be found in the outer enclosure of temples. The temples of the Chola period were no different from those of today in terms of the 'utter recklessness' with which they appear to sanction and absorb 'the basest superstitions... as well as the noblest and purest forms of worship and meditation'. The inclusion of non-Brahmana Nayanars and Alwars in the pantheon, particularly the pariah saint Nandan, could be the result of the persistence of the social-reformist influence of the bhakti movement. Many 'fanatical and repulsive' Saivite sects such as the Kalamukhas persisted and were even given royal patronage at the time of Sundara Chola and the later Chola period. In any case, the more impressed that people were with the countless idols in Thanjavur temple, the easier they would be for Rajaraja to command loyalty. A good number of ascetics led a 'life of pious, if not uneasy, poverty' and while accumulating religious merit, ensured the rich of 'a good berth in the other world' through the medium of charity and gifts to their *mathas*.

Besides Saivism and Vaishnavism, Jainism had a fair following notwithstanding the united onslaught by the main orthodox sects and 'enjoyed the patronage of princes and people' alike. The palli, Jain temple, was usually designated as tax free land. Stone inscriptions of the time of Rajaraja mention several land grants and gifts of lamps to Jain temples in several areas by the emperor and his sister. The joint project undertaken by Rajaraja in building the Chudamani Vihara in Nagapattinam, in collaboration with Srivijaya, is proof enough that Buddhism also thrived along with the other sects. Such was the prosperity of the Vihara that we have a story of Thirumangai Alwar, whom we had seen earlier collaborating with the Saivite saint Sambandar, of having defrauded the Vihara of a golden image of Buddha for building a temple wall at Srirangam. The city of Kanchipuram which was one of the great centres of the orthodox cults as well as Jainism, 'also accommodated a Buddhist colony'[45]. But on the whole, the 'Jains and Buddhists suffered a great decline', and many of the Jain centres in Kanchipuram, which apparently were weaving centres, 'were converted into Saiva ones dominated by the Kalamukhas'[46].

The unbounded ambition of the Cholas required 'an ethical system capable of sanctioning and integrating new values into a coherent and viable synthesis'[47]. The expansion of urban centres, the rise of powerful guilds and the expectations of the masses—who in the first instance made the prosperity and expansion of the Chola Empire possible—begged for a new deal. Rajaraja came up with an iconography with messianic appeal that touched all aspects of life – architecture, sculpture, painting and allied arts and crafts, and most importantly social organisation and religious practices. The temple at the centre of the royal city became the earthly centre of the cosmic order. It was certainly a glorious symbol of a powerful ruler's patronage and not 'a method adopted by an ambitious ruler to enhance his very uncertain power'[48], as some would like us to believe. But to set matters right, it would not be wise either to look at royal figures or dynasties as the only real agents of change, as 'those responsible for inspiring or instituting new religious and artistic forms', because admittedly, transformations are related to a 'complex and shifting backdrop of regional and local on-the-ground realities'[49]. In this respect, the agency of a variety of productive forces such as the peasants, craftsmen, artisans and the ubiquitous trader, cannot be ignored. Undeniably, the worlds of the trader, village landlord and craftsmen were different, but the temple brought them together on a certain plane.

7

A Bright Star in the Firmament

Abu Zeid, the ninth century Arab traveller, thought of the Chinese as more handsome than the Indians, nearer to the Arabs in their countenance, way of riding and in their manners. Nonetheless, Indian kings and the elite were not wanting in the lavishness of their dress or in the flamboyance of their lifestyle. Kings lived in splendour and Rajaraja must have been no exception, especially when gold bracelets, gem studded earrings and pearl necklaces jostled around in his treasury vaults. Zeid reported that the Indian elite 'wear two short veils and men as well as women wear golden bracelets, adorned with precious stones'[1]. The kings wore golden earrings studded with precious stones and golden neck collars studded with rubies and emeralds[2], a practice which is a fashion to this day among Indian women. Yet, the traveller believed that pearls were the most treasured, and assuredly so, if we go by the epics and poems of the period in the South. The nobility had a train of attendants including servants to fan the fly whisk and hold a parasol of peacock feathers to shade them from the sweltering sun when they went out on inspection rounds. Some kings went to the extreme of refusing to eat twice from the same dish and had fresh tables made for them every day with fresh dishes and plates and 'when their meal is over they throw the table, dishes and plates into the water'[3]. The plates in the South were of course made from banana leaves and hence didn't cause much of a drain on the state treasury. Invariably, the king's revenue was divided between hoarding, personal expenditure and charity to temples and public works, the ratio varying wildly according to his whims and fancies. From all accounts, Rajaraja managed his wealth judiciously, and made sure that the charity part was quite visible in the tall towers of temples and the perpetual lamps which lit their insides.

Taxes from agricultural land was the mainstay of Rajaraja's revenue. True, the war booty filled his coffers in torrents, while tax revenue came in like a regular stream. But wars were expensive as well, and there were only that many kingdoms, loaded with riches, to conquer. For that matter, 'virtually all campaigns at one level were plunder raids, but such raids could not have sustained a state as complex as the Chola kingdom'[4]. The Chola state could boast of a well-developed bureaucracy for revenue collection. The revenue department comprised various offices, functions and features[5]. In spite of a well-oiled administrative apparatus, the king believed in collecting taxes more by persuasion than by rapacious fiats and was content to claim a small portion of it while leaving the rest in the hands of local authorities to take care of maintenance and development of the village or town, if the inscriptions of the period are not fairy tales. The country was divided into revenue divisions called the *mandalam* and revenue districts, the *valanadu*, with the *mandalam* acting as an 'intermediary between the central treasury and local bodies'[6] providing greater accountability and control in revenue operations. The introduction of the *valanadu* inbetween the *nadu* and the larger *mandalam* might have been to weaken the kinship and regional ties in the *nadu*[7]. This is quite at odds with the enduring picture of Rajaraja's state as an imperial state, with a highly centralised bureaucracy and administrative apparatus. The real picture is closer to a state which was undoubtedly strong, but which delegated powers of revenue, administration, maintenance and dispensation of justice to local corporate bodies, the ur, *sabha, nagarattar* and the trade guilds. The emperor proved as adept at administration as previously he had been at vanquishing enemies.

Apart from regular taxes, the Chola kings levied a war cess, when required, and that might have been quite frequent. Parantaka I, in the year 945, ordained the assembly of the Thirukudamukkil to pay a cess of 3000 kazhanju[8] of gold, which was so hefty for the unfortunate body, that it was still arranging for it by selling their lands, after Parantaka had died and his son Gandaraditya had assumed power. This is at least one Brahmana *sabha* which had got into the bad books of the tax collector. But, surprisingly, there were many others which were fined, providing perverse pleasure for their administrative overseers. Ostensibly, the landed gentry paid three types of taxes, not necessarily all of them together, the tax to the king, tax to the *ur* or *nagaram* by residents in proportion to their land holding, and a citizenship tax which flowed into the general exchequer. For all practical purposes, most land taxes went to the village assembly and royal orders revealed the 'readiness of the central government to come to their aid' if taxpayers played hide and seek. Retribution was severe and direct. Again, in one more instance, all villages where Brahmanas and monks thought they were beyond taxes, had the honour of being pulled up by the king himself and their lands put up for sale by the village assembly[9]. In another instance, the *nagaram* of Tirunavalur in South Arcot district, defaulted on paying taxes and the *nagarattar* had to shell out the dues in paddy and gold[10]. The village assemblies had the power to remit taxes on individuals where they thought fit and recover dues with interest for the unpaid period. It was also possible for them to commute taxes if a bulk payment had been made 'equal to their value capitalised at current rates of interest'[11].

In effect, the Chola system of tax collection was a highly efficient delegated system, where the village assembly which collected the taxes was a corporate body formed of taxpayers themselves, an unthinkable prospect today. There was choice in tax matters and each town decided for itself what was best, but guided by custom and 'ancient time honoured standards', as in the case of several towns 'following the ancient standard of Nandipuram'[12], the home town of Sundara Chola. Local authorities imposed occasional contributions too. About twenty-five years before the birth of Rajaraja, an entire *nadu*, around Erode, agreed to pay a cess for installing a statue of Krishna in a Vishnu temple. The application of the cess to different sections of the population was innovative. Each household had to pay a half-panam, each of the bride and groom had to pay an eighth of a panam on the wedding day and one manjadi from a small amount of gold from each crematorium[13]. The cess on the crematorium looks strange but could have been passed off as a cess on the deceased for an easy entry to the other world! Those who went to the villages to collect the dues were also given food along with enough betel leaves to digest it. Avowedly, local authorities had much more say in tax collection, administration and maintenance than what we see in modern times. It appears that when 'ad hoc taxation was resorted to, the active consent of the taxpayer was sought beforehand'[14] again indicating a major departure from the taxation process of today. At least from the inscriptions it is evident that large tax riots were few and far between, if not totally absent, which is hardly surprising.

The impressive, and sometimes over-zealous, network of revenue collection from both agricultural and commercial activities discounts the view held by some historians that Chola wealth was essentially acquired through 'plunder raids'. True, war campaigns were raids of plunder, apart from extending the imperial empire, but 'such raids could not have sustained a state as complex as the Chola kingdom'[15]. To improve productivity, bring new areas under cultivation and increase the tax flow into royal coffers, Rajaraja continued with land grants, initially of wetlands and later including dry lands as well as state supported irrigation expanded. The two land owning groups, the Brahmanas and Vellalars, had 'superior rights over tenants and cultivators', although tenurial rights could not be given 'any easy descriptive label'[16] considering their wide range. Brahmanas who were granted *brahmadeya* land had the royal backing, and 'often possessed advanced knowledge of organising agriculture and other technologies', giving them a 'distinct edge' over existing landholders. If for no other reason, land grants to Brahmanas gave the emperor the satisfaction of being in the good books of that section of society 'who can deify those who are not gods and can dethrone existing gods'[17]. But, while Brahmana landholders pocketed many land grants from Pallava times, the overall area under agriculture too expanded, and not surprisingly 'non-*brahmadeya* villages far outnumbered the *brahmadeyas*'[18]. In the initial stages of Chola rule, private property was not common in non-*brahmadeya* villages but as the differentiation among peasants themselves and between landowners and the landless increased, individual land ownership increased in such villages. It is not uncommon to see names of 'non-Brahmana landed magnates included in Chola records'[19] with about 20 percent of names figuring in the records owning a considerable parcel of land. Progressively, as inscriptions reveal, as we go from the early Chola period to the later Chola period, an increasing number of non-Brahmana individuals raised their social status to the level of sellers or donors of land[20]. As would be expected, the practice of granting land to officials and the investment of war booty in the central delta region created rich landowning individuals[21]. Temples had also grown into 'huge landed magnates'[22] in this period. Brahmanas and *Vellalars* were the most prominent landowner groups in the early Chola period. The Vellalars enjoyed almost equal status with Brahmanas, but only just so, since their ritual status and that of the various other *jatis*, always had the Brahmana as the reference point[23]. Joint interests to protect their sphere of power relations from the growing clout of merchant and craft guilds could have driven the Brahmana and Vellalar landholders into each other's arms[24] as some believe, into the unlikeliest of alliances. But that is very farfetched considering that Brahmana *sabhas* operated independently of the non-Brahmana *urs* and therefore their independent domination over other groups in the countryside would not have gone unchallenged. In any case, land did not remain the preserve of Brahmanas and Vellalars. Chettis, Kaikkolars, Surudimans, Pallis and other ex-hill tribes increasingly lay their claims to land ownership[25]. Concurrently, 'the composition of the *nattars* also changed from a Vellala monopoly to include other communities'[26] in the decades after Rajaraja.

There were certain collective tasks imposed on village life, such as maintaining the services in a temple and the cost of feeding ten hungry Brahmana mouths, which could lead us to an exalted assessment that 'caste and group life formed no hindrance to social cooperation for common ends'[27]. Social exclusiveness and class antagonisms 'were not altogether wanting', but a system of 'social exemptions and privileges' kept these tendencies apparently under control. Sections of Vellalar peasants were exempted from local dues, scribes of Kanchipuram were a privileged lot since they engraved grants on copper plates and weavers from the city supplied the royal robes. In a few instances, the privileges stretched to outlandish limits. In Karuvur, one of the Chola monarchs was so thrilled with the work of stone masons that he made it a point to record on a temple wall that 'at your marriages and funerals, double conches may be blown and drums, etc., beaten, that sandals may be worn (*on the way*) to places which you have to visit, and that your houses may be covered with plaster'[28].

A particularly puzzling development is the emergence of supra-local divisions called the Right-Hand and Left-Hand castes[29], plausibly getting their titles when two sections of the population went to petition the king, 'with one party standing on the right hand side of the monarch, the other taking a position on the left'. Starting as a benign association of people engaged in certain occupations at the time of Rajaraja[30], they soon developed into warring factions, responsible for burning a village and 'looting the temple treasury' at the time of Kulottunga I, forcing the *sabha* to borrow fifty kazhanjus of gold coins to rehabilitate the village. Besides members of existing occupational *jatis*, others were also co-opted as in the twelfth century report where the emperor 'imported a large colony of holy Brahmanas' and the Left-Hand castes 'accompanied these Brahmana colonists as the bearers of their slippers and umbrellas'. Having established themselves in the village by this means they even entered into a tight compact among themselves vouching that they are like sons of the same parents, will fight for their rights together and stand apart from others using 'distinguishing symbols— the feather of the crane and the loose-hanging hair'. Whether or not the feathers made a difference, their unity and compact did them a lot of good. Much later 'the quarrels among these divisions often threatened to fill the streets of Madras with blood in the days of the East India Company'[31]. These two divisions could very well have their roots in the basic division of society in the Sangam period into the urban – cosmopolitan and trade oriented, and the rural – including in its fold the tribal clans with simpler economic organisations[32]. The critical feature of these divisions, however, is that unlike the caste system 'there was no relative ranking among the constituents, but shared substance and interests'[33]. In real fact, they were really not 'super castes' but groupings of established collectives, or special interest groups, 'capable of dealing with extra local problems beyond the scope and capability'[34] of a *sabha*, *nadu* or even a trade guild.

When land with existing cultivators was given as grant to temples or as individual or collective grant to Brahmanas, then the regime had a tough time working out 'the gift formula giving detailed expression to rights and privileges, and obligations, if any'[35]. 'Negotiations were required'[36] but there was no surprise about the outcome. Those with royal backing took the cake. When Sundara Chola, Rajaraja's father, announced a land grant to his favourite Chief Minister, Aniruddha, he drew up a detailed contract[37], leaving nothing ambiguous. If the new owner made their life miserable, the only option before the peasant families was to move to a new area and start from scratch, which was a forbidding task but a possible one. Recorded peasant revolts are scant in Rajaraja's period, possibly because of availability of alternate irrigated land. It would not be too great a stretch of imagination to understand that under such conditions landowners would have easily resorted to forced labour of their landless and extortion of their tenants only mitigated by the fact that the village elite would have required steady hands to harvest their crops[38]. The power hierarchy was quite straightforward, unlike the façade of modern times, with the king right at the top with his right to appropriate or reassign land, but which 'was exercised occasionally'[39]. Below him were the *nadus*, which were really a conglomeration of the villages, the urs. The landed magnates controlled the assembly of the villages. Under them were the sub-tenants and hired labour. The landed magnates 'sported bombastic titles and functioned as the state's agents'[40] but their most potent fears centred upon the availability of labour to do their menial work.

Notwithstanding the privatisation of land, 'village assemblies were crucial to the Chola administration'[41] and whether they always contributed to the villages being 'full of vigour and strength'[42] or not, they had existed from Pallava and Pandya times, and proved they were 'little affected by dynastic wars and the shifting of political power at the top'[43]. Government by primary assemblies of villages was certainly a working proposition in those times. Large villages were divided into streets or quarters and smaller assemblies existed within the larger one, since occupational groups such as carpenters, potters and smiths had their own issues to sort out. But both derived their authority from 'ancient custom and dharma'[44]. The village assembly had the widest range of functions, whereas the groups were limited to their range of operation. Periodic elections took place and the 'continuity of their life as corporations' was independent of their changing personnel'. The three types of assemblies, the ur, *sabha* and nagaram, were subject to periodical audit of their financial transactions by the officials of the king's government' but otherwise were left to themselves, provided they paid their taxes, which when not done attracted royal interference. Where some land in the village was gifted to Brahmanas, the *sabha* and the ur coexisted within the village. The incursion of Brahmanas into the placid life of a village would have stirred contradictory emotions. The members of the ur could have looked at the new occupants as land grabbers and resented the imposition of notions of ritual purity. On the other hand, they could have welcomed them for the 'rise in land values', for providing cash for 'financing projects of public utility'[45] and for bringing learning and technology into the village, however far-fetched this may sound. Nothing prevented a village from having more than one assembly, as in the case of Sattamangalam, which had two assemblies, one occupied by the Saivite and Vaishnavite sects and the other by the Jaina palli, both cooperating in maintaining the village tank and undertaking to pay taxes.

The Brahmana *sabhas* generally had a 'more complex machinery of local administration' than the non-Brahmana urs, perhaps dictated by the larger size of the former and the better availability of educated administrators. The celebrated Uttaramerur, for instance, had thirty wards in about 922 and many sub-committees called *variyams*, filled with elected representatives fulfilling some basic requirements[46]. In a big departure from today's electoral system, the elected representatives performed honorary work and were working people, giving a part of their spare time to administration. Interestingly, there was a gold committee assisted by a gold assay committee in the village administration, perhaps to assess and take care of donations in gold, of which there were many, to the nearby temple. The right to sit on the council was limited by a 'property qualification of a house and a small plot of land'[47]. Men between the ages of thirty-five and seventy could contest, but those who had served for one year on the council had to sit out for the next three years. Overzealous collection of taxes by the committees was abhorred and expenditures beyond the stipulated limit had to be sanctioned by the *mahasabha*. Each *sabha* had its own constitution delineating the process of selection, election and recall or rejection of candidates, though the uneven pace with which they were developed across villages, made them appear simple and piecemeal. The resolutions of these *sabhas* had the sanctity of a king's order, while the king's government itself interfered in the internal affairs of the *sabha* only in rare instances, till the late Chola period. It is only much later during the reign of Rajaraja III that the assemblies had to ward off intrigues by officials of the king's government and declare factions installed by them as traitors to the village![48] Where mercantile interests overshadowed those of the rural landowners, the *nagaram* became the more dominant assembly, but in most cases they co-existed with the urs peacefully. The 'striking feature' of the functioning of these assemblies is that rules were made and kept flexible through 'amendments from time to time' and great care was exercised 'to ensure that factions were kept at a minimum'[49]. Not for nothing have historians averred that, in effect, these councils 'are a permanent memorial to the best side of early Indian politics'[50] perhaps till date. And yet, the villages were not exemplars of class peace, given the wide chasm between the landowners and the rest, and that elections alone do not count for equity any more than endowments to temples for piety.

With the need to bring propertied households under the tax bracket, Rajaraja consummated 'an accurate survey of land' so that government books reflect land rights on the ground. Encroachments were severely dealt with and changes in land measurement due to altered course of rivers were periodically updated. Most notably, giving due importance to the basic necessities of the village, land set apart for the sacrificial square and houses occupied by potters, blacksmiths, goldsmiths, washermen and other artisans were exempted from tax as were riverbanks and cremation grounds[51]. There were twelve different classifications of land, each attracting a tax rate in keeping with its location and fertility. The standard rate was fixed at 100 kalams[52] per veli[53] of land for temple lands, 'working out to something like a third of the gross produce'[54]. Villages can opt for a permanent settlement at a fixed tax rate, as when Rajendra fixed in perpetuity the dues to be paid to the temple of Mahadeva by the *devadana* village of Pazhaiyanur[55]. A particular tax that no one complained about was for a system of safeguarding property from theft, especially when the village or town people were asleep. Each village and ward in towns maintained a patrol, called the *kavalkaran*, who in turn for regular payments guaranteed the security of the area, a 'system which survived in some measure almost till the other day in Tamil country'[56].

An enormous number of taxes, cesses, duties and octrois figure in the Chola lingo, but many of them were specific taxes, leaving out just a few which were applied as standard dues across the Chola region. To estimate the incidence of tax in a complex system where 'central and local, compulsory and optional' taxes prevailed, did produce complications. While the local authorities were the best to judge the tax rate that would be appropriate for their constituency, the 'widespread practice of assigning revenues to members of the official nobility, to feudatory chieftains, to temples and so on' ensuring equally rigorous and just rates of taxation would have been quite difficult. The only option for the taxpayer was to appeal to the centre against local excesses, which took endless time for resolution, or literally migrate from the locality, a reality not unfamiliar even today.

Protests against exorbitant levies did happen and customary laws were invoked such as when at a later period than Rajaraja, a new tax on cows and she-buffaloes was nullified, and the government share of forest tracts and dry lands was fixed at one-fifth of the produce and one-third for rice lands irrigated by tanks, vetoing demands from some quarters. The customary rate of tax on 'the cultivation of hill tracts by hunters, the vedars, was fixed at a modest rate of one cloth (a saree) for 1500 *kulis*[57]. This unusually generous offer would have been made to expand land under cultivation by enticing tribals to become a part of the village community and lend their hands. Notwithstanding that, such attempts to reinstate customary rates of taxes may not have always restrained the monarchy, 'in the popular consciousness there was a clear limit to the taxing power of government'[58] in the Chola polity.

Farmers foregoing their property because they could not pay back their loans were not at all as frequent in the regime of Rajaraja as they are today. The Chola state fixed taxes partly based on custom and partly 'on the consent, tacit or express, of the groups affected'[59], a practice unimaginable in modern times where an entire battery of tax officials prey on their victims like vultures who smell their carrion from miles away. A good part of the income of the Chola state was the land tax collected in cash or kind, which grew substantially with the regime nurturing agricultural growth and expanding irrigation. As trade expanded and cities flourished, customs and octroi, taxes on crafts and services, and on gifts of nature which was converted into useful products by man, such as from mines, forests and salt-pans also swelled the royal treasury. In the non-monetary form, 'the corvée was exacted with more or less regularity'. Taxes on commercial activities and professions were comprehensive and 'levied on virtually every aspect of economic activity outside agriculture'[60]. Tolls were collected on goods in transit on highways, shops paid taxes based on sales, and the large merchants, the Chettis, as well as foreign merchants were not exempt. Goldsmiths, weavers, oil mongers, blacksmiths and potters came also under the taxman's insatiable gaze. Taxes collected by the town's corporate body, the nagaram, included 'flowers in shops, lime trees, dry crops, red water-lilies, areca nut, betel leaves, saffron, ginger and sugarcane'[61] almost making it appear that nothing under the sun escaped the taxman's net. It appears from inscriptions in the core administrative areas of the empire that there were a phenomenal 422 terms which referred to a tax or due[62]. Yet, many believe that the existence of a complex tax structure does not prove that the Chola state was an imperial state. The range mentioned is not just 'to inventory a mélange of taxes' as Stein ridicules, 'but to spuriously establish that the Chola state possessed the undeniable attribute of a powerful state, whose arm extended to the entire realm'. According to him, as opposed to the 'richly documented vigour of local institutions', notwithstanding the elaborate tax rules, the Chola 'central government' has a poorly documented and often tortuously argued existence[63]. While this is a fallacy , we will be veering to the other extreme if we liken the Chola state to modern states and take Sastri's description of a 'Byzantine Royalty' as gospel truth. But as far as one can tell, the efficiency of Rajaraja's administration did not fail to touch ordinary subjects and his munificence, along with the rest of the elite, did not fail to keep the temple lamps perpetually glowing.

Modern governments collect taxes without empathy for the taxpayer, but in the Chola Empire 'it was not merely the king's government that collected revenue in the form of taxes; local bodies and other agencies of a communal or professional character also raised levies' bringing the tax collector into a closer relationship with the working population. The emperor gave free rein (and taxpayers' money and endowments) to the corporate bodies of the village and town to manage local affairs as well as the neighbourhood temple. Salaries of high-ranking officials were generally directly paid through other revenue items so that what reached the king's treasury was, after paying other administrative expenses, entirely at the disposal of the king. This was no small amount, going by the expensive palace establishment 'including the numerous queens and their retinues'[64].

Some say that Rajaraja's empire was built on booty plundered through conquests, while others believe that his rise was due to the flowering of productive sections of society. Even a perfunctory glance at the complex administrative apparatus and the exhaustive taxation rules are proof enough that the empire had grown out of living on war booty in his time. Either way, it cannot be denied that the emperor rose in popularity to become the most beloved king of Thamizhagam and the Chola Empire, among the brightest stars in the subcontinent's firmament.

8

CELEBRATING LIFE

Architecture, sculpture and the arts of the Chola period, even though taking a religious form and mythical content, have a striking connect to material life. 'A slender, poised image of the goddess Parvathi', Siva's consort, can very well be confounded with a portrait of the Chola queen, Sembiyan Mahadevi, 'idealised as divinity and portrayed in the guise of a goddess'[1]. 'Verismilitude certainly was not the ruling principle' of the times. Stretching the point a bit further, these were not portraits of likenesses, but portraits which celebrate life with all its beauty and perfection. The two portraits of Rajaraja, one sculpted and the other painted, likewise, 'portray a generic idealised figure with locks piled high in imitation of his favourite deity, Siva'[2].

For a while, the unsettled state of the Tamil country, when conflicts raged between the Pallavas, Cholas, Pandyas, Chalukyas and Rashtrakutas, all striving for supremacy, temporarily halted any notable architectural enterprise during the last centuries of the first millennium. The Cholas finally emerged triumphant, but preoccupied as they were in dynasty building, the architectural productions attributed to them before the tenth century are not many, nor are they large, and 'they imply a local rather than an imperial development'[3]. In a power greedy world, a monarch has to provide a periodic demonstration that his sword remains sharp. But once he had settled scores with the kingdoms of the south and north, Rajaraja should be credited for hanging up his sword, in the literal sense, and turning his attention to the improvisation of architecture, sculpture and literature. The Thanjavur temple was 'apparently the most ambitious production of its kind hitherto undertaken by Indian builders, it was a landmark in the evolution of the building art in southern India'[4]. The next great building effort was by Rajaraja's son, Rajendra I, who built the temple of GangaikondaCholapuram, 'a monument evidently erected in a spirit of emulation, to excel in richness and grandeur, its predecessor'. But, unlike the father's temple, this one 'now stands in a solitary state, except for the mud huts of a village straggling around it, as centuries ago the tide of life receded from these parts, leaving it like a great stranded shell'[5]. The neglect of this historic temple by the authorities can only be put in attenuating terms that 'nature, with its artistic hands, has endeavoured to veil its abraded surfaces, not always for its structural good, with festoons of foliage, so that it appears as a lovely grey-green pile slumbering amidst the tangled verdure of a wide neglected garden'. With these two imposing monuments and a number of modest temples, the dynasty seems to have remained content. Once the dynasty became a spent force in the twelfth century, no especially remarkable buildings appeared on the scene thereafter.

Exotic stone and bronze sculptures and colourful frescoes, retaining their brilliance even after centuries of neglect, adorn the numerous Chola temples that have survived until now. Most artistic remains are of a religious nature, but secular art must have thrived 'for literature shows that kings dwelt in sumptuous palaces, decorated with lovely wall paintings and sculptures'[6], though they have vanished because palaces were built of the the more delicate bricks and wood. The sculpture of Nataraja, particularly, is indeed 'imbued with an intensity of religious feeling rare in the art of the world', but it is the realism and earthiness of the surviving art which 'remind us rather of this world than the next', and bring to life in our imagination 'the warm bustle of the Indian city and the turbulent population of the Indian forest'[7].

A striking aspect of the art and architecture of the Chola period, if one spares particular attention to the massive Thanjavur temple that Rajaraja erected, is that they celebrate life, without inhibition. A comparison with western art brings out the best in Chola art. Gothic architecture and sculpture are vertical, the spire and arch pointing upwards, the statues of gods and saints unusually large, 'their poses are generally restful, and they rarely smile'[8], leave alone express any other emotion. This is unsurprising because they were 'deliberately designed to lead the worshipper's thoughts away from the world of flesh to the things of the spirit'[9]. But Chola architecture and art have a diametrically opposite approach to life, far away from the concept of a burning purgatory and the even more fiery hell. The temple towers are solid and ornate and display vivacious beauty. Both the gods and the demigods, the countless pantheon, 'are young and handsome; their bodies are rounded and well nourished'[10]. They display all the human emotions, *navarasa*, with remarkable facial and bodily detail, some appearing grim and wrathful and others smiling, so much so that 'the artists' idea of portraiture, especially of royalty and sainthood, tended toward idealised visions of the quality, character, and stature of the subjects rather than a precise likeness of their physical features'[11]. The dancing form of Siva, with his streaming hair, and his Tripurantaka form mounted on a racing chariot, exude an electrifying feeling that cannot be missed even by the balmiest. The female form, without exception, conforms to the South Indian standards of voluptuousness, poise and beauty. The idealised portrait of Sembiyan Mahadevi as the goddess Parvati, now in the Freer Gallery, is 'stylistically idiosyncratic in its proportions, in the marked and even exaggerated slope of its shoulders, in the naturalistic handling of its full heavy breasts, and its solemn, thoughtful expression'[12]. One thing can be said for certain. For a region where asceticism held sway for many centuries before Rajaraja, the temple architecture, sculpture and art of his times are a complete and calculated retreat from anything ascetic. But, as we shall see in the next chapter, even the South Indian brand of asceticism was a whole new experience compared to the practice of Buddhist and Jain monks. The Chola craftsmen gave shape to the ingenious iconography that the bhakti saints had painted with their mind's eye. Rajaraja's craftsmen must have 'worked according to priestly instructions and increasingly rigid iconographic rules' but there was nothing religious about their art for 'they loved the world they knew with an intensity which is usually to be seen behind the religious forms in which they expressed themselves'[13]. The figures in the niches of the Thanjavur temple walls and the frescoes within the inner ambulatory do not portray 'so much a ceaseless quest for the Absolute as a delight in the world as the artist found it, a sensual vitality, and a feeling of growth and movement as regular and organic as the growth of living things upon earth'.

Having said this, a cursory review of the development of architecture in Thamizhagam from about the 6th century and the emergence of the distinctive 'Chola style' in temple architecture would be in order. Before the rise of the Cholas in the 9th century, the Pandyas and Pallavas had established a certain precedence of style and quality in architecture. The rock-cut temples of the Pallavas, which stand in monumental glory even today, deserve particular mention. In the first half of the 7th century, Vichitra Chitta, the Pallava King Mahendravarman, according to the Mandagapattu inscription written in Grantha, 'records his achievement with boyish glee ... that he caused a temple for Brahma, Ishwara and Vishnu to be made without the use of brick, timber, metal or mortar'[14]. Before his time, temples were built of wood joined by metal nails and raised over plinths of brick and mortar[15]. It is precisely because of the non-use of perishable material that the stone temple of those times has survived the ravages of many centuries. None of the earlier brick and timber temples have survived. But the Pallava temples must have borrowed the forms and motifs that earlier temples used. The great Pallava temples such as the Shore Temple at Mamallapuram, and the Kailasanathar and Vaikunthaperumal temples at Kanchipuram are magnificent testimonies to the grandeur of Pallava architecture. They 'show the rapid advances in architectural in the two centuries after Mahendravarman'[16]. Be that as it may, stone temples were still not proliferous in the Tamil region until the kings of the Vijayalaya line emerged on the scene. A noteworthy aspect of these temples is that they 'marked the zenith of Pallava art'[17]. The *garbhagrha* of the Kailasanathar temple is a composite structure containing sub-shrines built on to its walls

Fig. 12 – Queen Sembiyan Mahadevi

Fig. 13 - Kailasanathar Temple at Kanchipurama

141

and corners. The early Chola temples departed from this in the manner that the sub-shrines are detached from the main sanctum and 'arranged as separate shrines around it in the courtyard'[18].

The Cholas, who came after the Pandyas and Pallavas, would have definitely benefited from the cultural treasures which they appropriated from earlier regimes, as they did of their gold and silver. This is undeniably evident in the architecture of the temples and palaces constructed by the Cholas. Moreover, improvements in technology and crafts along with a surplus economy permitted the Chola emperors to undertake massive building projects as we arrive nearer to the time of Rajaraja. Rock-cut temples give way to temples built using stone structures. From modest stone temples in the early Chola period, the temples reach gigantic proportions in the mid-Chola period around the time of Rajaraja and his son Rajendra I. Public structures other than temples — palaces, hospitals, public utility buildings, houses and all other types of civil architecture — have disappeared today, leaving only a few traces 'as in the instance of Uttriramerur, where we get to see the unbroken continuity of the town plan, even the names of streets in important centres from those days to ours'[19]. The golden palace that the murdered prince and brother of Rajaraja, Aditya Karikala, built in Kanchipuram for his father Sundara Chola to spend his retirement days, and where he died in grief after his son's death, earning the name of *pon maligai thunjina thevar* (the king who slept in the golden palace), has left behind no traces.

Hundreds of temples had sprung up all along the inland and coastal trade routes throughout Thamizhagam thanks to the systematic activity of the Alwars and Nayanmars from the 6th century onwards. The temples were located in the *nagarams* and *managarams* and near the headquarters of the *nadus*, for this is where they could get material and financial sustenance and draw their devotees from the local populace. The location of the shrines and the activity of the bhakti saints during the centuries preceding Rajaraja's rule were closely correlated with the location of trade and craft centres and the royal palaces. Superficially, however, it appeared that the 'saints' pilgrimages and celebratory songs about hundreds of holy places mapped the country much as the king's institutions did; they literally sang places into existence'[20]. Those temples[21] which had been consecrated by the hymns of the Devaram and Divyaprabandham attracted the attention of the Chola rulers for renovation and rebuilding. 'Music, sculpture, painting and philosophy were a part of this creative upsurge, and 'these overflowed into the numerous Hindu colonies across the sea'[22]. The temples were not only great specimens of art and architecture, they were also 'as utilitarian as dams and canals. Public works like the latter were often administered under the auspices of temples from the middle Pallava through at least the Vijayanagar period'[23].

During the initial period of the Chola expansion, those difficult years from 850 upto the ascension of Parantaka I, the stone temples were 'unpretentious structures hardly to be distinguished from those of the later Pallavas in the decline'[24]. It would appear 'that Pallavas excelled in sculpture and Cholas above all were architects, their style distinguished by simplicity and grandeur'[25]. This has proved to be not entirely true, since Chola sculptors were 'no less noteworthy than the Chola architects', brilliantly evident in the way they manipulated large masses of metal to produce exquisite bronze sculptures 'unsurpassed for their beauty and for the technical skill'[26]. The stone temples were popularly called the *kattralais* (temples fully created out of stone structures). They had a certain common architectural form and motif in the way that their walls bear inscriptions, the size of the *garbhagrham* and *mahamandapam*, the cornice supported on a hamsa frieze, the absence of niches on the exterior walls of the sanctum and so on.

Many brick and mortar temples were replaced by stone temples right through the Chola period. During the time of Uttama Chola, his mother, the scholarly dowager queen Sembiyan Mahadevi, rebuilt the brick temple with stone at Thirukodikaval in today's Thanjavur district. She was a woman with such a remarkable sense of historic documentation, that when she replaced brick temples with those built of stone, 'she ensured that all the original dedicatory inscriptions were re-engraved on the new

143

stone structures, alongside her own record'[27]. Likewise, Rajaraja rebuilt the Thirumalavadi temple. Temples with a more pronounced Chola style started appearing first in the period from the coming to power of Parantaka I, the grandfather of Rajaraja. But it must be remembered that this heralding of a new style rested on the earlier Pallava-Chalukyan tradition in the building of structural temples and rock-cut temples. Though the early Chola temples were small structures they 'display a freshness and spirit in marked contrast to those last productions of the declining style of the Pallavas'[28]. But opinions differ. The Thiruvaliswaram temple to the west of Thirunelveli in the south of Tamil Nadu, is considered 'typical of Pandya temples'[29] by some while others declare that it is 'a beautiful specimen of Chola art of the middle period in the Pāndyan region,' it having 'been built by the Cholas during their imperial sway... started in the days of Parantaka I near his military station of Brahmadesam and completed by Rājarāja I during his early days after the conquest of Pandi *Nadu*' and a standing proof that 'In India, Art follows the flag'[30].

The Vijayalay-Choleswaram temple of Narthamalai is one such temple built in this exquisitely fresh style. The temple stands majestically on a hill and is surrounded by seven small attendant shrines, of which six are intact. The subshrines are 'all cut-stone replicas of the main shrine' with a nandi in front 'which has left no trace'[31]. Again, the commetaries on its style differ as the sun from the moon. It has been described as the 'grandest of the early Chola structural temples... the forerunner of the glorious monuments of the Cholas'[32], yet there is no evidence that the Chola kings had anything to do with either temple, since inscriptions clearly identify the pioneers of the building and renovation of this temple as local chiefs of the Pudukkottai region[33].

The temple at Thirukattalai best illustrates the style adopted in this transition period. It was a loving creation of Aditya, the son of Vijayalaya, who frenziedly 'built all-stone temples of Siva on both banks of the Kaveri from the Sahayadri to the sea'[34] presumably so that people in his kingdom could bathe themselves in devotion as profuse as in the monsoon rains.

The central shrine consists of a square *garbhagraham*[35] and an *ardhamandapam*[36] besides a *mukhamandapam*[37], an almost square *vimana* overlooking them. Siva, Vishnu and Brahma adorn the niches on the tiers of the *vimana* and 'above the cornice there runs a frieze of rampant *yalis* with projecting *makara* heads at the corners'[38]. There are seven sub-shrines around the main shrine. A small *gopura* rises above the front gateway to the temple. The Nageswara temple at Kumbakonam takes us closer to the most important phase of temple building during the period of Rajaraja and his son. Notable in this temple is the Ardhanarishvarar[39] figure at the back of the *garbhagraham*. Fine portrait figures adorn the niches. Scenes from the puranas and epics now start appearing as friezes on the walls of the temples.

One can say that Chola temples proper started appearing only in the period from Parantaka to Rajaraja, his great-grandson. The distinct Chola style is reflected in the 'emphasis on the central shrine which dominates the whole group of sub-shrines by its position and its architecture'[40], a key aspect of the Chola iconography. The exterior of the main shrine is rendered much simpler than its predecessors, 'fretful detail is eliminated' and plain space around the shrine receives more importance. The *vimana* and the *ardhamandapam* are given distinct treatment. The dominating lion motifs in pillars in the corners of the temple gradually disappears under the Chola style.

A whole host of temples, the Koranganatha temple at Srinivasanallur, the Agastiswara temple of Kiliyanur, the Mahalingaswami temple of Thiruvidaimarudur, the Muchukundeswara temple of Kodumbalur – all of them belong to this period from the beginning of the reign of Parantaka I up to the ascension of Rajaraja.

It is during the middle Chola period (985-1070), which covers the reign of Rajaraja and his son Rajendra I, when Chola art predictably 'reached and passed its meridian'[41]. Rajaraja was quick to adopt the temple building culture set by his precedents and even quicker to raise it to new heights. The number of temples built, and their spatial distribution vastly increased during this period keeping pace with the expansion of the empire and the overflowing treasury with the spoils of war and taxes of the hard working. Embittered and frosty relations continued with the Chalukyas and Lanka, but that did not deter father and son from building stupendous structures. Towering above all the temples of this period are the temples of Thanjavur and Gangai-konda-Cholapuram, 'which constitute a landmark in the history of Indian architecture'[42]. To put these two behemoths in perspective, 'in comparison with the temple of Koranganatha they are as cathedrals to a parish church'[43].

The temple built at Thanjavur during the reign of Rajaraja surpassed all earlier temples in effort and size by a wide margin and invested the crown with an immense amount of ritual dignity. It was a remarkable manifestation of the engineering acumen of Chola builders, acquired painstakingly over decades. Clearly there was never a dull moment in his reign. The building of the temple commenced in 1003 and by 1006, within three short years, the construction must have been sufficiently well ahead for Rajaraja to have offered golden flowers to the deity, the first of his profuse gifts, after returning with his pockets full from the war against the Chalukyan king, Satyasraya. In 1010, he dedicated the *kalasa* (the copper dome) above the *vimana*, signifying the completion of the last stage of the temple. This was a most ambitious undertaking, and as we had observed earlier, 'quite in keeping with the vast power and growing extent and resources of the Chola Empire'[44].

From all accounts, 'the eleventh century was the grandest period of temple building activity in India'. It was the age when India witnessed the highest achievements in temple architecture. Among them are those of Khajuraho built by the Chandelas, the most conspicuous of these being the Khandariya Mahadeva; and the Lingaraj of Bhubanesvar in Orissa. About this time some Hindu and Jain temples were also built at Osia in Rajasthan, and again two Jain temples, in marble, at Mt. Abu. 'Even among these, the Rajarajesvaram holds the pride of place'[45]. Undoubtedly, this temple at Thanjavur is the most colossal of Indian temples of the time, with Chola architects, masons and sculptors going much farther than they thought they ever would.

The *vimana* soared to a breath-taking height of 190 feet above the sanctum, dwarfing the Siva temples we saw earlier, and even putting the central tower of the 11th century Lingaraja temple to shame. Various sections of the temple, the *vimana*[46], *ardhamandapam*, *mahamandapam* and the massive Nandi[47] structure, taller than a man mounted on an elephant, are all housed within a walled enclosure of 500 feet by 250 feet. A tall *gopuram*, the Rajarajan *thiruvasal*, stands at the entrance to the temple in the east. All along the inside perimeter of the walls on all four sides, runs an elevated pillared cloister. Situated at intervals in this cloister are a set of thirty-five subshrines. There is also a second gopuram in front acting as the gateway for a front enclosure. The vertical base of the *vimana* is an 82 feet long square structure rising to a height of 50 feet. Above it rest thirteen structures of diminishing area making it a pyramid with its apex reducing to one-third of the base[48]. A massive cornice juts around the lower portion of the vertical structure. There is a circumambulatory path all around the sanctum housing a massive *linga*. The temple walls are embellished with expansive and exquisite mural paintings. Eighty-one of the 108 *karanas*[49], posed in *Bharatanatya*, are carved on the walls of the second *bhumi* around the *garbhagriha*. There is a shrine dedicated to Amman dating to the 13th century. Although the Thanjavur region has no hills or rocky outcrop, the temple complex was entirely built of stone, which meant that huge rocks of stone were quarried from Mammalai near Thiruchi and hauled to the site. It is estimated that the *vimana* alone took up some 17,000 cubic metres of masonry. The entire temple complex with its vast enclosure and two gateways would have consumed almost 50,000 cubic metres of masonry[50]. Even the 'distinctive' imperial style of the Vijayanagara Empire of the 15th century merged local Deccani architectural features with those of the Southern Tamil areas of the empire, specifically elements that the imperial Cholas had conjured[51]. If Rajaraja had moments of regret in his life over his campaigns of plunder, the soaring towers of the Thanjavur temple would have been expiation enough.

The temple acquired the sanskritised name Brihadeeswaram much later under the rule of Marathas and their vassals, the Nayaks. Rajaraja preferred to call it the *Rajarajesvaram* and the chief deity Siva in Linga form as *Peruvudaiyar*. The king thought it fit to engrave on its expansive walls, elaborate administrative and financial procedures concerning the day-to-day administration of the temple. The inscriptions provide, apart from a comprehensive history of the times, a full enumeration of all the metallic images set up in the temple. These 66 icons have been described, in a masterly manner, providing the minutest details of size, shape and composition, offering a mine of information for the art historian.

Considering the size of the subcontinent, Indian temple architecture is amazingly uniform but for the two chief styles of architecture and the numerous schools which claim the temple as theirs. Historians have divided the styles into Indo-Aryan and Dravidian. But since the styles have been influenced by the location and not so much by the race, due to intermingling, it is better to distinguish them as Northern and Southern. The Northern style usually employs a tower with a rounded cupola and having a curvilinear outline. The Southern style follows a square or rectangular base and a truncated pyramid erected over the base[52]. Architecture in the Pallava and Chalukya times, as we had seen earlier, 'show the gradual emancipation of the architect from the techniques of carpentry and cave architecture' to shaping a stone and then shifting to temples erected using stone structures.

Inscriptions and literature of the Cholas show that kings lived in grand and ornately constructed palaces having multiple storeys, sprawling gardens, fountains surrounded by high walls. But their architectural remains have vanished. Colonial historians and some Indian historians have therefore stressed on the religious and mystical aspect of Indian architecture, sculpture and art. But in the temple building phase of the Pallavas, Pandyas and the Cholas, from the 6th century onwards, we find an intense vitality which could only spring from the energy of the new and expanding productive forces and notable achievements in agriculture, metal smelting and stone sculpting. As we have seen in the earlier chapter, the construction of the temple at Thanjavur required meticulous planning, mobilisation of massive resources and well-trained architects and masons.

As with architecture, the sculpture of the Chola period, even though taking a religious form and mythical content, has a striking connect to material life. It manifested itself as decoration on the walls, pillars, roofs and other convenient spots. What distinguished the Chola sculptor was that he 'appreciated the value of plain spaces' nor did he go to town with 'filigree work on his ornamentation'. He worked on hard rock and 'depended on bold strokes and flowing lines for his effects'. While rules of iconography were followed, the art is 'still fairly free' and there is little that is 'mechanical and hidebound'[53]. In sharp contrast with his Pallava predecessors, the Chola artist evolved 'a new and attractive conception of life and beauty' clearly evident in the sculptures of the Chola ladies who are portrayed as 'picturesque and realistic human figures, full of feminine grace and the joy of life'[54]. Strikingly, and surprisingly, it has been observed that excellence in sculpture preceded that of architecture and technology. Unlike technology and architecture which attained their peak at the time of Rajaraja and Rajendra, the superiority of the sculptures on the walls of the Koranganatha temple at Srinivasanallur and the Nageswara temple at Kumbakonam are so pronounced as to 'enforce a revision of the common view that Chola sculpture attained its high water mark in their time. Though the sculptures in the two temples precede the accession of Rajaraja by more than a century, 'we have nothing else like them either before or after'[55]. Nevertheless, the sheer numbers of sculptures in the Thanjavur temple make amends for this disparagement.

While stone images of deities are the most common, the Tamils preferred metal over stone in making images for worship in the temple and at home. Apparently, it is especially during the Chola period, 'that the greatest Indian works of art in metal were made, by a school of bronze-casters which has not been excelled in the world'[56]. Bronze statues varied in size but many of the best specimens are large and heavy, 'their pedestals fitted with lugs for carrying in processions'. The Tamil craftsmen produced metal statues capable of exuding a terrific aura of grace and emotion. In spite of the severe iconographical constraints imposed on them, they 'succeeded in producing works of such great beauty and often of considerable individuality'[57]. Although the emergence of stone Nataraja images is attributed to Chola queen Sembiyan Mahadevi, bronze Natarajas seem to have been already cast by the Pallava period, prior to the Chola period when they were widely patronized[58]. The hagiographic texts on the Saivite and Vaishnavite saints had strikingly picturesque legends. The craftsmen made the best of them and produced livelier objects that the texts themselves would envy. The physical features and the contours of the face, limbs and the uncovered parts of the body revealed the depth of understanding of human anatomy among the sculptors. Figures representing kings, queens, saints and lesser gods often decorated the space around the central sanctum in temples.

Thanjavur was a major centre for the production of metal sculptures. As opposed to the hollow metal figures of the North, the Southern craftsmen made solid metal figures. Traditionally, northern craftsmen were believed to have used an alloy of eight metals while the southern ones used an alloy of only five (gold, silver, copper, tin and lead)[59]. The iconography did not differ between stone and metal. The South followed the practice of clothing and ornamenting the statues of gods and taking them around the temple square in processions. The most overwhelming number of statues depicted are of Siva, particularly the Nataraja (the Lord of Dance) form. Statues of Krishna, Vishnu, their consorts, the Alwar and Nayanmar saints and even Buddhist images were the next in line.

One major difference between the sculptors in the Chola and the earlier Pallava period is that the former moved away from the bas-reliefs, the large engravings on stone, to sculptures in high relief or stand-alone round sculptures. The rich iconography of the Nayanmars and Alwars had developed to a considerable level of sophistication by the time of Rajaraja. This is not to say that they totally gave up stone sculptures. As we had seen, the stone sculptures at the Srinivasanallur and Nageswara temples exceled the Pallava ones and the ones to come later. The Chola bronze sculptures used the *cire perdu* process[60]. The Thanjavur temple inscriptions throw some light on the technique and the type of images produced – solid, hollow or semi-hollow with thick sides.

Among the Chola bronzes, the Nataraja image in its various forms, holds pride of place. While hundreds of images can be found in temples and museums in Tamil Nadu today, many of them have emigrated to museums and private homes abroad. We have to rely upon this rather long quote from a foreign author to bring out the ecstatic and almost apocalyptic expression of the sculpture.

'Whether he be surrounded or not by the flaming aureole of the *tiruvasi* (*prabhandmandala*) —the circle of the world which he both fills and oversteps —the king of the dance is all rhythm and exaltation. The tambourine which he sounds with one of his right hands draws all creatures into this rhythmic motion, and they dance in his company. The conventionalized locks of flying hair and the blown scarfs tell of the speed of this universal movement, which crystallizes matter and reduces it to powder in turn. One of his left hands holds the fire which animates and devours the worlds in this cosmic whirl. One of the god's feet is crushing a Titan, for "this dance is danced upon the bodies of the dead," and yet one of the right hands is making the gesture of reassurance (*abhaya mudra*), so true it is that, seen from the cosmic point of view, and *sub specie aeternitatis*, the very cruelty of this

Fig. 14 - Statue of Nataraja, Chola style

universal determinism is kindly, as the generative principle of the future. And, indeed, on more than one of our bronzes the King of the Dance wears a broad smile. He smiles at death and at life, at pain and at joy, alike, or rather, if we may be allowed so to express it, his smile is both death and life, both joy and pain ... From this lofty point of view, in fact, all things fall into their place, finding their explanation and logical compulsion. Here art is the faithful interpreter of the philosophical concept. The plastic beauty of rhythm is no more than the expression of an ideal rhythm. The very multiplicity of arms, puzzling as it may seem at first sight, is subject in turn to an inward law, each pair remaining a model of elegance in itself, so that the whole being of the Nataraja thrills with a magnificent harmony in his terrible joy. And as though to stress the point that the dance of the divine actor is indeed a sport (*leela*)—the sport of life and death, the sport of creation and destruction, at once infinite and purposeless—the first of the left hands hangs limply from the arm in the careless gesture of the *gajahasta* (hand as the elephant's trunk). And lastly, as we look at the back view of the statue, are not the steadiness of these shoulders which uphold the world, and the majesty of this Jove-like torso, as it were a symbol of the stability and immutability of substance, while the gyration of the legs in its dizzy speed would seem to symbolize the vortex of phenomena?'[61]

Metal artefacts of the Chola and Pallava periods have different characteristics[62][63]. It appears that the Nataraja bronzes found in Kunniyar in Thanjavur district and the one languishing in the British Museum in all likelihood belong to the Pallava period and not to the Chola period as originally believed. Technical finger printing study suggested that the Nataraja bronze, depicting Siva dancing the *anandatandava* with the lifted leg extended in bhujangatrasita karana, might have been a Pallava rather than a Chola innovation[64].

An interesting fact is that since early Pallava bronze images of Nataraja were a copy of wooden images, the limbs are not spread out and the scarf hangs downwards. In the Chola bronzes, the sculptors having recognised the greater tensile strength of the metal, dared to bring a lot more dynamics to the limbs, scarf and locks, which was not even remotely possible for the Pallava sculptor. Due to improved technology well-rounded stone and bronze images were made during the reign of Parantaka and Rajaraja. They are attributed to the efforts of queen Sembiyan Mahadevi, the mother of Rajaraja's uncle Uttama Cholar, who ruled before him[65]. In fact, such was the queen's exemplary personality and integrity that the royal family commissioned a bronze portraiture of her. Her image of power and eminence was so overpowering that the artist 'envisioned her as comparable to none less than Parvati, the great goddess'[66]. It would have been difficult to recognise the queen in this image, in which the queen and the goddess mingled and merged, 'but when the image was carried out in processions during her birthday celebrations, all would have recognised her'[67].

Siva was not the only privileged god to be cast in bronze and preserved for eternity. Other popular gods such as Muruga, the son of Siva – who takes after the north Indian god Skanda – as well as Parvati, Siva's consort, and Vishnu in his various forms were also favourites of the bronze-casters, reflecting their popularity at that time. Vaishnava bronzes of Vishnu in the *samabhanga*[68] pose, with the body in perfect equilibrium, and Lakshmi and Rukmini in the *tribhanga*[69] pose, in the temple at Srimadevi in Thirunelveli district, might be products of the Rajaraja period. Similarly, a group of three bronzes of Rama, Lakshmana and Sita with Hanuman in an attitude of worship is 'obviously one of the finest products of the best age of Chola bronze-casting of that time'[70].

As in the case of architecture and sculpture, Chola painting was also a continuation and embellishment of the work done earlier during the Pallava and Pandya regimes. But unlike architecture and sculpture, we see extensive references to the excellence of Chola paintings in literature but only a few have survived. Paintings are much more susceptible to decay due to time, weather and chemical reaction. As if that is not enough, many paintings have been overlaid by later dynasties. The best specimens of Chola paintings have survived in the circumambulatory, *paradakshina*, around the central sanctum of the Thanjavur temple.

South Indian paintings differ from the ones in the Ajanta caves in the aspect that the former uses a coarser lime mortar for the base with a finer coat of limewash above it. The Thanjavur paintings use the fresco technique in the sense that the painting was done over this fine coat of lime when it was still wet. This allows the pigment to penetrate and as the coat of lime dries, it reacts with the ambient carbon dioxide to form a thin protective layer. Unlike the paintings in the Deccan and Lanka, the mineral colours are not mixed with glue or gum to bind them to the surface. Lime was used for white shades and wood charcoal or lamp black for black. Pigments for other colours were of mineral origin. Ultra-marine was used for blue and mixed with lime to obtain lighter shades. Ochres were used for yellow, brown and red. Mixing ochres in different proportions produced different shades. Limited colouring materials were used to give permanent effects. Obviously, the painter's imagination was restricted by the limitations of the technique. As the fresco dries, the pigments lose some brightness. The Thanjavur painters 'understood this so well as to achieve a fine harmony of colour'[71] with terrific results. The biggest challenge would have been to complete an entire panel before the lime dries, so that joints are avoided. The artists seem to have done with great gusto with a group of them working together to complete a single panel and several groups working to complete the wall in this short stretch of time. Considering that some of the panels were 60 sq ft, this was a stupendous job. 'To put so much detail of dress and ornament, and to achieve so much decorative effect even in the disposition of the figures under such limitations of time as the fresco process imposed required great skill of the artists indeed'[72].

We need to examine a few of these panels closely to appreciate the sublime imagination of the artist and the mythical stories which formed their basis. One such panel is the Kailasa scene involving Siva and Sundaramurthi Nayanar and a host of other celestial beings. The panel depicts Siva seated in the yogasana position on his inevitable tiger skin upholstered seat with the ever-present Nandi in the couchant position. There are a group of rishis in the front contrasting completely with a group of divine apsara maidens dancing at another end. As if to excel this rich imagery, there is another ingenious scene at the bottom. The two friends, Sundarar seated on an elephant and Cheraman, his compatriot Nayanmar, riding a high-speed horse are seen racing each other to reach Kailasa first. The decorations on the elephant and steed and the creative attire of the protagonists are breathtaking. Again, we see the contrasting scene of the riders being welcomed by both the severely clad rishis on one side and the diaphanously clad apsaras on the other. As we had seen in the earlier chapters on architecture and sculpture, the Thanjavur paintings are full of life. The imagining of Kailasa as a place offering spiritual and sensual solace is superb[73].

Patently, the enormous resources required to build the Brihadeeswara temple and adorn it with sculptures and frescoes would have made the royal treasury significantly lighter. But the temple and its treasures were ostensibly open to all thanks to the vigorous bhakti movement of the previous centuries.

Fig. 15 - A mural painting at Brihadeeswara Temple

One of the panels showing the Emperor, escorted by his three queens and worshipping Lord Nataraja, is considered a masterpiece of the Chola artist, who 'was as versatile in handling the human form as in portraying Nature in all her facets'. Here the artist was thrown the challenge of not only representing the relationship between the Lord and the Emperor in an acceptable arrangement, but also the relationship between the Emperor and his queens. He must have been extremely thankful that the entourage was limited to only three of the Emperor's queens, though. The wall of the enclosure is simple. But the artist solves the problem in contriving that 'the Chit *Sabha* is shown in magnified dimensions to accommodate the figure of Nataraja which dominates the scene and the Kanaka Sabha shown respectfully smaller, accommodates Rajaraja and his three queens'[74].

The figure of the dancing Nataraja, called Adavallan appropriately, 'is exquisite in workmanship and enormous in proportions, comparable to the actual size of some of the man-sized bronzes of Nataraja cast in this period, with emphasis on poise and balance. The Dhatura flower is enchantingly natural, while the cobra wriggles and dangles from the divine body in all its sinuousness and colour'[75].

Another panel recreates the scene that we admired in an earlier chapter, when Siva dressed as a bearded old man disrupts Sundarar's marriage and claims that his grandfather had pledged him to serve Siva. The Sabha members exhibit conflicting emotions while the old man pulls out a palm leaf manuscript as evidence while Sundarar shoots a baffled look at his tormentor. On one side marriage preparations are in full swing. On the other side, the final act of the drama unfolds[76].

The 'grandest composition in the whole series' is the panel portraying Tripurantaka, the form of Siva most endorsed by the Rajaraja regime. Siva is standing on the deck of his chariot in the alidha pose, his left knee bent, the weight of his body thrown on the forward placed right leg. His eight arms carrying different missiles, his 'vibrant frame and defiant expression' suggest a disaster for the victim. Brahma, chastened by Siva and bereft of his fifth head, is seen at the wheels of the chariot. In front is a bloody battlefield between the asuras and Siva's ganas. Added to the grim battle scene is a painting of Durga on top, riding on a lion and impaling an asura with her spear, while her lion is holding another by his neck[77].

The Tripurantaka iconography was carried forward at least for another 150 years when Rajaraja II built the Darasuramlwars Temple near Kumbakonam in the twelfth century. It has been regarded as the most beautiful Chola monument of this period, 'a sculptor's dream re-lived in stone, which is unequalled in its technical perfection and exuberant ornamentation'[78]. According to tradition, the temple was constructed by the divine architect Vihwakarma himself, with a difference, in that the mukhamanadapa has been very ingeniously 'designed to simulate a chariot (ratha) on two wheels drawn by two horses and serves as an entrance to the temple by way of lateral stairways on the east and west'[79]. But, unlike the period of Rajaraja I when the Tripurantaka icon announced his consummate victory over the Pandyas, Cheras and Lanka, the structure in Darasuram in the form of Tripurantaka's chariot was perhaps 'a last great effort to regain control

Fig. 16 - Image of Tripurantaka

over the three southern enemies by invoking help from the Destroyer of the Three Cities' by Rajaraja II who was desperately trying to control the turbulence from his vassals and renewed threats from the South. But what is even more interesting, is that, just as in the Brihadeeswara Temple, the Buddha finds a prominent place, sitting cross-legged[80] on a double-petalled lotus under a tree, 'regarded as the most outstanding image among these panels'. His right hand is in the gesture of preaching knowledge[81] while the left rests on his lap[82]. It is possible that the Buddha was drawn in as the heretic avatar of Vishnu, the Mayamohin, according to legend, but the importance given to the figure is equal to that of the other gods figuring in the Tripurantaka legend.

The sculptures and paintings are far from being stereotyped, and a conscious attempt at modelling is evident. The celestial beings, apsaras and gandharavas, 'have a certain bend of body as if they had floated into shapes on waves of an invisible sea'. Seated figures of women exude charm. The dancing forms are full of action and expression. 'The hair is done into elaborate coiffures with some ringlets falling on the face' and the figure accentuated with flowers, buds and ornaments. The eyes, eyelids and noses have expressive and sensitive shapes. The drapery of female figures usually consists of a sari of diaphanous muslin, decorated by floral patterns or horizontal lines. 'The bust is generally bare except for a piece of cloth worn over the left shoulder and passing between the ample bosoms under the right arm'. In the panel at Rajeswaram, for instance, depicting Rajaraja and his three queens worhsipping Lord Natarja, 'what is noteworthy, among others, is the fine handling of the drapery of the queens who are shown wearing fine quality saris with lines and dots and decorative designs on them. The legs are revealed through the fineness of the diaphanous drapery'[83]. Not to be left behind, the menfolk are of strong build, bearded, moustached and with knots of hair on the head.

It is impossible to ignore the thoroughness with which the icons have been elaborately described. The name of the deities, the composition of the metal, the height and weight of each unit, their physical attributes— all these particulars have been provided in the inscriptions, something unparalleled in the history of any ruler in our land or elsewhere. The loss of most of these icons, vessels, ornaments in 'gold and precious stones, corals and pearls of fantastic numbers, variety and value', 'is a sad tale of a vanished glory whose shadow alone we can now see and read from the mute records inscribed on the temple walls'[84] painstakingly documented by the indefatigable labour and the mature scholarship of some of the greatest epigraphists[85] of our period.

A little-known chapter in the history of South Indian Art is the spread of this celebration of life beyond the subcontinent's shores to the Indo-China region.

9

DELIGHTFUL POTPOURRI OF
LITERARY SPACES

As in architecture and the arts, during the rise of the imperial Chola power, we see 'a more copious flow of literary effort'[1], no doubt realised by the fresh energy released by the new productive forces and the general expansion of the economy. While Rajaraja had earned a special place for himself in the history of India as a great builder, he turned out to be a great patron of the arts and the written word as well. In this he had many predecessors. The earlier lineage of Cholas, in the Sangam age, had seen many 'princes ... take a good part as patrons of poets and sometimes as authors'[2] themselves. After the Cholas waned during the 'dark' Kalabhra period, for a period of four or five centuries, the Pallavas and Pandyas became the main patrons of art and literature, until the Cholas gained the upper hand. There is no evidence of an umbilical cord connecting the earlier Cholas with those of the Vijayalaya line, but the propinquity between the Sangam literature and those produced during the period of the imperial Cholas cannot be altogether dismissed. The reign of Rajaraja intersects two great periods for Tamil literature. During the period between the 6th and 9th centuries, before Rajaraja sat on the tiger emblazoned throne, the great hymns of the Saivite and Vaishnavite canons were created, Kumarila and Sankara composed their didactic works, and Buddhists and Jains worked on their immortal epics and ethical treatises[3]. The period after Rajaraja is studded with great poets such as Kamban and Ottakuthar, and the prodigious development of philosophy and theology by Ramanujar and Arunandi.

With the rise of the imperial Chola state, there was 'a broadening of the channels of literature and a more copious flow of literary effort'. The devotional hymns of the Nayanmars and Alwars 'evolved in ever increasing complexity'. It was a new experience altogether, which was 'not only a development *en train* towards more complex metrical forms, but also a transformation of the ancient themes and situations of the Sangam age settings into religious-philosophical, polemic or simply devotional genres'[4]. Such was the impact of the new literature that even the language used in inscriptions became 'highly ornate and poetic' compared to the 'meagre and arid prose of the inscriptions of the earlier times'[5] though at the time of Rajaraja the presentation style of the inscriptions was standardised. These eulogies, called *meykeertis*[6], in Tamil, were written in both Sanskrit, the language of learning, and Tamil, the language of the people. But it was Tamil which gained most in this period, with a considerable number of documenters and inscribers trained in the language. The inscriptions used such 'stately diction', 'easy flow of the verse' and the 'animated narration of historical incidents' that they easily found themselves among the best specimens of literature of the times. Besides imperial *meykeertis*, there are others which recount the career and achievements of officials such as the Chidambaram and Thiruvadi inscriptions[7]. These compositions handle various metres of poetry with consummate skills and 'the somewhat complex laws of Tamil prosody are observed with an easy grace'[8]. They were no doubt composed by court poets and the great number of inscriptions would have definitely provided a great impetus to poetry and literature connected to the narration of historical incidents and the glorification of kings. This trend started with the reign of Rajaraja and a veritable cornucopia of literary works emerged. The names of a number of these works have been preserved in these inscriptions, but the literary works themselves, sadly, have disappeared. Nevertheless, they do provide us with a picture of the extent of popular interest in literary productions and the kind of literature which were acclaimed. What gave historians inconsolable grief is that a drama and a *kavya* on the emperor which would have 'contained several allusions, if not accurate descriptions, of some of the most striking episodes of Rajaraja's life'[9] were among the vanished lot. The drama went by the name of Rajarajeswara-natakam, which were ostensibly enacted in the great Thanjavur temple, the emperor's *chef d'oeuvre*, during festivals. The latter was a narrative on the emperor's achievements, called Rajaraja-vijayam, which was to be read out at temples. If they had survived today, they would have been the equivalent of the brilliant account of Nunes and Paes on Krishna Devaraya. If Rajaraja had wished, he could have commanded the empire's poets to write not one but many epics on himself and rolled a golden coconut for each verse, as a later Chola emperor did, but he was either pleasingly diffident compared to other emperors or too preoccupied with administrating the empire to spend his gold. Sadly, many other inscriptions attest the existence of widespread literary activities of a popular nature, but much excellent work has been lost beyond recovery. Ostensibly, the works which have survived 'have been the result more of caprice and accident than of deliberate choice'[10].

The transition of bardic poetry of the Sangam age into bhakti devotional hymns went through a lot of productive churning, turning out some exquisite poetic material in the process. The Sangam bards were generally held in 'high esteem' and presumably 'belonging to all cases of society'[11]. These men and women—at least 20 women minstrels could be counted—were recruited from many different communities, received bardic training and became professionals'. They travelled in groups, rich and poor alike, in search of patrons. They were so filled by 'passion balanced with courtesy, transparency by ironies and nuances of design' that 'the Tamils, in all their 2000 years of literary effort, wrote nothing better'[12]. But there had to be a break from early classical tradition and conventions, and that came in the early centuries of the first millennium. Transitions were visible in various anthologies such as the *Kalittogai* and the *Paripadal*. Here we can see the introduction of the Vaishnavite legends which branded the *Paripadal* as a 'Sanskrit plagiat' within the Sangam texts and their authors 'the fifth column'[13] of Sangam literature and Vedic philosophy and theology getting reflected in a language other than Sanskrit. The precursor of the bhakti hymns which started appearing in the sixth century, is however, the 'guide' poem, the *Thirumurugattrupadai*, in which the god Murugan appears as a 'blend, as a syncretic god' and the poem itself manifesting the 'welding of two cultures, the indigenous Tamil with the Sanskritic and Brahmanic'. It is a marvellous work of art and a poem of transition, marking the end of the classical age and the beginning of the period of bhakti, which lent character to the iconography of the Chola Empire. A verse giving a picture of the lush forest in the rainy season ends with the idea of devotion.

The forests,

cool and fragrant after first showers,

pouring down from gigantic clouds,

pregnant with waters sucked up from the sea

scattering heavy drops upon the firmament

whose darkness is dispelled

by the sun and the moon.

The forests,

darkened and overspread

by the dense leaves

of the red kadambu tree.

He has a garland of its flowers

on his chest[14].

Though not created exactly during Rajaraja's tenure, the *Seevaga Sinthamani*, one of the five greatest epics, the *mahakavyas*, in Tamil, needs to be looked at as representative of the times. It has been billed as a great work 'so replete with credible incidents, so wrought up by the vigour of literary talent, so interspersed with remarks involving the keenest introspection into the grounds of human action...'[15] Its author is the Jain poet Thirutakkadevar and the work was apparently composed in the 10th century. Tradition has it that after doing a full course on Tamil and Sanskrit, the author turned an ascetic and went to Madurai to find a place among the Sangam poets.

But the latter were circumspect about the capability of Jain ascetics, to write anything other than religious, leave alone on love, on which topic the Madurai poets were unrivalled pundits. The ascetic poet took up this challenge and even convinced his guru that producing an erotic poem would not harm his spiritual grounding. Embarking on this task, like the proverbial eager beaver, the poet composed the epic on the life of Seevagan and won the generous plaudits of his guru. But to Thirutakkadevar's dismay, 'this did not give the quietus' to the Sangam critics who unable to find faults with the merits of the poem, resorted to character assassination, accusing the ascetic of an active sex life without which he could not have produced such sensuous work. The ascetic was now caught in a bind. Just when he managed to prove that an ascetic could write a sensuous poem on an epic scale, he had to now backtrack and prove that he remained an ascetic after all. Thirutakkadevar was then forced to demonstrate his commitment to asceticism by going through an ordeal. This could not be but a tale, but the fact that the epic is acknowledged as a part of the chaste Jaina Puranas has flummoxed many.

It is the story of Seevaga, a Prince, whose father is killed by the treachery of his minister. The boy escapes with his mother and grows up into a man versatile in all the arts of war and peace, a veritable superman. His stormy youth is marked by many adventures, and through many valorous acts he acquires an astonishing number of eight wives, providing a more apt name to the epic, *Mana-nul*, the *Book of Marriages*. To achieve this brilliant feat, or acquire a bundle of worries, if one looks at it the other way, the Prince uses a variety of arts from archery to the curing of a snake-bite 'to win a new bride for his harem with every feat'[16]. All these adventures culminate into happy marriages and finally he becomes the monarch of a splendid kingdom and takes his revenge against the treacherous minister. But he is shaken out of complacency 'by an incident, trivial in itself, but full of deep significance to him'[17]. He sees 'in a moment's flash' the futility of the human material life and seeks peace in asceticism. It is a remarkable poem containing 3145 stanzas of four lines each, in the *agaval* metre, a very flexible type and most suited for narrative poetry. The poet's work is fantastic, and his 'style is elegant and ornate, and much influenced by courtly Sanskrit'[18]. Not only that, 'one moves in a world of typical court-poetry, and in a universe where the supernatural mingles freely with the natural'. The stories of the hero's love conquests are dealt with in great graphic detail, the poet excelling in *double entendre* with so much effect that 'for some hopelessly prudish critics, these episodes are unbearably sensuous'[19]. If some critics were repulsed by the epic, one should not be surprised, because it had an assortment of incidents that sounded uncomfortably lascivious. The poem was hailed by earlier generations of European scholars, with Beschi calling the author a 'prince among Tamil poets' and Pope equating it to 'at once the Iliad and Odyssey of the Tamil language'. It is accepted as great poetry and is believed to have 'furnished the model for even the genius Kamban'[20], who at a later date composed the Ramayana in Tamil. Fortunately for the author, the empire was not a citadel of prudish readers. All said and done, the verdict has been that the epic 'makes delicious, often intoxicating reading'[21]. In a trendsetting manner, the epic popularised a new form of poetry metre called the *viruttam* which successfully replaced the older *agaval* and *venpa* metres[22].

Two other epics, the *Valaiyapathi* and the *Kundalakesi*, a Buddhist Tamil work, were composed more or less at the same time, but they survive as only fragments cited in other works. *Valaiyapathi*, particularly, had a social message against casteism, and it is indeed a pity that the text of this epic has perished. Other works such as *Nilakesi, Soolamani, The Crest Jewel, and Udayanan Charitram* are all Jaina works composed in the tenth century. They point unmistakeably to a strong Jaina presence in popular literature around the time of Rajaraja. Among the Buddhist works figure *Kundalakesi*, which is a dramatic story of a maiden of the Chetty (merchant) caste who makes a wrong judgement when she falls in love with a murderer and who finally makes amends by pushing him over a cliff. The Jaina work *Nilakesi*[23] was a 'counter-blast against the Buddhist *Kundalakesi*'[24] indicating a vigorous ongoing polemic between the two sects. In fact, *Nilakesi* does highlight the nature of controversies between the two heterodox sects and there must have been quite a number of such polemic works, regaling patrons and readers of the time.

It is into this delightful potpourri of literary spaces that the *bhakti* saints of Thamizhagam entered like a storm around the 6th century and went on to embellish Tamil literature till at least the 9th century. The vigorous Jaina and Buddhist activity in literature, along with monasteries and pallis that Rajaraja supported is indicative of a fair amount of religious freedom and communal harmony at his time, and debunks the accounts of intolerance shown by the *bhakti* saints towards these 'heretic' sects. But, speaking realistically, the *bhakti* saints seem to have acquiesced, but none too graciously, to the continuing influence of the 'heterodox' sects in Tamil literature, as their constant pummelling of the Jains and Buddhists in their hymns reveal. The next great blast of exquisite Tamil literature starts from a few decades after Rajaraja, led by great poets such as Jayankondar, Kambar, Ottakuthar and Pugazhendi.

As hinted earlier, the arrival of *bhakti* hymns did presage a lowering of royal patronage for the classical poems of the Sangam era. The Sangam poems were just not the stuff to be recited in temples. The hymns of the *bhakti* saints captured the imagination of the people in such a way that they left little room for their more colourful elder cousin, to make any new inroads. The Chola kings 'enlarged and rebuilt extant Siva shrines and built great structural temples in stone, particularly in the places visited by Nayanars'[25], who were most active from the sixth to the ninth centuries. These temples called the *padal pettra sthalam*, a place sung by the saints, became the rallying centre for the empire. While the Pallavas had started the practice, the Chola kings went full hog and employed singers to sing the hymns of Nayanmars during ritual worship in the temples. Private corporate bodies also provided endowments for the hiring of dancers and musicians to make the hymns popular. The Nayanmars themselves became a central piece in the establishment of the iconography of the empire. As we had seen earlier, it would be naïve to think that the Nayanmars wished these temples into fame by singing for them. The temples dotted the trade routes and were rallying points for an already established trade or artisan centre and its existence depended on their charity. It is easy to spot this pattern of the Chola kings.

The fact that both the Saivite and Vaishnavite canons were compiled around the tenth century cannot go unnoticed here. In the late 10th century or early 11th, the hymns of the three great poets Sundarar, Appar and Sambandar, were compiled in seven volumes, to be collectively called the *Thirumurai*, the *Sacred Text*, and revered since then as the primary scripture of the Tamil Saiva sect. More texts were added to this in the next few centuries to provide a larger volume called the *Devaram*. The story of the canonisation of the *Thirumurai* is told in the fourteenth century work, the *Thirumuraikanda Puranam*, the story of the discovery of the *Thirumurai*. According to the narrative here, Rajaraja requested the poet Nambiyandar Nambi[26], hailing from a town called Naraiyur, to "reveal" the hymns and lives of the Saiva saints of the world. Siva's son Ganesa himself assisted the poet to discover the *Thirumurai* hymns in manuscript form, 'half eaten by white ants', from a sealed vault near the golden hall of the great Siva temple in Chidambaram. The choice of the temple and the dramatic fashion in which the manuscripts were recovered, under divine supervision, does hint at a calculated step to gather the hymns into a canon around which the empire's subjects can be rallied. This brilliant move gave Rajaraja plenty of skin in the game of statecraft. While Nambi could only find the hymns of the great saints and compile them, the musical tradition of the hymns was missing. He could 'reconstruct the melodic and rhythmic aspects of the hymns'[27] with the help of a female descendant of a musician who had accompanied Sambandar, in his times. 'The story of the discovery of the hymns in written form and the reconstruction of their ancient music modes, the pan, 'suggest that prior to the 11th century there may have been a break in the oral tradition through which the Saivite hymns were transmitted'[28]. The miraculous communication from Ganesa and by Siva himself, established the authenticity of the hymns as 'revealed' scripture. The hymns in the *Thirumurai* can certainly be counted as among the best poetic works of the times, but their impact far outstripped the other works, particularly when Rajaraja hit upon the brilliant idea of compiling them into a canon. The recovery legend certainly established the 'Chola monarch as the great patron of Saivism, and of Chidambaram as "The Temple", the *koyil*, as the greatest centre of Saivism'[29]. It is very likely that the hymns which survived the ravages of time are only a fraction of the original corpus[30]. The entire canon was actually completed in the 12th century, while the Cholas were still reigning, with the 'grand, public canonisation of the *Periya Puranam*, the *Great Story*, a narrative of the lives of the sixty three nayanars as the twelfth book of the *Thirumurai*'[31], by the great poet Sekkizhar.

From all accounts, the 10th century was certainly a productive time for compiling religious canons. Another fantastic legend, though less dramatic than that of the Saivite canon, surrounds the Vaishnavite canon. The saint Nathamuni[32] compiled the hymns of the twelve Vaishnava saints and arranged for their recitation, in what would appear as a déjà vu later when Nambi dug up the Saivite hymns from the vaults of a temple. According to a legend, Nathamuni heard visitors from Nammalwar's birthplace at Kurukur recite ten stanzas, while he knew that the saint had compiled nothing less than a thousand. Even when listening to these meagre hymns, his spirits took flight. He promptly dashed to Kurukur, where he appealed to Vishnu, meditated as a yogi and finally, when 'he recited 12,000 times Madhurakavi's praise poems about his master, Nammlawar'[33], then both magically appeared to him in a vision and did a knowledge transfer of the Alwar's four works. The canonisation of Nammalwar's work is significant considering that he was a Shudra saint and thus 'a non-Sanskritic, non-brahmanical religious literature became central to brahmana orthodoxy'[34] in the South. Inscriptions belonging to Rajaraja's reign mention endowments of land for the maintenance of reciters of the Alwar's poems in temples, making it clear that Vaishnavism was not ignored in spite of the preference for the Saivite iconography of the imperial Cholas. Nathamuni must have lived during the time of Parantaka I, the great-grandfather of Rajaraja, and Nammalwar would have also witnessed the Chola resurgence during his times.

Nathamuni's compilation was called the *Four Thousand Divine Compositions*, the *Nalayira Divyaprabandham* in Tamil. For the Vaishnavite sect, they were equal to the four Vedas, just as the *Devaram* had a higher standing than the Vedas for the Saivites. 'The singers of the Tamil hymns led the temple processions, walked before the god; and the Vedas followed behind'[35]. It might look like a queer coincidence that the religious canons of the two greatest sects of the region were compiled within a few decades of each other during the reign of the imperial Cholas and close to Rajaraja's time, but it was not.

The compilation of the Saivite and Vaishnavite hymns received the blessings of the Chola royalty driven undoubtedly by the need for fashioning the iconography of the all-powerful empire, but in this endeavour, the Chola kings and particularly Rajaraja kept the domination of Sanskrit at bay. It was a cause célèbre for the Tamil people both in the religious and literary domains and would have won the loyalty of the populace, something an oppressive state could have scarcely earned. Tamil is the one Indian mother tongue with a long literary tradition going back to the second half of the first millennium BCE. It is noteworthy that in the North the 'only literary languages by the time of the Guptas were Sanskrit and its Prakrit relatives'[36]. None of them was a language of transaction for the people. Even the great Kalidasa while regaling the king's court in chaste Sanskrit must have used a spoken dialect in his hometown Ujjayini. Regional languages of today such as Bengali, Marathi and various forms of Hindi did not have any literary form until after the 10th century.

By Rajaraja's time, the Sanskrit *kavya* style of poetry had considerable influence on Tamil poetry, but never replaced it as a literary language. This in spite of the fact that 'Sanskrit had antiquity, hieratic pan-Indian prestige; it was the lingua franca of pundits, philosophers, epic poets, lawgivers, courts and kings. Sanskrit was culture'[37] plain and simple! But not in the land of Rajaraja in his time, or for that matter, at any other time in the South. True that the great 12th century Vaishnavite saint, Ramanuja, never wrote a word in Tamil or cited a Tamil text, but this was an exception. The *meykeertis* of Chola times had a Sanskrit portion, more out of compulsion to follow tradition, but the portion in Tamil excelled in its composition, and was very much a part of the top stratum of the Tamil literary corpus.

From the 6th century onwards, the *bhakti* saints had won the hearts of people through their captivating Tamil hymns[38]. By compiling these hymns into a canon and providing endowments for singers, Rajaraja did yeoman's service to the Tamil language. For very obvious reasons, Tamil was dear to writers, poets, philosophers and theologians in the Tamil country. 'Tamil alone had a full-grown literary courtly tradition as well as oral and village folk traditions – which 'qualified' Tamil as a real alternative, in the culture of the time'[39]. The works of Sankara and Kumarila, both philosophers from the South, did create burbles in the sea of South Indian literature, but their choice of Sanskrit and the didactic and philosophical nature of their works did not enjoy the popularity that *bhakti* poems did. Considering that 'Tamil devotional sects resisted Sankritic culture'[40], clipping the spread of Vedic orthodoxy would not have been an imposing task for the emperor. However, women writers and poets were hard to come by. Their agency was still buried under grimy layers of male domination and social inequity, with the exception of Andaal and Karaikal Ammaiyar who entered the list of *bhakti* saints through sheer grit and determination.

A vigorous attempt was made by many authors to adapt Sanskrit and northern literary works to Tamil. An important work in this genre is the Tamil adaptation of the *Brhatkatha*, the *Great Story* in the Paisachi language, ascribed to Gunadya, a poet in the Salivahan court of the 1st century. While the Ganga ruler, adapted this in Sanskrit in the 7th century, the Tamil version was done by Konguvelir, a Kongu chieftain, somewhere in the 9th century and goes under the name *Perungathai*, or *Udayan Charitram*. 'The work is a torso of nearly 16,000 lines' and is 'the first of the Jaina narratives in Tamil which have for their topic the story of a man driven to religious life and asceticism through satiation with the good things and pleasures of life'[41]. There are many striking parallels between *Perungathai* and a later Jaina epic, *Seevaga Sintamani*, which we had the pleasure of looking at closely earlier in the chapter. We can see this constant tussle between asceticism and the pleasures of material life in the poems and literary works of this period. Ostensibly, rapid urbanisation and expanding productive forces compelled the writers and poets to address the problems of this world than that of the other.

While the *bhakti* hymnists and the writers of epics moved away from the Sangam genre, there is a persisting effect of the genre in the works of the Chola period. The classical Tamil poetry of this period 'reworks oral folk materials. Many genres, especially epics and *bhakti* poems, blend Sanskrit and Tamil traditions, and within Tamil, bridge the 'high' and 'low'"[42]. Periyalwar's lullabies, poems on Krishna's pot-dances, the pounding pestle songs of Manickavachagar[43], songs that accompany games like *ammanai* (jacks) and *untipara* (a game of tag or toss) are part of Tamil folklore to this day[44].

A curious genre, called the *parani*, emerged in later years. It is puzzling why it became popular much later when all the ingredients for the genre were present in the wars that Rajaraja waged against the southern and northern kingdoms. One can make a plausible assumption that the genre started earlier, considering that it had strong ties to the *puram* war poems of the Sangam age, and that the works done up to the period of Rajraja were lost. The *Kalingattuparani*, composed during the reign of Kulottunga I, by the inimitable poet Jayamkondar is the 'earliest and the best of the poems accessible to us'[45] in this genre. It is horror and fascination in equal parts, though the horror half lingers longer. The survival of this work in its entirety is certainly due to its supreme merit; and for that reason, it may have buried many other inferior works in the genre into oblivion. The hero of the poem is a warrior who has killed a thousand male elephants on the field. It is a war poem par excellence; and a 'poetic expression of gruesomeness and horror'[46] notwithstanding its narrative on some of the most unlikely situations and improbable happenings. It has the place of the 'gothic novel' in Tamil literature and can easily trounce today's horror stories in its macabre quality. It is about the Kalinga war waged by the King around 1110, when the Chola army crossed the Vengi territory, destroyed an elephant corps, torched Kalingam, made mincemeat of the enemy army and in the end 'subdued the seven Kalingas'[47], all for the innocuous reason that the Kalinga king forgot to pay his annual tribute. This war, by all accounts, is a repeat of the Kalinga war during the earlier Mauryan times, no less ferocious. According to tradition, unlike Ashoka who repented the carnage, the Chola emperor, Kulottunga I, was so impressed with the poem, that he rewarded the poet 'by rolling a golden coconut at the end of each stanza'[48]. Considering that there are about 500 stanzas, the poet would have laughed all the way to the bank. The poet in question does not hesitate to paint the most gruesome pictures such as the stanza where it describes the devils sniffing at their hands bathed in rivers of flowing blood, or when the goddess Kali promises her devils a feast since she is sure that the war is going to be a massacre. When the ghouls are worried whether they will indeed be able to taste the gruel prepared from corpses, Kali assures them that the feast will be double the size of the war in Lanka. The goddess is a 'horrible apparition and is served by terrifying rites'. Her devil worshippers are lean and famished. The killed warriors lie spread-eagled on the battlefield with their mouths prised open by enemy spears, as if they were blowing trumpets. Arrows are pulled out of the wounds with their heads stained with blood and fat. The devils pounce upon the corpses and cook their gruel from the 'blood, bones, fat and marrow of the dead'. The poet finds a place for fiendish humour amidst the gruesome scenario when he describes the 'Brahman devil gaping with his mouth ajar at the tasty soup of stinking corpses and begs for it like a religious beggar; the Jaina devil eats only once a day and will be given only strained soup; the Buddhist devil will be given only the brains of the dead'[49]. In this devilish commentary on the cruel deeds of men, the first part of the poem describes the love-hungry women of the Chola country; it then goes onto present the demoniac havoc caused by their husbands; and finally it sympathises with the bereaved women of the defeated kingdom. The poem is filled with similes and metaphors such as when the arms and legs of the emaciated devils are compared to the thick forest of tall Palmyra trees, and the two armies falling upon each other like two oceans. We have a devil here using the wrenched-out arm of a corpse as a ladle and a devil there using the elephant's cut off trunk as a water container. On the whole, 'the impression it leaves is that of a fantastic nightmare of devils and corpses, sex-hungry women and weeping widows'[50]. The poem is certainly a glorification of the 'expansionist imperialism of the Cholas' and this is revealed in the panegyric stanzas praising the gruesome wars waged by Karikala, Parantaka and Rajaraja while they blasted their way towards an imperial dynasty.

The literary genre called the *ula*, the procession, was developed by Cheraman Perumal, the Saivite poet, in the 8th century and was certainly popular during Rajaraja's time. In this variety of poems, the patron, who is usually a king or god, goes in procession around the streets of a city, in a carriage of polished teak and gilded metal pulled by the best Arabian horses or the most majestic elephants, and women of seven different age groups fall in love with him. But unfortunately, the love is one-sided for a king can take only that many wives[51]. In the reign of the imperial Cholas, this became a very productive (for the poet) and an important genre (for the patron). Ottakkuttar, the emperor of poetry, who served three Chola kings, a century after Rajaraja, composed an *ula* on each one of them, compositely called the *muvarula*, the *ulas* on the three kings. They are not only the poet's best, but also the best among *ulas*. They provide some historical data but more importantly perform two unconnected feats, 'they manifest grandeur and colour, and offer some lovely description of women'[52].

Rajaraja's reign was certainly at the crossroads of a vigorous literary movement. The bardic Sangam poems, the great epics and the mesmerising hymns of the *bhakti* saints had already been composed when he rode to power. On the other hand, great poets such as Jayankondar, Kambar and Ottakoothar and the great philosopher Ramanujar were yet to appear on the scene. Historians, however, are still puzzled by the absence of major literary works produced during a time which saw the tallest temple being built and the most exquisite sculptures carved.

Epilogue

About 6 kms from Kumbakonam, in Udayalur village, lies Rajaraja's grave in an unattended quiet spot. For a king who built the largest empire of South India, the grave is too self-effacing compared to the glittering mausoleums erected for later day emperors and politicians. Belying the gospel that 'all those who take the sword shall perish with the sword', the emperor died in peace. Rajaraja's reign lies somewhere in the middle of what is called 'the early medieval period', covering a period of seven centuries between 600 CE and 1300 CE, 'framed by the Gupta empire at one end and the consolidation of the Delhi Sultanate on the other'[1]. Between the Sangam age of the early centuries of the first millennium and the 6th century, a 'period of darkness' enveloped the Tamil country for about three centuries. The darkness was more the imagination of the Cholas, Pandyas and the Pallavas who were subdued by the Kalabhras, possibly a regime following Buddhism and Jainism, considering their opposition to *brahmadeya* rights of Brahmanas and to the existing Sangam age kingdoms. Later records express their revulsion that this was a period of 'the onslaught of evil kings, the *kali arasar*, and the dominance of 'heterodoxy'[2]. But it was more likely a period of the 'breakdown of earlier tribal forms' followed by a transition to new socio-economic arrangements. It was a period when there was 'flux and instability' due to the decline of the three traditional kingdoms – the Chera, Chola and Pandya, a clash of interests among new aspirants to social and political authority and competition among 'brahmanical, Buddhist and Jain religions for patronage'[3].

The Pallavas and Pandyas were the first to come out of this 'darkness' and divide the Tamil land between them up until the ninth century. The scions of the ancient royal line of the Cholas 'found themselves compelled to seek service and patronage under their more successful rivals'[4], until Vijayalaya retrieved the Cholas to the path of an imperial empire. The fealty status that the Cholas had to endure for three long centuries was now foisted back on their former masters. The Pandyas, Pallavas, Cheras, Eastern Chalukyas, Gangas and Banas now ate out of the Chola bowl for the next three centuries. During the period of the bad fortune of the Cholas, several princes and chieftains claiming Chola ancestry spread out far and wide in quest of fortune, but finally the Chola Empire consolidated around their good old capital of Uraiyur, which they had abandoned centuries back. The Chinese pilgrim Xuanzang who visited Amaravati and Kanchipuram in the seventh century mentions a Chola kingdom in Kurnool and Cuddapa districts of present-day Andhra, tracing their descent from Karikala. They had connections with the Chalukyas and played a role in the hostilities between the Pallavas and Pandyas. Evidently, numerous dynasties existed in Andhra and Karnataka with links to the early Cholas of the Tamil country, providing grist to the mill that the Cholas who revived the fortunes of their tribe actually came from outside the Tamil land. From all accounts, the Tamil Cholas had not gone into oblivion during this period, for the hagiography of the Saivites produced in the 12th century, the *Periyapuranam*, mentions a Pandya king married to a Chola princess and also a Chola prince married to a Pandyan princess. So, the 'darkness' that enveloped the Cholas from the third to the ninth centuries may best be described as a state of 'suspended animation'[5]. Beyond doubt, some of them had found a second home in the north of the Tamil country, and those who had stayed behind 'bent low before every storm that passed over them and bided their time'[6]. In any case, from Rajaraja's ascension it can be said with certainty that South India stepped out of the era of kingdoms and chieftains into the era of imperialism, not of the variety we know of today, but of a type that needs to be located in the 'medieval'[7] period.

At the time of Rajaraja, Buddhism and Jainism were still popular. The imprint of these sects on the *bhakti* movement was clearly evident when 'they leaned towards rejecting the established order of society as stratified in the caste structure'[8]. Earlier, Achuthavikkanta, the king of the Kalabhras was believed to be a follower of the Buddha and there were committed adherents to Jainism among the Pandya and Pallava rulers. Buddhadatta, a 5th century monk who might have lived in the Kalabhra age, 'gives testimony to the construction ... of two large monasteries in the Chola country'[9]. The 7th century Pallava monarch, Mahendravarman, was initially a patron of Jainism until he was drawn to the Saivite faith by the saint Appar. Thirumangai Alawar, who must have lived in the 8th century, is believed to have looted the large Buddha image made of solid gold from the Nagapattinam monastery, as confirmed by the Guruparampara[10]. Rajaraja himself rebuilt the Buddhist monastery at Nagapattinam in a joint venture with the Srivijaya Empire and also committed a number of endowments to Buddhist viharas and Jain pallis. The compilation of the Vaishnavite canon was completed in the reign of Parantaka I while Rajaraja himself oversaw the canonisation of the Saivite hymns under the able guidance of Nambiyandar Nambi. A massive renovation of stone temples in the Chola country was taken up during the Chola period, thus reaching 'a secure position of ascendancy'. The massive Thanjavur temple, the southern Meru, represented the cosmic centre of the imperial empire, and the Saivite iconography became the rallying symbol, within which all other forms of theistic belief were accommodated, in a tremendous effort at religious syncretism. It took another century for the Saivite hagiography to be completed by the classic poet Sekkizhar[11], but the lives of the Saivite and Vaishnavite saints were already revered legends and found ample reflection in the iconography of the time. Rajaraja deserves particular credit in popularising the Saivite and Vaishnavite hymns as the Vedas of the South and giving them space in temple worship or even a higher status in recitation ahead of the Vedic chants. Not only did Rajaraja tolerate religions and sects other than his own, he 'patronised all persuasions in equal measure' and this general attitude is evident in the decoration of the Siva temple with themes and motifs from Vaishnavism and Buddhism. Notwithstanding 'the stories of the persecution and extirpation of Jainism and Buddhism, so freely retailed in the hagiography'[12] of the sects, 'religious differences of the time, such as they were, did not tend to produce social discord, and a general attitude of mutual tolerance, if not respect, seems to have been well sustained'[13]. Appar, the great Saiva saint, who was initially a Jaina monk, repents his life as a Jain in many of his verses:

I was a deadly snake, dancing to the tunes

Of evil men.

Filthy, foul-mouthed, I wandered aimlessly,

Begging for food, eating with both hands,

Truly a wretch![14]

Yet, such invectives, not even embroidered to sound polite, did not do much damage to intra-sect relationships. As stated earlier, though these sects came across as hostile to Buddhism and Jainism, they 'were nevertheless influenced by these religions'[15]. While rivalries existed, between Buddhism, Jainism and the *bhakti* sects, society during Rajaraja's time was not riven by religious and communal acrimony, considering the absence of authoritative accounts to the contrary. In fact, it is difficult to recall any other remarkable instance in the history of the South when sectarian strife produced such exquisite literature and poetry. Notwithstanding the accusation against 'evil men' of other religions, religious identities in the 11th century 'were restricted to the renouncer, and often centred on the monastery'[16]. Forsaking worldly life were prerequisites for entering a *matha* or a monastery, but these identities turned out to be the exclusive preserve of saints and renouncers. The Pallava monarch getting converted from Jainism to Saivism by the Saivite saint Appar is not an instance of religious conversions as we see today but 'initiations into the order by a preceptor, either as an ascetic or a renouncer, or as a listener/worshipper'[17]. Votaries of tradition may believe that the *bhakti* movement was the precursor of Hinduim in the South. However, this is a moot point. In an excellent presentation on the *Pre-history of Hinduism*, Devadevan argues that 'the theory and history of Hinduism, and its practice, were brought into existence by the upwardly mobile, literate, and mostly male intelligentsia of the nineteenth century'[18]. For the majority, religion 'remained an area of interplay, accommodation, contestation of a localised kind, and experimentation in seeking the emotional and psychological responses'[19] rather than as an instrument of communalism that one sees it today. Murderous communal rampages by the ruling establishment are a recent phenomenon, which were inconceivable at the time of Rajaraja, religious differences being limited between the organised mathas and sanghas.

An honoured place was held by many Nayanmars and Alwars who were not of the priestly class by birth and the popularity of legends of Nandanar, the pariah saint, revealed an aspiration that rejected brahmanical values. The *bhakti* movement had already run its course in the Chola region by the time of Rajaraja, but its impact lingered very strongly. The ideas expressed in the *bhakti* hymns and the extent to which the movement expanded social access to temples establish the view that it was a social movement within a religious shell, with Vaishnavism and Saiavism 'being a religious form given to movements that would have surfaced in any case'[20]. Most notable is that its leadership consisted of learned Brahmanas, Vellalars, Kallars and other non-Brahmana castes and Shudras. It did not overturn the caste system, but it did 'create a religious community within which traditional social distinctions could be transcended, at least with regard to the relationship between the bhakta and his/her god'[21]. Detractors of the *bhakti* movement have argued that with its focus on devotion and loyalty, it was an ideology well-suited for the feudal state[22]. Whether devotion to a deity made a person more loyal to the state is a moot point, but the movement took the emphasis away from rituals and sacrifices to 'personal worship' involving offerings of 'flowers, fruit and grain' as 'part of the ritual of puja'[23] in place of sacrifice of animals. It was no wonder that this struck root in the populace and 'was more comprehensible' to the common devotee than the 'complicated Vedic and other rituals performed by kings under the guidance of their priests'[24].

The creation of the iconography of the imperial Chola state based on Saivite and Vaishnavite temples reciting *bhakti* hymns and popularising legends surrounding them and the emergence of temples as landed magnates and administrative centres have been derided as an effort to entrench the feudal setup. But the questioning of prevailing hierarchies and the expansion of the social contours of the sacred space, do not gel with the characterisation of temples as 'feudal'. In fact, under the Cholas, some of the *bhakti* centres became leading, political or pilgrimage centres and evolved into huge urban complexes, either around a single large temple or with multiple temples together forming parts of an urban complex. The Thanjavur temple 'legitimised the sovereignty of the emperor while at the same time bringing various socio-economic groups into the orbit'[25] of the urban centre with the temple as the centre. The economic and structural activities within and around the temple contributed to urban growth complemented by expansion of trade and the largescale settlement of craftsmen and artisans in these centres. In the final analysis, however, Rajaraja's statecraft enshrined power, administrative efficiency and economic development and not just the religious ideas of Saivite supremacy.

Undoubtedly, the Chola state at the time of Rajaraja was a hereditary monarchy. Disputed successions were not uncommon as in the case of the murder of the king's elder brother by his uncle. The ravages that followed conquests were brutal and 'war was not, as so often made out, the pleasant diversion of a few professionals which left the normal course of life in the country untouched'[26]. The inhabitants of northern Lanka and Vengi would have certainly vouched for this in Rajaraja's time. But dreams of empires come true only when they are backed by a ruthless army and single-minded purpose. The Vedic conception of the state, *rajya*, as an organisation with seven limbs, the angas, was known and accepted. By the 6th century, the *Thirukkural*, 'introduced a slight but significant change, making the remaining six elements subject to the king'[27] in an acknowledgement of the end of ancient republics and the birth of new states of the rulers and the ruled. There is very little reference to *Arthasastra* and *Nitisastra*, in Tamil didactic or political works, and a lot more clarity and precision on the concepts of polity must have flown from the 'ten verses' in which Thiruvalluvar, author of the *Kural*, 'deals with the essentials of *nadu, rashtra*'[28]. The concluding declaration states the principle of the state in clear terms:

> *'Though blest in every other way, it avails nothing to a nadu,*
>
> *if there is no peace between the people and the king'.*

179

The remarkable statement that the king's treasury is replenished from three sources — land tax, customs and tolls, and conquest — displays the 'shrewd practical wisdom' of the author. Obviously, this 5th century philosopher-poet commanded great respect even during the time of Rajaraja.

Like all kings of his age, Rajaraja must have been in all essential respects 'an autocrat, whose autocracy was tempered by the maxims of the wise and the occasional intercession of the minister'[29]. Maxims were certainly not in short supply, and Rajaraja must have relied on the cautious statements of poets and authors in their works. There is no reason to believe that the *Kural*, much of which is 'devoted to systematic treatment of the affairs of the state' would have been far divorced from practice. The warning to kings, for instance, against the corrupting influence of unlimited power must have seriously troubled Rajaraja in his sleep.

'The king with none to censure him, bereft of safeguards all

Though none his ruin work, shall surely ruined fall'.

Rajaraja continued the land grants to Brahmanas, a process started many centuries back by rulers who required Vedic endorsement of their rule and a safe passage to heaven in the afterlife. Some hold the extreme view that he allowed a Brahmana-Vellala alliance to solidify at the expense of his own authority over the Chola region, but others have dismissed this as highly fanciful. In spite of the fact that many *brahmadeyas* were given an autonomous status, where the Brahmana donees 'were free to do as they pleased and where the writ of the state did not apply', in reality, these kind of villages 'must have formed a small proportion of settlements'[30]. Royal power strengthened the economic power of only a section of the brahmana community, for not all Brahmanas were land holders or affluent. The landed Brahmana elite controlled villages but were far removed from the status of feudatories and high officials who often had their own army and treasury. Neither were they tax collectors who passed on the taxes to the king, except in the case when they were members of the *sabha*, but this status applied to all landholders organised into corporate bodies. By all accounts, the insertion of Brahmana donees into the village community did introduce a new element in village life, considering their tax-free status and ownership bestowed over the immediate natural resources. The elite of *brahmadeya* villages were organised into the powerful *sabhas* just as the elite of the non-brahmana villages formed the urar. One would assume that small peasants, tenants and sharecroppers would have experienced the same oppression in both types of villages. The Vellalars, were given the Shudra tag, but unlike in the north, 'the tag did not carry with it connotations of a lowly social status and discrimination'[31]. Within the second category of the Shudra, most of the occupational and service groups, the *jatis*, were placed. Social differentiation through diversification of economic activities and occupational differences in the kind of work performed, were interwoven in this process[32]. Nammalwar, a Vellala Vaishnavite saint put the caste system of the time in excellent perspective in his verses:

The four castes

Uphold all clans;

Go down, far down

To the lowliest outcastes

Of outcastes;

If they are the intimate henchmen

Of our land

With the wheel in his right hand,

His body dark as blue sapphire,

Then even the slaves of their slaves

Are our masters[33].

This view that 'the social world is still seen as a hierarchy, but as one ordered by men's relation to god, not by birth'[34] could very well describe the popular perception of the caste system in the emperor's time. The charge that the emperor aggravated caste disparity is not an easy one to lay at his door. Village life in the Chola realm cannot be reduced to its seamy underside alone. Particularly, the Right and Left-Hand divisions, which arose as some form of supra castes due to the increased mobility of artisans and craftsmen, were in a manner of speaking, quite unique in a subcontinent steeped in caste hierarchy. The celebrated self-government of the Chola villages does have its admirers around the world even today.

The *nadu*, the locality consisting of several settlements, both rural and urban, were indisputably more powerful than individual villages. The elite members of the corporate body which governed the *nadu*, the *nattar*, would have lorded over the village elite just as present-day trade moguls lord over the village gentry. The village assemblies were supplemented by other bodies representing carpenters, blacksmiths, goldsmiths and weavers[35], certainly providing a hint that these organisations of lower caste groups did have a say in the general affairs of the *nadu*. In the final analysis, the institutions which really thrived enormously during the middle and later Chola periods were the *nagarams*, towns, and their elite body, the *nagarattar*, who were merchants, moneylenders and landholders rolled into one[36]. The higher their profits, the more lavish were their gifts to temples and institutions. Like present day city dons, they must have been close to, if not living, in the corridors of power and controlling the merchant and artisan guilds. The focus of political and economic power 'shifted conspicuously from the *brahmadeya* to the temple'[37] perhaps depriving the rural Brahmana elite of some power. For all we know, the Brahmana priests and landholders would have easily traded places with the prosperous merchants, if given a chance.

To buttress the imperial status of the Cholas, the king's procession followed the same path as the one followed by the temple idol, which was taken out on specific occasions, to enthral the devotees. An entire genre of literature, called the ula, became popular during this time, to establish this identity of the king with the divine. The palace and the temple had similar accessories and staff. Whether the *devaraja* cult[38] of the South-east Asian kings followed from the *ula* identity or the other way about, is still to be established. It is a fact, though, that 'by the eleventh century, landed elites were beginning to build temples on a large scale, and tacitly making claims to divinity'[39]. Temples were built in which the deity was named after the patrons. 'The builders of the temple placed themselves in a mirror image relationship with their deities', just as Rajaraja named the Brihadeeswara temple as Rajarajeswaram, as if suggesting that 'I am the reflection of god on earth, without altogether ruling out the reverse possibility that god is indeed a reflection of my personality'[40]. Chola temples earlier to this were 'of a sepulchral nature that were built over the remains of kings who died in war'[41] or at sacred sites. But Rajarajeswaram was not a sepulchral temple since it was named after a living king.

Rajaraja's son and successor, Rajendra I, took the process of Chola territorial expansion even further. His military victories against Mahinda V and against the Pandyas, Cheras and Western Chalukyas are legendary. A successful naval expedition in 1025 against the kingdom of Sri Vijaya established the strategic hold of the Cholas over trade in the Indian Ocean. There was no end to military conflicts, but the 'Cholas held their own till the time of Kulottunga I (1070-1122)'[42] when trade flourished with Sri Vijaya and China. Chalukyas and Hoysalas were at the throat of the empire constantly and the Cholas revived again under Vikrama Chola (1118-35) after which the supremacy of the imperial Cholas waned until they disappeared at the end of the 13th century.

It will not be an overstatement to say that Rajaraja Chola left a stupendous legacy behind him, which has not lost its sheen even after a thousand years. His reign holds a vital place in the history of Thamizhagam. His thirty long years of rule constituted the formative period of the Chola Empire. Victory in wars can get you on the throne, but they are not enough to keep you there. It is beyond debate that 'in the organisation of the civil service and the army, in art and architecture, in religion and literature, we see at work powerful forces newly liberated by the progressive imperialism of the time'[43]. The productive forces that emerged, the nagarams which flourished, the in-land and overseas trade networks that were established, the high standards of art, literature and craft that were attained, makes him

183

an extremely popular emperor. Women of the upper class and saints enjoyed honour and privileges in the empire, as we had seen in many instances. The state did not play on the religious divisions among the people. The thousand-year-old administrative system and the principle of self-administration that he encouraged are relevant even today, of course after rendering them modern. That altogether would be right approach to take to the great stories, legends and achievements of this great empire and its accomplished architect – the emperor and the entire talent he commanded from every corner of the empire.

The earlier years of Rajaraja, when he subdued rulers of the South and North, with an iron hand mark the more aggressive part of his reign. In the bigger part of his reign, however, he is eulogised for the prosperity he brought to his realm and the encouragement he provided to the new productive forces to sprout and blossom. He could be reproached as over ambitious and ruthless but name an emperor who wasn't! His achievements during the calmer years of his regime were a rare characteristic in other kingdoms in contemporary times. By the time he rested his head in his grave, no one remembered that he had had a great-grandfather who killed his Pallava suzerain and usurped his kingdom and a brother who was fond of spiked heads.

GLOSSARY

Ainnurruvar – Members of a powerful merchant guild, the Five Hundred

Alwar – A Vaishnavite saint

angadi – market or bazaar

Anjuvannam – A guild early Arab Muslim traders of the west coast

bhakti – devotion

brahmadeya – royal gift of land to brahmanas by kings

chetti – generic term for a merchant

cheri – living quarters or colonies

devadana – donated to temples

devakoshta – a niche in the wall of a temple

erivirapattana – warehousing centres on trade routes used by itinerant merchants protected by armed guards

grantha – Tamil script used for Sanskrit transcriptions

Ezham – Sril Lanka

Kadaram – modern Kedah in Malaysia

kalam – about 100 kgs of paddy

kasu – two kasus made one kazhanju

Kammalar – craftsmen belonging to the Vishwakarma caste

kazhanju – gold weight of 80 grains

managaram – big city

mandalam – Revenue divisions

manjadi – eight manjadis were equal to one kasu

meykeerthi – means "true fame" in Tamil, a eulogy at the beginning of inscriptions

nadu – self-administered peasant localities and its assembly

nagaram – trading and craft centres, urban production centres and their assembly

nagarattar – members of the nagaram, merchants

Nanadesis – merchant guilds with trans-regional trade affiliations

nattar – corporate body which governed the nadu,

paraiyar – people of low caste

prashasti – eulogy in Sanskrit at the beginning of inscriptions

sabha – Assembly of a brahmadeya village

Sankarapadi – Oil merchants

Saliyar – Weavers

Thamizhagam – The Tamil speaking region

ur – A non-brahmadeya village and also the assembly of the village

urar – members of the ur

valanadu – Revenue districts

valangai-idangai – Right- and Left-hand divisions

variyam – administrative committee

Vellala – land-owning caste

vihara – Buddhist monastery

vimana – structure above the garbhagrha or the inner sanctum

yavana – Romans, Greeks

SELECT REFERENCES

I have depended on many books, papers, texts and reports for writing this book. They gave me a wealth of information on and insights into the world of Rajaraja. I welcome readers to experience the journey I went through.

The most important work I had referred to extensively, is that superb volume on *The Colas* by Professor K. A. Nilakanta Sastri. It is a landmark work in the realm of the social, political and cultural history of Tamil Nadu during the period of Chola dynasty from 850 to 1279 starting from Vijalaya Aditya I down to Rajendra III, up to the end of the dynasty. It is celebrated all over the world as a pioneering work in South Indian history, excellently researched and well presented. The first edition was published in two volumes, first in 1935 and the second in 1937 followed by a revised edition in 1955 which has been reprinted a few more times by the University of Madras. The 1955 edition is the one I used, and it is available on the internet.

Champakalakshmi's *Trade, Ideology and Urbanization: South India 300 BC to AD 1300* is an excellent collection of essays providing a regional perspective of urbanization in Thamzihagam based on empirical studies of specific urban centres within a socio-historical and cultural context. The discussion on the development of the iconography of the Chola Empire is entirely illuminating.

A.L. Basham's *The Wonder That Was India* is an excellent study of Indian history, culture, literature and languages. His translations of Sanskrit and Tamil poems are exquisite. His understanding of the origins of languages and scripts is marvellous. I have borrowed some of his translations in this novel.

Romila Thapar's *Early India: From the Origins to AD 1300* has an informative section on the Cholas in the Chapter on Authorities and Structures, but I wish it had not been that brief, considering the historical importance of the Chola Empire.

A History of Ancient and Early Medieval India: From the Stone Age to the 12th century by Upinder Singh, gave me an excellent introduction to original sources of documentation of the history of India. It has a clear and balanced assessment of the imperial Chola State and the progressive nature of the *bhakti* movement.

Burton Stein's *Peasant State and Society in Medieval South India* is a good account of peasant society and local institutions and investigates into the nature of the state during the Chola period. Though his theory of the segmentary state has been rejected, there is much useful information in his analysis of institutions.

I would certainly recommend readers to go through the papers edited by Karashima in *A Concise History of South India: Issues and Interpretations*. The volume is well illustrated with maps and images and incorporates new archaeological evidence and historiography to present fresh perspectives.

The Cilappatikaram: The Tale of an Anklet, Penguin Classics, is an excellent English translation by R. Parthasarathy of one of the world's masterpieces and perhaps India's finest epic in a language other than Sanskrit. I relied on the original as well as the translation for the description of life in ancient South India and the precedence it set for an interpretation of justice in the Tamil country.

Rethinking Early Medieval India, which is a nice collection of essays edited by Upinder Singh on the period, raises questions about the periodization itself, with specific focus on the Tamil country related to the nature of political systems, and rural and urban economy and society.

Tamil Literature by the European scholar, Kamil Zvelebil, established how the Tamil language can claim one of the longest unbroken literary traditions of any of the world's living languages. Its classification of Tamil literature not by time, but by specific literary types, is exquisite.

S.R. Balasubrahmanyam is acknowledged as an outstanding living authority on the subject of South Indian monuments and art in general and of the Cholas in particular. He has published four volumes on Chola temples based on a systematic, scientific survey of these monumental works of art. The third in the series, titled *The Middle Chola Temples* deal with the Middle Chola period, from Rajaraja I to Kulottunga I, and covers the history of over a hundred temples, making it a must read.

Indira Viswanathan Peterson, in her work *Poems to Siva: The Hymns of the Tamil Saints* eloquently renders the Saivite hymns of the *Devaram* into English, interpreting vivid and moving portraits of the images, myths, rites, and adoration of Siva. It is a rich source book for the study of the Saivite hagiography and works.

Likewise, *Pattupattu: Ten Tamil Idylls*, translated beautifully by J.V. Chelliah are among the best poems in the Sangam literature. One of the songs in the collection, the *Maduraikkanchi*, establishes Madurai as a great city and a major centre of crafts and trade as far back as the first millennium BCE, confirming the onset of the urbanisation process at a very early date in the South.

The book titled *Rajaraja Cholan*, authored by Sa. Na. Kannan, the only comprehensive book on the Emperor that I had come across, is a good compilation in Tamil, but not a very detailed one.

I have referred to many other papers, journals, articles, monographs and the like. There is no space to describe them here, but they have all contributed immensely to this work. I am greatly indebted to these authors.

BIBLIOGRAPHY

Balasubrahmanyam, S. R. 1975. Middle Chola Temples: Rajaraja I to Kulottunga I (A.D. 985-1070). Thompson Press (India) Ltd. Faridabad, Haryana.

Basham, A.L. 1967. The Wonder that was India, Rupa & Co, New Delhi.

Bharati, Gopalakrishna. Nandanar Charitram (translated by PR Ramachander). http://translationsofsomesongsofcarnticmusic.blogspot.com/2013/01/nandanar-charitram-of-gopala-krishna_1266.html

Brown, Percy. 1959. Indian Architecture (Buddhist and Hindu Periods). Fourth Edition. Taraporevala Sons & Co, Bombay

Caldwell, R. Rev. 1881. Political and General History of the District of Tinnevelly. Government Press. Madras.

Chandni Bi, Dr S. Women's World in the Chola Period's through Epigraphy, Indian Journal of Archaeology Vol. 3/NO. 4/October 2018 – January 2019.

Chakravarti, Uma. [1989] 1999. The World of the bhaktin in South Indian Traditions-The Body and Beyond. Manushi, Vol 10, Nos. 50-52.

Champakalakshmi, R. 1996. Trade, Ideology and Urbanaisation: South India 300 BC to AD 1300. OUP, Madras.

Chelliah J.V. 1985. Pattupattu: Ten Tamil Idylls (Tamil verses with English trsnslation). Tamil University Reprint. Thanjavur.

Cutler, Norman. 1987. Songs of Experience: The Poetics of Tamil Devotion. Indian University Press. USA.

Dehejia, Vidya. The Very Idea of a Portrait. Ars Orientalis, Vol 28, pp 40-48, Freer Gallery of Art, University of Michigan.

Devadevan, Manu V. 2019. A pre-history of Hinduism. De Gruyter.

Dorai Rangaswamy, M.A.. 1958-59. The Religion and Philosophy of Tevaram: with Special reference to Nampi Arurar (Sundarar). University of Madras, Madras.

Epigraphia Indica. Volume XVII. 1923-24. The Director General of Archaeological Survey of India. New Delhi. 1983

Gorringe, Hugo. 2005. Untouchable citizens: Dalit movements and democratisation in Tamil Nadu. Sage Publications. New Delhi.

Grousset, René. 1931. The Civilizations of the East: India. (Translated from the French by Catherine Alison Phillips). Tudor Publishing Company. New York.

Gurukkal, Rajan. 2010. Social Formations of Early South India. Oxford University Press. New Delhi.

Hardy, Friedhelm. 1983. Viraha-bhakti: The Early History of Krsn Devotion in South India. Delhi: OUP.

Hultzsch, E. 1991. South Indian Inscriptions: Volume II, Tamil Inscriptions. Archaeological Survey of India.

Kannan, Sa. Na. 2011. Rajaraja Cholan. Kizhakku Pathippagam. Chennai.

Karashima, Noboru (ed.). 2014. A Concise History of South India: Issues and Interpretations. OUP. New Delhi.

Karashima, Noboru et al. 2011. Nagaram: Commerce and Towns AD 850-1350. Rethinking Medieval India: A Reader (ed. Upinder Singh). OUP. New Delhi.

Karashima, Noboru and Sen, Tansen. 2009. Appendix II: Chinese texts Describing or referring to the Chola Kingdom as Zhu-nian in Nagapattinam to Suvarnadwipa: Refelctions on the Chola Naval Expeditions to Southeast Asia, edited by Hermann Kulke, K. Kesavapany, and Vijay Sakuja. Institute of Southeast Asian Studies. Singapore.

Kingsbury, F. 1921. Hymns of the Tamil Saivite Saints. Oxford University Press.

Kosambi. D.D. 1962. Myth and Reality: Studies in the Formation of Indian Culture. Bombay. Popular Prakashan.

Kulke, Hermann. 2011. The Early and the Imperial Kingdom. Rethinking Medieval India: A Reader (ed. Upinder Singh). OUP. New Delhi.

Mahalakshmi, R. 2014. Temples and sculpture. In Noboru Karashima (ed.), 2014, A Concise History of South India. OUP. New Delhi.

Mahalakshmi, R. 2014. Women in premodern South Indian society. In Noboru Karashima (ed.), 2014, A Concise History of South India. OUP. New Delhi.

Mahalakshmi, R. Intimately Bound: Woman and Family in early Tamil History, c. 300 BCE – 1300 CE. Centre for Historical Studies, Jawaharlal Nehru University. New Delhi

Mahalingam, T.V. 1969. Kancipuram in Early South Indian History. Asia Publishing House. Bombay.

Mahalingam, T.V. 1955 South Indian Polity. University of Madras.

Mevissen, J.R. Gerd, The Stone Chariot at Darasuram and the Myth of Siva Tripurantaka, from Studies in South Indian History and Culture, Editor Dr. R. Nagaswamy

Mukund, Kanakalatha. 2015. The world of the Tamil merchant: Pioneers of international trade. Penguin Random House India. New Delhi.

Nagaswamy R, Dr. Tamil Coins: A Study. Institute of Epigraphy, Tamil Nadu State department of Archaeology, Madras, 1981

Narayanan, M.G.S. Further studies in the Jewish Copper Plates of Cochin, The Journal of Indo-Judaic Studies. http://www.mei.org.in/uploads/jijscontent/59-1534436177-jijsarticlepdf.pdf

Omvedt, Gail. 2011. Understanding Caste: From Buddha to Ambedkar and Beyond. Orient BlackSwan. Hyderabad.

Orr, Leslie C. Cholas, Pandyas, and 'Imperial Temple Culture' In Medieval Tamil Nadu

Orr, Leslie C. Processions in the medieval South Indian temple: Sociology, sovereignty and soteriology, from South Indian Horizons (F. Gros Felicitation Volume) pp. 437–470

Orr, Leslie C. 2000. Donors, Devotees and Daughters of God: Temple Women in Medieval Tamilnadu. OUP. New York.

Percival P. 1857. The Tamil Epic Chintamani, Madras Journal of Literature and Science. Madras: Madras Literary Society and Auxiliary of the Royal Asiatic Society.

Peterson, Indira Viswanathan. [1989] 2007. Poems to Siva: The Hymns of the Tamil Saints. Motilal Banarsidass Publishers. Delhi.

Pillai, Manu S. 2018. Rebel Sultans: The Deccan from Khilji to Shivaji. Juggernaut Books. New Delhi.

Rajagopal, Govindaswamy. 2016. Beyond Bhakti: Steps Ahead ... Sun International Publishers. New Delhi.

Rajalakshmi, R. 1983. Tamil Polity. Ennes Publications. Madurai.

Ramanujan, A.K. 1993. Nammalvar: Hymns for the drowning. Penguin Books. New Delhi.

Ramanujan, A.K. 1985. Speaking of Siva. Penguin Books. England.

Ramaswamy, Vijaya. Metal Crafts in Peninsular Indian History (with special reference to Tamil Nadu).

Sastri, K.A. Nilakanta. 1975. A History of South India from Pre-Historic Times to the Fall of Vijayanagar. OUP, New Delhi.

Sastri, K.A. Nilakanta. [1955] 1975. The Colas. Madras University. Madras.

Sastri, K.A. Nilakanta. 1987. The Colas. In R.S. Sharma; K.M. Shrimali (eds.). A Comprehensive History of India: AD 985-1206 (https://ia801608.us.archive.org/0/items/in.ernet.dli.2015.459498/2015.459498.A-Comprehensive_text.pdf). People's Publishing House. New Delhi.

Shwartzberg, Joseph B. A Historical Atlas of South Asia, p. 34, Digital South Asia Library

Singh, Upinder. 2013. A history of ancient and early medieval India: From the stone age to the 12th century. Pearson. New Delhi.

Sinopoli, Carla. M. From the Lion Throne: Political and Social Dynamics of the Vijayanagara Empire. Journal of the Economic and Social History of the Orient, Vol. 43, No. 3 (2000), pp. 364-398

Stein, Burton. 1999. Peasant State and Society in Medieval South India. New Delhi: Oxford University Press.

Srinivasan, Mathi, Dr. 2000. Thiruvaimozhi, Nalayira Divyaprabandham (Tamil original with explanatory notes in Tamil). Sri Varagi Printers. Chennai.

Srinivasan, Sharada. 2004. Shiva as cosmic dancer: On Pallava origins for the Nataraja bronze. World Archaeology, Special Issue on 'Archaeology of Hinduism' 36(3): 432-50.

Srinivasan, Sharada. 2016. Tamil Chola Bronzes and Swamimalai Legacy: Metal Sources and Archaeotechnology. Journal of Metals, Vol. 68(8): 2207-221. DOI: 10.1007/s11837-016-1959-1.http://rdcu.be/nbyZ:

Subrahmanian, N. 1996. Sangam Polity: The Administration and Social Life of the Sangam Tamils. Madras. Asia Publishing House.

Tamilmudi, Pulavar. 2005. Thiruvasagam (commentary in Tamil). Gangai Puthaka Nilayam. Chennai

Thapar, Romila. 2015. The Penguin history of early India from the origins to AD 1300. Penguin Books, Gurgaon.

Tirumalai, R. Collected Papers. Department of Archaeology, Madras, 1994.

Yamashita, Hiroshi. 2014. Language and Literature. In Noboru Karashima (ed.), 2014, A Concise History of South India. OUP. New Delhi.

Zvelebil, Kamil. 1974. A History of Indian Literature, Vol 10 (Tamil Literature). Otto Harrasowitz. Wiesbaden.

Zvelebil, Kamil. 1968. Introducing Tamil literature. Hoe & Co. Madras. https://ia800906.us.archive.org/6/items/dli. jZY9lup2kZl6TuXGlZQdjZI3kuQy.TVA_BOK_0009568/TVA_ BOK_0009568_Introducing_Tamil_literature.pdf

ATTRIBUTION

1.   Map showing the extent of the Chozha empire during Rajendra Chohja I (1030), son of Rajaraja - per http://cw.routledge.com/textbooks/9780415485432/15.asp, 'THE CŌḶAS' by K. A. Nilakanta Sastri and other histories of South Asia consulted. Attribution: https://commons.wikimedia.org/wiki/File:Rajendra_map_new.svg: The original uploader was Venu62 at English Wikipedia.derivative work: Gregors, CC BY-SA 3.0 <http://creativecommons.org/licenses/by-sa/3.0/>, via Wikimedia Commons

2.   Map of Chozha mandalams based on the map provided by Noboru Karishma (who credits Y. Subbarayalu) in 'A Concise History of South India' (2014). Some elements missing from Karashima's map have been sourced from Subbarayalu's book directly. The spellings are as per Karashima (2014). Neither of the sources noted above explicitly date the map (to the 11th century). But the map is displayed in the context of the establishment of the Chozha mandalams in the reigns of Raja Raja Chola (985 – 1014) and Rajendra Chola (1014 – 1044). Attribution: By Cpt.a.haddock - Own work, CC BY-SA 4.0, https://commons.wikimedia.org/w/index.php?curid=63066896

3.   Chronology chart of the Chozha Dynasty (adapted from 'A History of South India', K.A. Nilakanta Sastri, P. 190)

4.   Statue of Rajaraja - Attribution: https://commons.wikimedia.org/wiki/File:Rajaraja_cholan_statue.jpg , dixon, CC BY 3.0 <https://creativecommons.org/licenses/by/3.0>, via Wikimedia Commons

5.   The 13-storeyed vimana (tower) of the Brihadeeswara Temple – Credit: G.V. Balasubramanian

6.	Statue of Nataraja, Chozha style - Attribution: https://commons.wikimedia.org/wiki/File:Shiva_Nataraja_Tanjore_Bruxelles_02_10_2011_01.jpg, Vassil, CC0, via Wikimedia Commons

7.	Coins of Uttama Chozha – Attribution: http://coins.lakdiva.org/medievalindian/uttama_chola_ag.html at http://lakdiva.org/coins/The silver was scanned at 600 dpi and displayed at 300 dpi. It was purchased on ebay in Sept 2002., CC BY-SA 2.5, https://commons.wikimedia.org/w/index.php?curid=827515

8.	Image of Tripurantaka – Attribution: Benjamín Preciado Centro de Estudios de Asia y África de El Colegio de México - Own work, CC BY-SA 4.0, https://commons.wikimedia.org/w/index.php?curid=14531178

9.	A typical inscription from Brihadeeswara Temple in Thanjavur – Attribution: By Nittavinoda - Own work, CC BY-SA 4.0, https://commons.wikimedia.org/w/index.php?curid=68139543

10.	Royal seal of the Chozha dynasty – Credit: Raghavan Srinivasan

11.	A mural painting at Brihadeeswara Temple – Attribution: https://commons.wikimedia.org/wiki/File:Mural_Paintings_in_Brihadeeswara_Temple_01.jpg , Sugeesh, CC BY-SA 4.0 <https://creativecommons.org/licenses/by-sa/4.0>, via Wikimedia Commons

12.	Child bhakti saint Sambandar – Credit: Raghavan Srinivasan

13.	Queen Sembiyan Mahadevi as goddess Parvati, India, state of Tamil Nadu, Chola period, ca. 998 Bronze; height 92.1 cm (36 1/4 in.), Freer Gallery (Washington D.C.) – Attribution: Kosigrim - Own work, Public Domain, https://commons.wikimedia.org/w/index.php?curid=53305834

14.	*Sri Vimana* of Brihadeeswara Temple – Outer wall detail, Credit: G.V. Balasubramanian

15.	Kailasanathar Temple at Kanchipuram, Credit: G.V. Balasubramanian

16.	Decorative elements on the outer wall of the *Sri Vimana*, Credit: G.V. Balasubramanian

ENDNOTES

1. The Great One Who Measured the Earth

[1] Sastri quotes Kennedy who concludes that maritime trade between South India and the West dates from the 6th or even the 7th century BCE.

[2] A sect which worships Siva

[3] A devotional and social reform movement which first started in the South around the 6th century CE and was represented by the twelve Alwars and sixty-three Nayanmars

[4] This description is ascribed to the poet Kamban or to the poetess Auvaiyar. Kottaikarai means fort-bank.

[5] Sastri, The Colas, 20

[6] EI, xi, 338 – A set of plates discovered in Cudappah district, called the Malepadu Plates, a chief named Chandraditya in Bastar, a feudatory of the Naga king, claimed that he was a descendant of Karikala Chola and flaunted the lion crest.

[7] Mamulanar mentions an invasion of the South by the Moriyar (Mauryas) and also the wealth of the Nandas hidden under the Ganges at Pataliputra.

[8] Ancient Tamil poems like the Akananuru and the Narrinai narrate that the Mauryan invasion was repulsed by the Tamil kings

[9] Pillai, Rebel Sultans, 5

[10] Caldwell, Tinnevelly, 12

[11] Basham, The Wonder that Was India, 465

[12] Tamil Nadu Archaeological Department (TNAD) report known as Keeladi-An Urban Settlement of Sangam Age on the Banks of River Vaigai,

[13] Sastri, 23

[14] For the tamil people, Elara is Manuneedhi Cholan, the Chola king who dispensed justice guided by Manu

[15] Sastri quotes from Geiger's Mahavamsa

[16] Satri quotes from Mahavamsa xxi, 21-6

[17] Sastri, 24

[18] The subjoined set of copper-plates discovered in 1905 and made by Rajendra I in the 6th year of his reign, has been fully described in the Director-General's Archaeological Survey Report for 1903-04, pp. 233-5. Its contents are discussed in the Madras Epigraphical Report for 1916, Part II, paragraphs 11 to 20. The plates and the massive seal on which they are hung weigh 8 maunds, 2 visses and 20 palams. The Thiruvalangadu plates consist of thirty-one copper-sheets.

[19] Copper plate records have been an important mainstay of the historians of the Chola Empire. Some of the copper plate charters are considerably long with writing engraved on a comfortable sized, good quality copper plates. These were strung together by a thick copper ring with a circular seal burnt on them. The Leyden Grant plates describe events in the 21st year of Rajaraja's reign. They take their name after the Leyden Museum in the Netherlands, which holds these plates captive, much to the ire of the Tamil people. Other plates which have contributed significantly to the reconstruction of the history of Rajaraja are the Thiruvalangadu and the Karandai plates of the time of Rajendra I, his son and successor. The Leyden Plates have 443 lines on 21 plates, Thiruvalangadu Plates have 816 lines on 31 plates and the spectacular Karandai Plates have 2500 lines on 55 large plates, each measuring 16" x 9".

Chola copper plates, have tiger, fish and the bow seals all together. These are the emblems of the Chola, Pandya and Chera dynasties respectively. The fact that they were all used together in the copper plates of Chola times indicates the political supremacy of the first over the other two. It can be safely said that when all three symbols appeared together on a coin or copper plate, it belonged to the Cholas. Coins were in gold, silver and copper.

[20] The prashastis are eulogistic inscriptions written in form of poetry or ornate prose, generally composed by court poets.

[21] The language and script employed in inscriptions varies with time and place, but Tamil was the most commonly employed language followed by Sanskrit, and in some cases Telugu and Kannada

[22] South Indian Inscriptions (SII) - No. 205.— The Thiruvalangadu Copper-Plates Of The Sixth Year Of Rajendra-Chola I

[23] Singh, A History of Ancient and Early Medieval India, 559

[24] ibid

[25] The so-called Sangam period has a long duration of about 6 centuries from 300 BCE to 300 CE and even beyond. Hence, the Sangam works cannot be entirely relied upon for constructing an authentic chronology, considering that they have thrown up several different internal chronologies and that these works were collected and systematised much later in the eighth to ninth centuries CE.

[26] The king of Urayur, Ilamcetcenni married a Velir princess who gave birth to Karikala. Ilamcetcenni died soon after. Due to his young age, Karikala's right to the throne was overlooked leading to political turmoil in the country. Karikala was exiled. When normality returned, the Chola ministers sent a state elephant to look for the prince, who was found hiding in Karuvur. His political opponents arrested and imprisoned him and set the prison on fire. Karikala reportedly escaped the fire and, with the help of his uncle Irum-

pitar-thalaiyan, defeated his enemies. Karikala's leg was burnt in the fire earning him the name of Karikala, the one with a burnt leg.

[27] Among all the hagiographic Puranas in Tamil, Sekkizhar's Tiruttondar Puranam or Periyapuranam, composed during the rule of Kulottunga Chola II (1133-1150) stands first. It is an account of the lives of the 63 Saiva saints called Nayanmars. It is considered as the fifth Veda in Tamil.

[28] Sastri, The Colas, 8

[29] Ibid. 30

[30] Ibid., 116

[31] Epigraphia Indica, Vol 18, P. 51, Kanyakumari inscriptions of Virarajendra Deva

[32] The Kalabhras, or kalappirar, were rulers of all or parts of the Tamil region sometime between the 3rd century and 6th century, after the ancient dynasties of the early Cholas, the early Pandyas and Cheras disintegrated. Information about the origin and reign of the Kalabhras is uncertain and scarce. The Kalabhra era is sometimes referred to as the "dark period" of Tamil history.

The Kalabhra dynasty lasted up to the last quarter of 6th century when Simhavishnu, the Pallava King, consolidated his rule up to the Kaveri river, south of which the Pandyas by then were already in power.

According to Burton Stein, the Kalabhra interregnum may represent a strong bid by non-peasant (tribal) warriors for power over the fertile plains of Tamil region with support from the heterodox Indian religious tradition (Buddhism and Jainism). This may have led to persecution of the peasants and urban elites of the Brahmanical religious traditions (Hinduism), who then worked to remove the Kalabhras and retaliated against their persecutors after returning to power. In contrast, R.S. Sharma considers "Kalabhras as an example of a peasant revolt" – with the support of tribal elements. But all these theories are hampered by the fact that there is a profound lack of evidence regarding Kalabhra rule.

[33] SII, No 205

[34] Sastri, The Colas, 8

[35] Ibid., 110

[36] Ibid., 113

[37] Ibid., 120

[38] Anbil Plates, verse 18, EI Vol 15, p. 68 - A set of still earlier copperplates was discovered by Mr. T.A. Gopinatha Rao at Anbil. They belong to the time of Sundara-Chola Parantaka II., the father of Rajaraja I, and have been edited by him in the Epigraphia Indica.

[39] Satri, 114

[40] Ibid.

[41] Ibid., 116

[42] Ibid., 122

[43] SII, No 205

[44] The set of Leyden Plates is a copper and bronze charter of the Cholas. Its inscriptions have been meticulously engraved in twenty-one copper plates that are held together by a massive bronze ring. The ring is closed with the impressive seal of King Rājendra Chola I (1012-1042). The construction weighs no less than 30 kgs and symbolizes as it were the power of the king who had the charter made. https://Leydenspecialcollectionsblog.nl/articles/a-world-treasure-of-great-weight-the-charter-of-king-raajendra-chola-i

[45] Melpadi, is a village six miles north of Tiruvallam in North Arcot district.

Rajaraja built the Choleswara Temple here and named it as Arinjaya-Iswara, after his grandfather's name.

[46] SII, No 205

[47] Sewell, A Forgotten Empire, 145

[48] Sastri, The Colas, 143

[49] Epigraphia Indica, Vol xxi, p. 167

[50] Sastri, The Colas, 157

[51] SII, No 205

[52] Sastri, 168

[53] Singh, A History of Ancient and Early Medieval India, 559

[54] Ibid., 560

[55] Sastri, The Colas, 168-169

[56] Karashima, Nagaram: Commerce and Towns AD 850-1350, 147

[57] SII, Inscriptions Collected During The Year 1906-07, https://www.whatisindia.com/inscriptions/south_indian_inscriptions/volume_23/introduction.html

[58] Karashima, Nagaram: Commerce and Towns AD 850-1350, 147

[59] ibid

[60] Singh, A History of Ancient and Early Medieval India, 560

[61] The Devaram denotes the first seven volumes of the Thirumurai, the twelve-volume collection of Śaiva devotional poetry. These volumes contain the works of the three most prominent Tamil poets of the 7th and 8th centuries: Sambandar, Appar, and Sundarar

[62] Thevaradiyar (servants of god) were temple dancers paid a monthly salary by the royal court

[63] Sastri, The Colas, 4

[64] Ibid., 5

[65] Sastri, A History of South India, 15

[66] Archaeological Survey of India, translation of original inscription from Mulbagal in Karnataka.

2. Kings of the Sea Waited on Him

[1] SII, Thiruvalangadu copper plates, vv 61-63

[2] Ibid.

3 Sastri, A History of South India, 163

[4] SII, Vol 2, Introduction

[5] ibid

[6] Sastri, The Colas, 157

[7] As quoted by Sastri in 'The Colas', 158

[8] Thiruvalnagadu Plates, v. 72

[9] Ezham, spelled Eezham, is the native Tamil name for the South Asian island country now known as Sri Lanka. The earliest use of the word is found in a Tamil-Brahmi inscription as well as in the Sangam literature. The Tirupparankunram inscription found near Madurai in Tamil Nadu and dated on palaeographical grounds to the 1st century BCE, refers to a person as a householder from Eelam

[10] Stein, Peasant State and Society in Medieval South India, 345

[11] SII, Vol II, Introduction - The Tiruvalangadu plates, which provide a lengthy account of Rajaraja's campaigns, do not mention this battle at all. They begin with the war against the Pandyas and report that Rajaraja seized the Pandya king Amarabhujanga and that the Chola general captured the port of Vizhinjam. It is surmised that Kandhaloor or Kandhaloor-Salai was near Vizhinjam.

[12] SII, Vol II, Part I, No. I - An inscription on the wall of the Thanjavur temple reads: "On the twentieth day of the twenty-sixth year (of the reign) of Ko-Rajakesarivarman, alias Sri-Rajarajadeva, who — while (his) heart rejoiced, that, like the goddess of fortune, the goddess of the great earth had become his wife, — in his life of growing strength, during which,

having been pleased to cut the vessel (kalam) (in) the hall (at) Kandhaloor".

[13] The discovery of a copper plate dated 868 and belonging to the time of the Ay chieftain Karunanthadakkan provides evidence of the establishment of a Vedic education centre, modelled on the one at Kandhaloor Salai. An earlier work in Prakrit called kuvalyamala composed in the 8th century describes Kandhaloor Salai as a university which had students from several countries, taught many subjects and followed strict disciplinary rules.

[14] Battle of Kandalur Salai - https://en.wikipedia.org/wiki/Battle_ of_Kandalur_Salai#:~:text=The%20battle%20of%20Kandalur%20 salai,at%20Kandalur%20in%20south%20Kerala.&text=The%20 Brahmin%20warriors%20of%20the,military%20monks%20of%20 medieval%20Europe.

[15] Stein, Peasant State and Society in Medieval South India, 348

[16] Ibid., 349

[17] Stein, 38

[18] Thapar, Early India, 365

[19] Narayanan, The Jewish Copper Plates of Cochin, 19-21

[20] Ibid., 25-26

[21] SII, Vol 2, Introduction

[22] The battle won Rajaraja fame in all the eight directions as announced by an inscription on the north wall of the Vishnu temple at Ukkal.

> Hail! Prosperity! On the 124th day of the 24h year (of the reign) of the glorious king Rajaraja-Kesarivarman, alias Sri-Rajarajadeva, who, (in) his life of growing strength, during which,- (in) the belief, that, as well as the goddess of fortune, the goddess of the great earth had become his wife,- ... conquered by (his) army, which was victorious in great battles, ... Ilamandalam, (the conquest of which) made (him) famous (in) the eight directions, ...

(Source: SII, Vol iii, Part I, No. 9)

[23] The conquest of Ezham by Rajaraja have been repeated in inscriptions from the first tirumagal introduction in 1993, in which he refers to the "warlike Singhalas".

Hail ! Prosperity ! In the 29th year (of the reign) of the glorious king Rajakesarivarman, alias Sri-Rajarajadeva, who, in his life of growing strength, during which, - (in) the belief that, as well as the goddess of fortune, the goddess of the great earth had become his wife, - he was pleased to destroy the ships (at) Kandalur-Salai, and conquered by (his) army, which was victorious in great battles, Vengai-nadu, Gangapadi, Nolambapadi, Tadigaipadi, Kudamalainadu, Kollam, Kalingam, Ilamandalam, (which was the country) of the warlike Singalas, the seven and a half lakshas of Iratta-padi, and twelve thousand ancient islands of the sea, - deprived the Seliyas of (their) splendour at the very moment when Udagai,[16] which is worshipped everywhere, was (most) resplendent ... (Source: SII, Vol III, Part-I, Inscriptions at Ukkal).

[24] Sastri, The Colas, 172

[25] Ibid., 173

[26] Rajaraja built a stone temple of Siva and called it Vanavan Mahadevisvaram, after the name of his queen. It is more popularly known as Siva Devale and survives till today. The temple was constructed of granite and stone and has the same architectural style as the temples built between the tenth and twelfth centuries. The temple houses inscriptions from the early years of Rajaraja. Another temple called the Rajarajeswara was built at Mantota by an officer of the Chola state by the name of Tali Kumaran. (SII, iv, 1412)

[27] Sastri, 199

[28] The inscription on the south wall of the temple records the assignment of certain villages in Mummadi-Sora-mandalam. This inscription authoritatively confirms that that the conquest of external provinces, as in the case of Ezham, is not a mere military incursion but a more or less permanent colonisation of them. Minute details of measurement, which are

usually mentioned in connection with the villages of the Chola country, are absent in this case. (SII, ii, No.92, intro and paras 12-15)

[29] Thiruvalangadu Plates, v. 78

[30] V.77

[31] Tirumalai, Collected Papers, 26

[32] Ibid., 28

[33] The Valanjiyar

[34] Tirumalai, 46

[35] SII, Vol 2, Introduction

[36] Sastri, The Colas, 171

[37] As quoted from MGS Narayanan (2013). Perumāḷs of Kerala: Brahmin Oligarchy and Ritual Monarchy in wikipedia – 'Tiruppalanam and Tiruvenkatu (999 and 1000 CE) inscriptions mention the gift of an idol by king from the booty obtained in Malainadu and the treasures taken from the Chera king'.

[38] Sastri, The Colas, 175

[39] Ibid., 245

[40] Sastri quoting Dr S.K. Aiyangar Gangai-Konda, 541-2

[41] Sastri, The Colas, 177

[42] The reference could be to the income from the region 'Iratta-padi, (the revenue from from which amounts to) seven and a half Laksha' as found in the inscriptions at Mamallapuram, No. 40, https://www.whatisindia.com/inscriptions/south_indian_inscriptions/volume_I/mamallapuram.html

[43] Ibid., 182

[44] As quoted by Sastri from the Hottur (Dharwar) inscriptions dated 1007

[45] Thiruvalangadu Plates, v. 81

[46] Sastri as quoted in Annual Report on Epigraphy, 1904, para 17

[47] Sastri as quoted from 394 of 1911 ARE

3. Rise of Cities and the Expanding World of Merchants

---

[1] The First Spring Part I: Life in the Golden Age of India, Abraham Eraly

[2] Myos Hormos was an important ancient trading port, possible used by the Pharaonic traders of ancient Egypt and the Ptolemaic dynasty before falling into Roman hands.

[3] Ahananooru, 149

[4] Champakalakshmi, Trade, Ideology and Urbanisation, 12

[5] Ibid. 11

[6] Singh, A History of Ancient and Early Medieval India, 584

[7] Champakalakshmi, 17

[8] Ibid. 17

[9] Singh, 597

[10] Champakalakshmi, 38

[11] Nagaswamy, Tamil Coins, 31-32

[12] Singh, 597

[13] Mahalingam, Kancipuram in Early South Indian History, 171

[14] Nandikkalambakam, a ninth century literary work, praised Nandivarman II on his victory over Pazhayarai after defeating six armies

[15] Sastri, The Colas, 110

[16] Nagaswamy, Tamil Coins: A Study, 35

[17] Ibid., 110

[18] Ibid. 112

[19] https://www.independent.co.uk/arts-entertainment/travel-lost-empire-explored-cholas-once-had-great-power-world-has-forgotten-them-writes-david-keys-2321900.html

[20] Champakalakshmi, Trade, Ideology and Urbanisation, 337

[21] Quoted by Champakalakshmi from EI, 245 of 1911

[22] Singh, 599

[23] Mukund, The World of the Tamil Merchant, 126

[24] Ibid 127

[25] SII, Vol 4, No 223

[26] Singh, 597

[27] SII Vol 2, No. 4, 5 – Major villages and towns had a living quarters for artisans, the kammanacheri and labourers, the paraicheri

[28] Ramaswamy, Metal Crafts in Peninsular Indian History,

[29] Ibid. 13

[30] Quoted from Ramaswamy from Nachchiyar Tirumozhi of Andal (seventh century) stanza X in Hardy Friedhelm, Viraha Bhakti: The Early History of Krishna Devotion in South India, Oxford University Press, Oxford, 1983, p.423

[31] Ibid. 7

[32] Champakalakshmi, Trade, Ideology and Urbanisation, 347-48

[33] Sastri, The Colas, 157

[34] ibid, 653

[35] SII, Vol 2, Part III, No. 66

[36] Tirumalai, Collected Papers, 298

[37] Thapar, 355

[38] Singh, 597

[39] Brahmadeya, royal gifts of land to Brahmanas by kings has its origins from Vedic times. The Mahabharata gives wholehearted approval to this process and makes repeated exhortations to kings to gift land to brahmanas, because they can deify those who are not gods and can dethrone existing gods. The earliest indication of Brahmana settlements established by royal decree and given tax exemptions and privileges comes from the Arthashastra – Singh, 494

[40] Singh, 597

[41] Champakalakshmi, 63

[42] Singh, 598

[43] Karashima, 2014, 129

[44] Mahalakshmi, 2014, 159

[45] Karashima, Chinese texts, 295

[46] Archaeological excavations in Thanjavur, the capital of Rajaraja, have so far failed to locate the palace.

[47] Singh, 599

[48] Narrated by Upinder from a review of Vijaya Ramaswamy's detailed study of the weavers of South India between the 10th and 17th centuries – Textiles and Weavers in Medieval South India.

[49] SII, Vol 14, No. 128.- MADRAS MUSEUM PLATES OF UTTAMA-CHOLA

[50] The term Anjuvannam was wrongly interpreted as a group of five different communities or castes, but more probably, it is derived from Anjuman, used by early Arab Muslim traders of the west coast.

[51] A merchant organisation operating within specific regions as the designations 'Kodumbalur manigramam' and the distribution of their inscriptional references would show. They were apparently are descendants from a group of traders in Puhar, who after the decline of coastal trade, moved into the interior such as Uraiyur and re-emerged as an organised group of traders by the 9th century. (Champakalakshmi, 49)

[52] Singh, A History of Ancient and Early Medieval India, 600

[53] Quoted by Champakalakshmi from Kenneth Hall, Trade and Statecraft, 151

[54] Champakalakshmi, 215

[55] Mahalingam, South Indian Polity, 391

[56] Singh, 601

[57] Sastri, 211

[58] Champakalakshmi, 222

[59] Karashima, Chinese texts, 299

[60] Ibid. 298

[61] Ibid. 298

62 As narrated by Sastri from Chau Ju-kua

[63] Thapar, Early India, 365-66

[64] Singh, 602-03

[65] Champakalakshmi, 49

[66] Champakalakshmi, 217-18

[67] Ibid, 217

[68] Sastri, 614

[69] Nagaswamy, Tamil Coins, 32-33

[70] Nagaswamy, 38-40

[71] The kazhanju was a gold weight of 80 grains; two kasus made one kazhanju, and eight manjadis were equal to one kasu.

[72] Mukund, 120

[73] Champakalakshmi, 57

[74] 'The lost empire explored' - https://www.independent.co.uk/arts-entertainment/travel-lost-empire-explored-cholas-once-had-great-power-world-has-forgotten-them-writes-david-keys-2321900.html

4. Power to Share

---

[75] Sastri, The Colas, 447

[76] Ibid 446

[77] Leslie Orr mentions that George Spencer has argued that Chola military campaigns were more oriented toward plundering than imperial expansion and suggests that 'we have been misled by the language of territorial conquest in which the inscriptional claims about these raids were conventionally expressed' - Spencer 1976, 406

[78] Sastri, 447

[79] Stein, Peasant State and Society in Medieval South India, 255

[80] Sastri, 515

[81] Ibid 515

[82] Stein, 23

[83] Singh, A History of Ancient and Early medieval India, 588

[84] This expression appears from the time of Parantaka I

[85] This finds mention in the Thiruvalangadu Plates where Uttama Chola made a compromise deal with Sundara Chola that Uttama will be succeeded not by his own son but by Arulmozhi (Rajaraja). Thiruvalangadu inscription states: "Having noticed by the marks (on his body) that Arulmozhi was the very Vishnu, the protector of the three worlds, descended on earth, [Uttama] installed him in the position of yuvaraja (heir apparent) and himself bore the burden of ruling the earth ... " - https://www.newworldencyclopedia.org/entry/Raja_Raja_Chola_I

[86] Sastri, 448

[87] From an account by Zhao Rukuo who was a Chinese historian and politician during the Song dynasty. He lived in the later Chola period but

reconstructed many impressions of countries around China from earlier times.

[88] Sastri, 451

[89] ibid

[90] Tulabhara - an ancient practice in which a person is weighed against a commodity (such as gold, grain, fruits or other objects), and the equivalent weight of that commodity is offered as donation to a deity or a charitable cause

[91] Hiranyagarbha - an ancient ceremony involving the donation of a golden vessel by a donor in the expectation of a rebirth as a higher being

[92] Ibid, 453

[93] As quoted by Sastri from ARA, 1909-10, p. 16

[94] As quoted by Ramanujan from George L Hart's "The Nature of Tamil Devotion", Nammalwar, 107

[95] Orr, Processions in the Medieval South Indian Temple, 453

[96] Ibid., 450-51

[97] As quoted by Sastri from ARA, 1909-10, p. 16

[98] SII, Vol 2, Introduction

[99] Stein, 257

[100] Sastri, 455

[101] Ibid 456

[102] This is taken from Part I of the Zhufan zhi (Gazetteer of Foreign Lands), an early thirteenth-century ethnographic and geographical description of nearly sixty foreign countries known to the Chinese through maritime trade relations, as well as a couple of imaginary countries that appear to be based on Arab myths. The author, a Southern Song official named Zhao Rukuo

(or Zhao Rugua, 1170-1231), composed this text in 1224-1225 based on information gathered from earlier Chinese sources and from foreign merchants whom he had interviewed. He had never travelled out of south China but was stationed in the major port city of Quanzhou as a supervisor of maritime trade.

[103] Singh, 591

[104] Sastri, 458

[105] SII, Vol 2, No 91

[106] Ibid., No. 92

[107] Stein, 257

[108] Sastri, 459

[109] Quoted by Sastri from Ferrand, Voyage

[110] Sastri, 461

[111] Ibid 462

[112] SII, Vol 2, No. 82

[113] EI, Vol 18, P. 336

[114] Quoted by Sastri from Indian Antiquary

[115] Silappadhikaram, 341

[116] Silappadhikaram, 341

[117] Ibid.

[118] Translation by R. Parthasarathy, Silappadhikaram, verse 25.103-106

[119] Translation by R. Parthasarathy, Manimekalai, verse 7.8-12

[120] Sastri 474-476

[121] Ibid 486

[122] Singh, 592

[123] Ibid., 591

[124] Analysis of Heitzmann in 'Gifts of Power', 38-54 presented by Singh, 595-96

[125] Singh, 597

[126] Sastri, 595-598

[127] Thapar, Early India, 365

[128] Sastri, 598

[129] Champakalakshmi, 56

[130] Ibid., 229

[131] Stein, 181

[132] Ibid., 206

[133] Singh, 588

[134] ibid

[135] Thapar, 370-71

[136] Stein, 283

[137] Sastri, 187

[138] Stein, 303

[139] Sastri, 188

[140] Ibid, 187

[141] Thapar, 363

5. Donors, Rebels and Deviants

[1] Nagaswamy, http://tamilartsacademy.com/articles/article18.xml

[2] Dehejia, The Very Idea of a Portrait, 43

[3] Sastri, The Colas, 653

[4] Ibid., 449

[5] Ibid., 579

[6] Balasubhramanyan, Middle Chola Temples, 159

[7] Nagaswamy, http://tamilartsacademy.com/articles/article18.xml

[8] Sastri, 6

[9] Orr, 2000, 162

[10] Ibid., 554

[11] Ibid.

[12] Orr, 161

[13] Ibid.

[14] Mahalakshmi, 2014, 115

[15] Chakravarthi, 18

[16] Thapar, Early India, 355

[17] Singh, A History of Ancient and Early Medieval India, 619

[18] Chakravarthi, 18

[19] Mahalakshmi, 118

[20] Ibid., 119

[21] Vijaya Ramaswamy, https://www.india-seminar. com/2003/523/523%20vijaya%20ramaswamy.htm

[22] Ibid.

[23] Mahalakshmi, Intimately Bound…

6. The Dance of Siva

[1] Sastri, The Colas, 641

[2] Ibid., 635

[3] Thapar, 356

[4] Sastri, 635

[5] Singh, A History of Ancient and Early Medieval India, 508

[6] Brahma's downfall was tragic. Infatuated with Shatarupa, Brahmā had developed a fifth head to gaze at her. The enraged Siva cut off the fifth head for the reason that since Shatarupā was Brahma's daughter (being created by him), it was wrong and incestuous of him to become obsessed with her. As a punishment, he directed that there be no proper worship in India for the "unholy" Brahma. Of the three Gods of the Trimurti, this gave an upper hand to Vishnu and Siva. Apparently, ever since the incident, Brahma has been reciting the four Vedas, one from every mouth, in his attempt at repentance.

[7] Basham, The Wonder that was India, 300

[8] ibid

[9] Ramanujan, Nammalwar: Hymns for the Drowning, 104

[10] Basham, 300

[11] Ibid. 306

[12] Ibid. 304

[13] Singh, 611

[14] Basham, 310

[15] Ibid, 311

[16] Basham, 313

[17] Champakalakshmi, Trade, Ideology and Urbanisation, 424

[18] Another name for the Brihadeeswara temple, equating the ruler Rajaraja to the deity Ishvara

[19] Champakalakshmi, 425

[20] Ibid, 426

[21] Ibid., 428

[22] Ibid., 429

[23] Sastri, 653

[24] The demon Taarakaasura had three sons, Taarakaaksha, Kamalaaksha and Vidyunmali. The three asuras, after severe penance to Lord Brahma, were granted three invincible forts, made of gold, silver and iron, which would float around in space. The asuras travelled around the universe creating havoc for they could only be destroyed when the three forts came in a single line and are set on fire by a single arrow. Siva does exactly this, a feat that gave birth to Pasupatham. Queen Chembiyanmadevi, Rajaraja's grand-aunt, got many temples renovated and had bronze images of Tripurantaka installed in all of them, where special pujas were conducted. But the most important and most beautiful Tripurantaka is, undoubtedly, the large mural around the main shrine at the Brihadeeswara temple. (https://www.thehindu.com/society/history-and-culture/one-shot-that-felled-three-forts/article17844844.ece)

[25] Quote from Champakalakshmi on Schwindelr's interpretation of the repeated use of the Tripurantaka form of stone sculptures, frescoes and metal images.

[26] Mevisson, The Stone Chariot at Darasuram and the Myth of Siva Tripurantaka, 292-293

[27] Champakalakshmi, 431

[28] Mahalakshmi, 2014, 158

[29] Sastri, 654

[30] Champakalakshmi., 436

[31] Sastri, 636-37

[32] Ibid., 638-639

[33] He contributed four pieces of works to Divya Prabhandham, the Vaishnavite canon. These works consisted of 1,296 poems, making him the most prolific contributor to the 4,000 hymns written by the Alwar poet-saints

[34] Thapar, 357

[35] Indira, Poems to Siva, 20

[36] Dehejia, The Very Idea of a Portrait, 45

[37] Indira, 21

[38] Ibid., 20

[39] Ibid., 21

[40] Sastri, 636

[41] ibid

[42] Ibid., 643

[43] Ibid., 644

[44] Ibid., 646

[45] Ibid., 657

[46] Champakalakshmi., 398

[47] Ibid., 61

[48] Words of G.W. Spencer quoted by Champakalakshmi, 430

[49] Orr, 99

7. A Bright Star in the Firmament

---

[1] Eusebius, Ancient Accounts, 38

[2] Ibid. 98

[3] Ibid. 99

[4] Thapar, Early India, 371

[5] Karashima, 2014, 129

[6] Mukund, 77

[7] Karashima, 133

[8] Sastri estimates that in the Chola period, the kazhanju of twenty manjadis was equal to about 72 to 80 grains of gold, 613

[9] SII, No 9 - "(The land of) those landholders in villages of Brahmanas, in villages of Vaikhanasas, and in villages of Sramanas (i.e., Jainas) in Sonadu, in the adjacent districts included in Sonadu, in Tondai-nadu, and in Pandi-nadu, alias Rajaraja-valanadu,[5] who have not paid, on the land owned by them, the taxes due from villages, along with the (other) inhabitants of those villages, for three years, (of which) two are completed, between the 16th and the 23rd years (of my reign), shall become the property of the village and shall be liable to be sold by the inhabitants of those villages to the exclusion of the (defaulting) landholders. Also, (the land of) those who have not paid the taxes due from villages for three years, (of which) two are completed, from the 24th year (of my reign), shall be liable to be sold by the inhabitants of those villages to the exclusion of the (defaulting) landholders."

[10] SII, Vol vii, No. 1000

[11] Sastri, The Colas, 524

[12] Ibid. 524-25

[13] Ibid. 525

[14] Ibid 527

[15] Thapar, 371

[16] Ibid. 372

[17] Singh, 494

[18] Veluthat, Land Rights and Social Stratification

[19] Ibid. 126

[20] Karashima, 2014, 136

[21] Ibid., 137

[22] Veluthat quotes from Jha, Studies in Early Indian Economic History, pp. 74-89

[23] From a discussion of the findings of MGS Narayanan and Subbrayalu presented by Veluthat, p. 130

[24] Stein, 86 – when arguing for a Brahmana-peasant alliance, Stein treated the entire peasanstry as a homogenous lot, ignoring the differentiation within them, as 'peasants without lords'.

[25] Karashima, 137-138

[26] Ibid., 138

[27] Sastri, 548

[28] SII, Vol 3, Plate 25, inscription on the north wall of the pasupatiswara shrine

[29] Left-Hand and Right-Hand divisions are known as idangai and valangai repectively

[30] Rajaraja's army had valangai military units but there are no records of idangai associations

[31] Sastri, 550-51

[32] Subrahmanian, Sangam Polity

[33] Stein, 213

[34] Ibid., 180

[35] Sastri, 576

[36] Thapar, 372

[37] The Anbil grant of Sundara Chola recording the donations of land to the brahman Anirudha

Brahmadhiraja provides meticulous details of ownership rights: 'We marked [the boundaries of] the land thus defined by erecting mounds of earth and planting cactus. The several objects included in this land - such as fruit-yielding trees, water, lands, gardens, all upgrowing trees and down-going wells, open spaces, wastes in which calves graze, the village site, ant-hills, platforms [built around trees], canals, hollows, rivers and their alluvial deposits, tanks, granaries, fish-ponds, clefts with bee-hives, deep ponds included; and everything else on which the iguana runs and the tortoise crawls; and taxes such as the income from places of justice, the taxes on [betel] leaves, the cloths from looms, the kanam [of gold[on carriages, . . . the old tenants being evicted, everything that the king could take and enjoy - all these shall be made over to this man. He shall be at liberty to erect halls and upper storeys with burnt bricks; to dig wells, big and small; to plant southernwood and cactus; to dig channels in accordance with watering requirements: not to waste surplus water but to dam it for irrigation; no one shall employ small baskets [for lifting such water]. In this wise was the old order changed and the old name and old taxes removed, and an ekabhoga brahmadeya (land granted to a single brahman) under the name of Karunakaramangalam was constituted'.

'The Anbil Plates of Sundara Chola', in K. A. Nilakanta Sastri, The Colas (Madras, 1955), p. 577

[38] Thapar, 373

[39] Veluthat, 128

[40] Ibid.

[41] Thapar, 373

[42] Sastri, 486

[43] Ibid. 487

[44] Ibid.

[45] Ibid. 493

[46] Ibid., 496

[47] Basham, 107

[48] Sastri, 496-503

[49] Thapar, 377

[50] Basham, 108

[51] Sastri, 528

[52] I kalam is about 100 kgs of paddy

[53] I veli is roughly 26,775 sqm

[54] Sastri, 529

[55] Ibid 529

[56] Ibid. 533-34

[57] I kuli is approx. 7 cubic metres

[58] Ibid 539

[59] Sastri, The Colas, 520

[60] Mukund, 80

[61] Mukund, 82 quoted from Hall, Trade and Statecraft, 58.

[62] Karashima, 2014, 131

[63] Stein, 256

[64] Sastri, 521

8. Celebrating Life

[1] Dehejia, 41

[2] Ibid., 42

[3] Brown, 84

[4] Ibid., 85

[5] Ibid., 86

[6] Basham, The Wonder that was India, 348

[7] ibid

[8] ibid

[9] Ibid., 349

[10] ibid

[11] Dehejia, The Very Idea of a Portrait, 47

[12] Ibid., 43

[13] Basham, 349

[14] Sastri, The Colas, 693

[15] EI, XVII, P. 14-17

[16] Sastri, The Colas, P. 641

[17] Ibid., 693

[18] Ibid., 698

[19] Sastri, 694

[20] Ramanujan, 107

[21] The Saiva saints celebrate 274 holy places; the Vaishnavas, 108, of which 106 are terrestrial and 2 celestial, that is, Vishnu's paradise Vaikuntam, and the Ocean of Milk where he sleeps. The 108 places were called divyadesam, divine places, and 'patal pettra patikal', places that received a song.

[22] Sastri, A History of South India, 147

[23] Quoted by Ramanujan from Nicholas B. Dirks, 'Political Authority and Structural Change in Early South Indian History', 145-46

[24] Sastri, 694

[25] Quoted by Sastri from Jouveau-Dubreil, Archaeology du sud de l'Inde', I, p. 116

[26] Sastri, 694

[27] Dehejia, 43

[28] Percy Brown, Indian Art and Architecture (Buddhist and Hindu), p. 84

[29] Orr quotes Soundararajan, 90

[30] Orr quotes Balasubrahmanyam, 90

[31] Sastri, 695-6

[32] Orr quotes Balasubrahmanyam, 91

[33] Orr, 91

[34] Sastri, A History of South India, 159

[35] Garbhagrham is the sanctum sanctorum, the innermost sanctuary of a temple housing the idol of the primary deity.

[36] Ardhamandapam is usually an open—to provide light and air—four-pillared pavilion in front of the entrance door of the mandapa of the temple.

[37] Mukhamandapam is a pavilion or porch built in front of the doorway to the temple

[38] Sastri, The Colas, 702

[39] The Ardhanarishvarar is a composite form of Siva and Parvati. Ardhanarishvarar is depicted as half-male and half-female, equally split down the middle. The right half is usually the male Siva, illustrating his traditional attributes.

[40] Sastri, 703

[41] Sastri, 709

[42] Ibid., 710

[43] Brown, 85

[44] Sastri, 710

[45] Balasubrahmanyam, Middle Chola Temples, 37

[46] Vimana is the structure over the garbhagriham or inner sanctum in the temples of South India

[47] Nandi is the sacred bull calf, gatekeeper, and vehicle (vahana) of Siva

[48] Sastri, 712

[49] In Bharatanatyam, 108 karanas form the basic movements. There are beautiful sculptures of 81 of the 108 karanas inside the chamber of the first tier of the vimana (tower) above the sanctum. Siva, Lord of dance, is portrayed as performing these karanas. (https://www.thehindu.com/features/friday-review/history-and-culture/How-karana-sculptures-in-Big-Temple-were-discovered/article16044743.ece)

[50] Chola Splendour, https://frontline.thehindu.com/arts-and-culture/heritage/article30180994.ece

[51] Sinopoli, From the Lion Throne, 373

[52] Basham, 359

[53] Sastri, 723-24

[54] Quoted from Ajit Ghose by Sastri, 725

[55] Sastri, 724-75

[56] Basham, 377

[57] ibid

[58] Sharada Srinivasan, 2016, Tamil Chola Bronzes, 2218

[59] Singh, A History of Ancient and Early Medieval India, 641

[60] Lost-wax process, also called cire-perdue, is a method of metal casting in which a molten metal is poured into a mold that has been created by means of a wax model. Once the mold is made, the wax model is melted and drained away. A hollow core can be effected by the introduction of a heat-proof core that prevents the molten metal from totally filling the mold. The lost-wax method dates from the 3rd millennium BC and has sustained few changes since then. https://www.britannica.com/technology/lost-wax-process

[61] Grousset, The Civilization of India, 252-53

[62] Sharada Srinivasan, 2004, 447 – Sharada's analysis of 130 metal images using archaeometry revealed that the metal artefacts of the Pallava and Chola periods show different results. On this basis, several bronzes which were earlier described as "Chola bronzes" in all likelihood belonged to the Pallava period.

[63] Sharada Srinivasan, Tamil Chola Bronzes, 2016, 2208 – In this study, the South Indian bronzes have been classified under the prominent ruling dynasties of different periods as Early Andhra Pallava (c 200–600 CE), Pallava (c.600–875 CE), Vijayalaya Chola period (c. 850–1070CE), Chalukya-Chola (c. 1070–1279 CE), Later Pandya (c. 1279–1336 CE), Vijayanagara and Early Nayaka (c. 1336–1565 CE), and Later Nayaka and Maratha (c. 1565–1800 CE), drawing from classifications discussed by various historians. The archaeometric analyses for the fingerprinting, authentication, and stylistic reassessment involved 130 South Indian

representative bronze images.

[64] Ibid. 2215

[65] Singh, 642

[66] Dehejia, 43

[67] Ibid.

[68] The samabhanga, is a standing body position or stance used in traditional Indian art and Indian classical dance forms, where the body placed upright in perfect balance represents the serenity of the soul.

[69] Tribhanga is a standing body position or stance used in traditional Indian art and Indian classical dance forms, where the body bends in one direction at the knees, the other direction at the hips and then the other again at the shoulders and neck.

[70] Sastri, 734

[71] Ibid., 738

[72] Ibid., 739

[73] Ibid., 739-40

[74] Balasubrahmanyam, Middle Chola Temples, 33

[75] Ibid., 33

[76] Sastri, 740

[77] Ibid., 741

[78] Mevissen, The Stone Chariot at Darapuram, 289

[79] Ibid.

[80] The padmasana pose

[81] Jnanamudra

[82] Dhyanamudra

[83] Balasubrahmanyam, 33

[84] Ibid., 53

[85] Among them stands out E. Hultzsch and his band of fellow workers

9. Delightful Potpourri of Literary Spaces

---

[1] Sastri, The Colas, 662

[2] Ibid

[3] The Devaram, the Thiruvachagam and the bulk of the 'Four Thousand Sacred Hymns', the Nalayira Divya Prabandham of the Tamil Vaishnava canon belong to this period as also the Pandikkovai, Sulamani, Nandikalabagam and the Bharatavenba of Perundevanar – Sastri, 662

[4] Zvelebil, Tamil Literature, 105

[5] Sastri, 662

[6] Meykeerthi in Tamil means "true fame". During the rule of Rajaraja Chola it became common practice to begin inscriptions of grants with a standard praise for the king's achievements and conquests. This practice was adopted by Raja Raja's descendants and the later Pandya kings. The length of a meykeerthi may vary from a few lines to a few paragraphs. Only the start of a particular king's meykeerthi remains constant in all his inscriptions and the content varies depending upon the year of his reign the inscription was issued (as he might have made new conquests or new grants since the previous inscription was made). Meykeerthis do not mention a calendar year. Instead they mention the year of the king's reign in which the inscription was made.

[7] These inscriptions recount the career and achievements of Naralokavira, and official who served Kulottunga I, the great-grandson of Rajaraja

[8] Sastri, 663

[9] Ibid., 663-64

[10] Ibid., 665

[11] Zvelebil, 43

[12] Zvelebil quoting A.K. Ramanujam

[13] Ibid., 48

[14] Translation by Zvelebil, 50

[15] Percival, P, The Tamil Epic Chintamani, 49

[16] Basham, The Wonder that was India, 477

[17] Sastri., 667

[18] Basham, 477

[19] Kamil Zvelebil in his 'Tamil Literature' points to warning by some critics that the poem 'gives terribly dangerous stimulation to the senses' and that it 'should be banned for the young'.

[20] Sastri, 667

[21] Zvelebil, 138

[22] Yamashita, 151

[23] It is the story of Nilakesi, a demoness known from the Tamil folk region, who is converted by a Jaina ascetic and made a preacher of Jainism. The work is generally dated in the latter half of the tenth century and may have very well been composed in the time of Rajaraja

[24] Zvelebil, 139

[25] Indira, Poems to Siva: The Hymns of the Tamil Saints, 14

[26] Nambiyandar Nambi arranged the hymns of the three great Saiva teachers, Sambandar, Appar and Sundarar, as the first seven books. He then added Manickavachagar's Thirukovaiyar and Thiruvachagam as the 8th book, then 28 hymns of nine other saints as the 9th book, the Tirumandiram of Thirumular as the 10th book, 40 hymns by 12 other poets as the 11th book, then described the labours of the 63 saints, and added his story and hymns to the 11th book. The hymns of the seven books came to be known as Devaram and the whole Saiva canon, to which was added as the 12th book, Sekkizhar's Great Puranam, is known as Thirumurai, the Holy Book. – Zvelebi, 91

[27] Indira., 15

[28] Ibid., 16

[29] Ibid.

[30] It is said that termites had chewed a large number of hymns and that the hymns compiled by Nambi were just a fraction. Fabulous figures are quoted for the output of the saints. 'Atleast in the case of Sundarar, it is quite likely that the hundred hymns (a nice, round figure) represent only a part of his compositions. The legend of enormous numbers of writings being lost and subsequently recovered, but only in part, is a recurrent motif in the Tamil literary tradition, the most famous of such accounts being the legend of the three classical Sangams or academies, from whose literary works only a portion is said to have survived great floods or tidal waves'. (Indra, 16n)

[31] Indra, 17

[32] Though not an Alwar himself, Nathamuni was first in the line of the acharyas, teachers, who completed the work begun by the Alwars, the Viashnava saints. The Vaishnava canon consists of the works of 14 poets, out of which 12 are considered Alwars.

[33] Ramanujan, Nammalvar, xiii

[34] Ibid.

[35] Ibid., xiv

[36] Ibid., 126

[37] Ibid., 127

[38] The Buddhists and Jainas were the first de-Sanskritisers. Buddha enjoined his followers to use the local language. Ashoka used Prakrit in the inscriptions of his kingdom. These were effective measures against the domination of Vedic orthodoxy. The bhakti saints were propelled by the same motive. The influence of Vedic orthodoxy over Tamil language and culture had to be countered by something the people cannot resist. By encouraging Tamil

meykeertis, compiling the Saivite hymns and building a mammoth temple in the Dravidian style, Rajaraja followed the methods of Ashoka and was rewarded by popular acceptance.

[39] Ramanujan, 128

[40] Thapar, 356

[41] Zvelebil, 135

[42] Ramanujan, 129

[43] A bhakti saint, one among the most revered contributors to the Devaram

[44] Ramanujan, 129

[45] Sastri, 668

[46] Zvelebil, 207

[47] ibid

[48] ibid

[49] Ibid., 209

[50] Ibid., 212

[51] Zvelebil, 106

[52] Ibid., 198

Epilogue

---

[1] Singh, Rethinking Early Medieval India, P. I

[2] Champakalakshmi, Trade, Ideology and Urbanaisation, 37

[3] Ibid.

[4] Sastri, The Colas, 100

[5] Ibid., 106

[6] Ibid.

[7] Terms such as medievalism and feudalism are contentious issues and there is no agreement between historians on one common definition and their context in Indian conditions

[8] Thapar, 356

[9] Sastri, 107

[10] Sri Rangastavam by Parashara bhattar states "I bow to ParakAla kavi (Thirumangai aalzhwaar) won over philosophies such as Jainism to establish the complete philosophy of SriVaishnavism and used the jewels and images from them to build the third wall around Srirangam Temple"- https://en.wikipedia.org/wiki/Thirumangai_Alvar#As_a_Vaishnava_saint

[11] Sekkizhar was a thirteenth century Saivite saint and a contemporary of Kulottunga Chola II. He compiled and wrote the Periya Puranam (Great Narrative) in 4253 verses, recounting the life stories of the sixty-three Nayanars, the devotees of Shiva. Sekkizhar himself was later canonised and his work, the Periyapuranam became the twelfth and final book of the sacred Saiva canon.

[12] Sastri, 656

[13] Ibid., 657

[14] Appar, IV.5, verse 5

[15] Thapar, 350

[16] Devadevan, A Pre-History of Hinduism, 19

[17] Ibid., 20

[18] Ibid., 178

[19] Thapar, 351

[20] Ibid.

[21] Singh, 619

[22] The feudalism model has been applied to the Chola period by many scholars such as D.D. Kosambi, R.S. Sharma and R.N. Nandi

[23] Thapar, Early India, 350

[24] Ibid.

[25] Champakalakshmi, Trade, Ideology and Urbanisation, 207

[26] Sastri, 66

[27] ibid

[28] ibid

[29] Ibid., 67

[30] Singh, A History of Ancient and Early Medieval India, 592

[31] ibid

[32] Champakalakshmi, 377

[33] Nammalwar's Thiruvaimozhi, 3.7.9

[34] Ramanujan, 149-50

[35] Stein, 181

[36] Singh, 597

[37] Champakalakshmi, 62

[38] Ibid.

[39] Devadevan, Pre-history of Hinduism, 38-39

[40] Ibid.

[41] Karashima, 2014, 128

[42] Singh, 559

[43] Sastri, 168

INDEX

Praise for the Book

'A rousing attempt at piecing together the lives and times of the Tamil country's most remarkable medieval personality, Rajaraja Chola, who despite the rich artistic legacy, plethora of inscriptions and maritime ambitions has remained an enigmatic figure' - **Sharada Srinivasan, Professor, School of Humanities, National Institute of Advanced Studies**

'The author has recorded the magnificent rule of Rajaraja I, the Imperial Chola, who brought the entire southern Peninsula under his regime. The book is divided into nine chapters with unique and different captions ... This book is designed for the lay reader, not necessarily in chronological order ... with interesting facts arranged in appropriate places. The book provides an excellent comparative study of Chola sculpture, painting and literature' - **Prof. S.S. Sundaram, Professor & Head, Department of Indian History, University of Madras**

'Raghavan Srinivasan's book is a riveting scholarly work on how the glory of the Chola Empire was crafted brick by brick by the ruler as well as the ruled. It is an overwhelming story of exemplary kingly attributes nurturing people so that they bloom as a multi-hued, many-splendored civilization 1000 years ago. Srinivasan's book informs and delights in equal measure. It's a must have for history buffs' ... **Ashwini Bhatnagar, author, nominated for Best Non Fiction Book, 2020, at Tata LitLive awards for The Lotus Years, Political Life in India During the Time of Rajiv Gandhi.**

'A fascinating introduction to Rajaraja Chola, as impeccably balanced in terms of content, insight, interpretation and style as a Chola Nataraja itself!' - **Shyam Banerji, Author of Pandit Ajoy Charabarty: Seeker of the Music Within and Hindu Gods and Temples: Symbolism, Sanctity, Sites. He is also Curator, heritage studies and spaces'.**

'The era of Raja Raja Chola, consolidator and emperor, has been brought to life in this racy novel style book by Raghavan, written for the layman and non-specialist like myself, without being an agglomeration of names and dates, against the background of economic and political forces. It lives on in myriad edicts, copper plates, temples and inscriptions therein and is a huge amount of other information from which this is reconstructed.' – **Prof. B. Anathanarayan, Indian Institute of Science**

The fourth century BCE is full of dangers and opportunities. Old republics are giving way to empires and cities. 'Naastik' sects are challenging the established varna system. The intellectual life of India is bristling like new shoots after the monsoon. The domination of the Kshatriyas and the Brahmanas is being challenged. State power is up for grabs. And the Macedonians are at the gates!

Most people believe that Bharatavarsha is only a dream. But not the Yugantar, a brotherhood of the wisest and most selfless thinkers of ancient India.

Interesting turn of events bring ordinary people from different parts of the subcontinent into the fold of the Yugantar—a rebel blacksmith from Ujjayini, a Siddha doctor from Madurai; a doughty mariner from Muziris; a trader from Pataliputra and a widow nun from Kaushambi.

They represent a microcosm of the sub-continent. Each of them is drawn towards the Yugantar by a strange turn of events. Each has a prowess which the Yugantar can mould into a formidable force. They converge in Takshashila, the centre of learning and transformation. This is the story of how their wit and determination contribute to a united Bharatavarsha.